Annie's Favorite Thread Projects

In this book, you'll find the unique, the practical, the breathtakingly beautiful, in lacy finery to display, wear or give away. Discover for yourself that the lovely and legendary art of thread crochet is the expression of a creative spirit that knows no bounds!

Editorial Director
Andy Ashley
Production Director
Ange Van Arman

Editorial
Senior Editor
Jennifer McClain
Editor
Liz Field
Editorial Staff
Shirley Brown, Alva Lea Edwards, Donna Jones,
Nina Marsh, Donna Scott, Ann White

Photography
Scott Campbell, Tammy Coquat-Payne

Production Manager
Diane Simpson

Production Team
Joanne Gonzalez, Betty Radla, Minette Collins Smith

Product Presentation
Design Coordinator
Sandy Kennebeck
Inhouse Designer
Mickie Akins
Design Copy
Linda Moll Smith

Sincerest thanks to all the designers and other professionals
whose dedication has made this book possible.
Special thanks to Quebecor Printing Book Group, Kingsport, Tennessee.

Library of Congress Cataloging-in-Publication Data
ISBN: 0-9655269-2-5
First Printing: 1998
Library of Congress Catalog Card Number: 96-79700
Published and Distributed by
Annie's Attic, LLC, Big Sandy, Texas 75755
Printed in the United States of America.

Cover: *Pineapple Angel and Table Topper,*
pattern instructions begin on pages 14
and 18 respectively.

Contents

Dear Friends,

Have you noticed something? Needlecrafters everywhere are turning back to the traditions of fine handwork so familiar to our mothers and grandmothers. My own favorite, the glorious art of thread crochet, is suddenly new again!

Why is thread crochet so dear to my heart? I was born on a Kansas farm, just two wheat fields away from the humble homestead settled by my great grandfather. I grew up rooted in family heritage. And the pioneering women in my family were all accomplished needleworkers. Stitching magnificent creations of fine thread crochet, they furnished their homes with exquisite handwork and earned countless blue ribbons at the county fair.

I was just six when, fascinated with watching the expert crochet skills of my grandmother, I begged my mother to teach me how to "hook the thread like Ma-Maw." I'll never forget how excited I was when I made my first chain.

In the years since, even as I went on to found the needlecraft company known as Annie's Attic, crochet has remained my first love. At last, after over 20 years of publishing needlecraft patterns, I'm celebrating the timeless legacy of thread crochet in one exclusive volume!

In this spectacular collection I've included my personal favorites, and designs perennially popular with our customers, in easy-to-follow patterns for exquisite thread crochet you and your family will prize for generations!

I've filled the nine chapters of Annie's Favorite Thread Projects with a lavish variety of crochet as lovely as it is useful.

In "Pineapple Passion" you'll discover why the pineapple pattern is beloved by crocheters everywhere by stitching a refined apron, a dramatic tablecloth or a splendid angel. In "Christmas Creations" you'll thread the pristine beauty of crochet throughout jolly festivity with delicate snowflakes, ornaments and doilies Santa himself will admire.

With "Wedding Wonders" you'll embrace the lace and grace of thread crochet with a trove of sentiment—choice accessories that befit the glowing bride. Romanticism rules our "Bed & Bath" chapter with fabulous embellishments you'll make to adorn a lampshade, tray, bedspread and pillowcase. And "Gifts for Giving," whether a filet pillow, a flower-strewn bookmark or a pair of tender booties for baby, remind us that our kindred lives are linked together by providential design.

In "Country Home" prove with handmade accents of baskets, curtains, dolls and coasters that stunning, yet sensible interior decorating is within reach with a hook and thread. Lend elegance to the tabletop, spice up decor with playful doilies and dress up with mother and daughter aprons in our "Kitchen Creations"—a recipe for contentment!

Don't forget "Doily Delights," the first ambassadors of thread crochet, and of course, when it comes to "Fashion Favorites," no matter what look is in vogue, you'll find crochet is always chic!

As an expression of the artistic imagination and its loving impulses, thread crochet is pure delight. May you recapture the values of the traditional home with the blessing and abundance of enduring thread crochet!

Happy Thread Crocheting,

Annie

Pineapple Passion

The elegant Pineapple,
a perennially popular stitch
pattern, is picked a favorite by
crocheters for good reason. Long
considered a traditional symbol of
hospitality, this pleasant fruit of
friendship is transformed into family
treasure as it is passed from one
generation of crocheters to the next.
Always classic, the versatile pineapple
can be stitched, as here, into a refined
apron, a dramatic tablecloth,
or a glorious angel—all
reinventions of timeless
thread crochet.

Star Tablecloth

Designed by Dot Drake

Finished Size: 60" across.

Materials:
- ☐ 2,600 yds. size 10 white crochet cotton thread
- ☐ No. 8 steel hook or hook needed to obtain gauge

Gauge: Rnds 1–3 = 2¼" across.

Basic Stitches: Ch, sl st, sc, dc, tr.

Special Stitches:
For **shell**, (4 dc, ch 3, 4 dc) in next ch sp.
For **beginning shell (beg shell)**, sl st across to first ch sp, (sl st, ch 3, 3 dc, ch 3, 4 dc) in ch sp.
For **picot**, (sc, ch 3, sc) in next ch sp.
For **block**, dc in next st, 2 dc in next ch-2 sp, dc in next st, **or** dc in each of next 4 sts and chs.
For **V st**, (tr, ch 7, tr) in next st or ch sp.

TABLECLOTH
Rnd 1: Ch 8, sl st in first ch to form ring, ch 3, 23 dc in ring, join with sl st in top of ch-3. *(24 dc made)*
Rnd 2: Ch 6, skip next st, (dc in next st, ch 3, skip next st) around, join with sl st in third ch of ch 6. *(12 dc, 12 ch sps)*
Rnd 3: Ch 6, skip next ch sp, (3 dc in **back lp**—*see Stitch Guide*—of next st, ch 3, skip next ch sp) around, 2 dc in same st as ch-6, join. *(36 dc)*
Rnds 4–6: Working in **back lps**, ch 6, skip next ch sp, dc in each st across next dc group with 3 dc in last st of group, ch 3, skip next ch sp, (3 dc in next st, dc in each st across to next ch sp, ch 3, skip next ch sp, dc in each st across next dc group with 3 dc in last st of group, ch 3, skip next ch sp) 5 times, 3 dc in next dc, dc in each st around, join. At end of last rnd *(108 dc)*.
Rnd 7: Working in **back lps**, ch 6, skip next ch sp, dc in next 6 sts, dc next 3 sts tog, ch 10, skip next ch sp, (dc next 3 sts tog, dc in next 6 sts, ch 3, skip next ch sp, dc in next 6 sts, dc next 3 sts tog, ch 10, skip next ch sp) 5 times, dc next 3 sts tog, dc in each st around, join. *(84 dc, 6 ch-10 sps)*
Rnd 8: Working in **back lps**, ch 6, skip next ch sp, dc in next 4 sts, dc next 3 sts tog, ch 5, 9 dc in next ch sp, ch 5, (dc next 3 sts tog, dc in next 4 sts, ch 3, skip next ch sp, dc in next 4 sts, dc next 3 sts tog, ch 5, 9 dc in next ch sp, ch 5) 5 times, dc next 3 sts tog, dc in last 3 sts, join. *(114 dc)*
Rnd 9: Ch 6, skip next ch sp; working in **back lps**, dc in each of next 2 sts, dc next 3 sts tog, ch 5, skip next ch sp; working in **both lps**, dc in next st, (ch 1, dc in next st) 8 times, ch 5, skip next ch sp; *working in **back lps**, dc next 3 sts tog, dc in each of next 2 sts, ch 3, skip next ch sp, dc in each of next 2 sts, dc next 3 sts tog, ch 5, skip next ch sp; working in **both lps**, dc in next st, (ch 1, dc in next st) 8 times, ch 5, skip next ch sp; repeat from * 4 more times; working in **back lps**, dc next 3 sts tog, dc in last st, join. *(90 dc)*
Rnd 10: Ch 6, skip next ch sp; working in **back lps**, dc next 3 sts tog, ch 5, skip next ch sp; working in **both lps**, dc in next st, (ch 2, dc in next st) 8 times, ch 5, skip next ch sp; *working in **back lps**, dc next 3 sts tog, ch 3, skip next ch sp, dc next 3 sts tog, ch 5, skip next ch sp; working in **both lps**, dc

7

Continued on page 8

Continued from page 7

in next st, (ch 2, dc in next st) 8 times, ch 5, skip next ch sp; repeat from * 4 more times; working in **back lps,** dc last 2 sts tog, join. *(66 dc)*

Rnd 11: Ch 6, skip next ch sp, dc in next st, ch 5, skip next ch sp, dc in next st, (ch 3, dc in next st) 8 times, ch 5, skip next ch sp, *dc in next st, ch 3, skip next ch sp, dc in next st, ch 5, skip next ch sp, dc in next st, (ch 3, dc in next st) 8 times, ch 5, skip next ch sp; repeat from * 4 more times, skip last st, join. *(66 dc, 54 ch-3 sps)*

Rnd 12: (Sl st, ch 3, 3 dc, ch 3, 4 dc) in first ch sp, ch 5, skip next ch sp, **picot** *(see Special Stitches),* (ch 5, picot) 7 times, ch 5, skip next ch sp, *shell* *(see Special Stitches),* ch 5, skip next ch sp, picot in next ch sp, (ch 5, picot) 7 times, ch 5, skip next ch sp; repeat from * around, join with sl st in top of ch-3. *(6 shells, 54 ch-5 sps—picots are not worked into or counted as ch sps or as sts)*

NOTE: *In rnds 13–21, work beg shell (see Special Stitches) for first shell of each rnd.*

Rnd 13: *(Shell, ch 3, 4 dc) in next shell, ch 5, skip next ch sp, picot, (ch 5, picot) 6 times, ch 5, skip next ch sp; repeat from * around, join. *(6 shells, 24 dc, 48 ch-5 sps)*

Rnd 14: *Shell, ch 3, shell in next ch-3 sp, ch 5, skip next ch sp, picot, (ch 5, picot) 5 times, ch 5, skip next ch sp; repeat from * around, join. *(12 shells, 42 ch-5 sps)*

Rnd 15: *Shell, ch 2, dc in next ch-3 sp, ch 2, shell, ch 5, skip next ch sp, picot, (ch 5, picot) 4 times, ch 5, skip next ch sp; repeat from * around, join. *(6 dc, 36 ch-5 sps)*

NOTE: *For remainder of pattern, skip each ch-2 sp unless otherwise stated.*

Rnd 16: *Shell, ch 2, dc in last dc of shell, ch 2, dc in next dc, ch 2, dc in first dc of next shell, ch 2, shell, ch 5, skip next ch sp, picot, (ch 5, picot) 3 times, ch 5, skip next ch sp; repeat from * around, join. *(18 dc, 30 ch-5 sps)*

Rnd 17: *Shell, ch 2, dc in last dc of shell, ch 2, dc in next dc, ch 2, 4 dc in next dc, ch 2, dc in next dc, ch 2, dc in first dc of next shell, ch 2, shell, ch 5, skip next ch sp, picot, (ch 5, picot) 2 times, ch 5, skip next ch sp; repeat from * around, join. *(48 dc, 24 ch-5 sps)*

Rnd 18: *Shell, ch 2, dc in last dc of shell, ch 2, dc in next dc, ch 2, block *(see Special Stitches),* ch 4, skip next 2 dc, block, ch 2, dc in next dc, ch 2, dc in first dc of next shell, ch 2, shell, ch 5, skip next ch sp, picot, ch 5, picot, ch 5, skip next ch sp; repeat from * around, join. *(12 blocks, 24 dc, 6 ch-4 sps, 18 ch-5 sps)*

NOTE: *Blocks are not included in stitch counts except when there is a change in the number of blocks.*

Rnd 19: (Shell, ch 2, dc in last dc of shell, ch 2, dc in next dc, ch 2, block, ch 7, sc in next ch sp, ch 7, skip next 3 dc, block, ch 2, dc in next dc, ch 2, dc in first dc of next shell, ch 2, shell, ch 5, skip next ch sp, picot in third ch of next ch-5 sp, ch 5, skip next ch sp) around, join. *(12 ch-7 sps)*

Rnd 20: *Shell, ch 2, dc in last dc of shell, ch 2, dc in next dc, ch 2, block, ch 7, (sc in next ch sp,

ch 7) 2 times, skip next 3 dc, block, ch 2, dc in next dc, ch 2, dc in first dc of next shell, ch 2, shell, ch 5, skip next 2 ch sps; repeat from * around, join. *(18 ch-7 sps)*

Rnd 21: *Shell, ch 2, dc in last dc of shell, ch 2, dc in next dc, ch 2, block, ch 7, (sc in next ch sp, ch 7) 3 times, skip next 3 dc, block, ch 2, dc in next dc, ch 2, dc in first dc of next shell, ch 2, shell, ch 3, skip next ch sp; repeat from * around, join. *(24 ch-7 sps)*

Rnd 22: Sl st across to ch sp of first shell, (sl st, ch 3, 3 dc) in ch sp, ch 2, dc in last dc of shell, ch 2, dc in next dc, ch 2, block, ch 7, (sc in next ch sp, ch 7) 4 times, skip next 3 dc, block, ch 2, dc in next dc, ch 2, dc in first dc of next shell, ch 2, 4 dc in ch sp of same shell as last dc worked, *ch 3, skip next ch sp, 4 dc in ch sp of next shell, ch 2, dc in last dc of shell, ch 2, dc in next dc, ch 2, block, ch 7, (sc in next ch sp, ch 7) 4 times, skip next 3 dc, block, ch 2, dc in next dc, ch 2, dc in first dc of next shell, ch 2, 4 dc in ch sp of same shell as last dc made; repeat from * around, join with dc in top of ch-3. *(Joining dc counts as ch-3 sp—6 ch-3 sps, 72 dc, 30 ch-7 sps)*

NOTE: *In rnds 23–27, work beg shell for first shell of each rnd.*

Rnd 23: *Shell in next ch-3 sp, ch 2, skip next 3 dc, (dc in next dc, ch 2) 2 times, block, ch 7, (sc in next ch sp, ch 7) 5 times, skip next 3 dc, block, (ch 2, dc in next dc) 2 times, ch 2, skip next 3 dc; repeat from * around, join with sl st in top of ch-3. *(6 shells, 24 dc, 36 ch-7 sps)*

Rnds 24–25: *Shell, ch 2, dc in last dc of shell, ch 2, dc in next dc, ch 2, block, ch 7, (sc in next ch sp, ch 7) across to next block, skip next 3 dc, block, ch 2, dc in next dc, ch 2, dc in first dc of next shell, ch 2; repeat from * around, join. *(At end of last rnd, 6 shells, 48 ch-7 sps.)*

Rnd 26: *Shell, ch 2, dc in next dc, ch 2, block, ch 7, (sc in next ch sp, ch 7) 8 times, skip next 3 dc, block, ch 2, dc in next dc, ch 2; repeat from * around, join. *(6 shells, 12 blocks, 12 dc, 54 ch-7 sps)*

Rnd 27: *Shell, ch 2, block, ch 7, (sc in next ch sp, ch 7) 9 times, skip next 3 dc, block, ch 2; repeat from * around, join. *(60 ch-7 sps)*

Rnd 28: Sl st across to first ch sp, (sl st, ch 6, 4 dc) in ch sp, skip next 3 dc of shell, block, ch 7, (sc in next ch sp, ch 7) 10 times, skip next 3 dc, block, *shell, skip next 3 dc of shell, block, ch 7, (sc in next ch sp, ch 7) 10 times, skip next 3 dc, block; repeat from * around, ending with 3 dc in ch sp of first shell, join with sl st in third ch of ch-6. *(66 ch-7 sps)*

Rnd 29: (Sl st, ch 11, tr) in next ch sp, ch 7, skip next block, **V st** *(see Special Stitches)* in next ch-7 sp, (ch 7, skip next ch-7 sp, V st in next ch-7 sp) 5 times, ch 7, skip next block, *V st in next shell, ch 7, skip next block, V st in next ch-7 sp, (ch 7, skip next ch-7 sp, V st in next ch-7 sp) 5 times, ch 7, skip next block; repeat from * around, join with sl st in fourth ch of ch-11. *(Ch-11 and tr count as V st—42 V sts, 42 ch-7 sps)*

NOTE: *In rnds 30–65, work beg shell for first shell of each rnd.*

Rnd 30: (Sl st in next 2 chs, shell) in first V st, *[ch 3, picot in fourth ch of next ch-7 sp, ch 3, (shell in next V st, ch 3, picot in fourth ch of next ch-7 sp, ch 3) 6 times], (shell, ch 3, 4 dc) in next ch-7 sp; repeat from * 4 more times; repeat between [ ], 4 dc in same V st as first shell, ch 3, join with sl st in top of first ch-3. *(42 shells, 90 ch-3 sps, 24 dc)*

Rnd 31: *(Shell, ch 7, skip next 2 ch-3 sps) 7 times, shell in next ch-3 sp, ch 1; repeat from * around, join with sl st in top of ch-3. *(48 shells, 6 ch-1 sps, 42 ch-7 sps)*

Rnd 32: *(Shell, ch 3, picot in fourth ch of next ch-7 sp, ch 3) 7 times, shell, ch 3, sc in next ch-1 sp, ch 3; repeat from * around, join.

Rnd 33: *(Shell, ch 7, skip next 2 ch-3 sps) 7 times, shell, ch 3, skip next ch sp, dc in next sc, ch 3, skip next ch sp; repeat from * around, join. *(54 ch sps)*

Rnd 34: *(Shell, ch 3, picot in fourth ch of next ch-7 sp, ch 3) 7 times, shell, ch 3, picot in next dc, ch 3; repeat from * around, join. *(96 ch sps)*

Rnd 35: (Shell, ch 7, skip next 2 ch sps) around, join. *(48 ch sps)*

Rnd 36: (Shell, ch 4, picot in fourth ch of next ch-7 sp, ch 4) around, join.

Rnd 37: (Shell, ch 9, skip next 2 ch sps) around, join.

Rnd 38: (Shell, ch 5, picot in fifth ch of next ch-9 sp, ch 5) around, join.

Rnd 39: (Shell, ch 11, skip next 2 ch sps) around, join.

Rnd 40: (Shell, ch 5, picot in sixth ch of next ch-11 sp, ch 5) around, join.

Rnds 41–46: Repeat rnds 39 and 40 alternately.

Rnd 47: (Shell, ch 13, skip next 2 ch sps) around, join.

Rnd 48: (Shell, ch 7, picot in seventh ch of next ch-13 sp, ch 7) around, join.

Rnd 49: *(Shell, ch 13, skip next 2 ch sps, (dc, ch 5, dc) in next shell, ch 13, skip next 2 ch sps; repeat from * around, join. *(24 shells, 24 ch-5 sps)*

Rnd 50: (Shell, ch 6, picot in seventh ch of next ch-13 sp, ch 6, 9 dc in next ch-5 sp, ch 6, picot in seventh ch of next ch-13 sp, ch 6) around, join. *(24 shells, 216 dc)*

Rnd 51: *Shell, ch 11, skip next 2 ch sps, dc in next dc, (ch 1, dc in next dc) 8 times, ch 11, skip next 2 ch sps; repeat from * around, join.

Rnd 52: *Shell, ch 5, picot in sixth ch of next ch-11 sp, ch 5, dc in next dc, (ch 2, dc in next dc) 8 times, ch 5, picot in sixth ch of next ch-11 sp, ch 5; repeat from * around, join.

Rnd 53: *Shell, ch 9, skip next 2 ch sps, dc in next dc, (ch 3, dc in next dc) 8 times, ch 9, skip next 2 ch sps; repeat from * around, join. *(192 ch-3 sps)*

Rnd 54: *(Shell, ch 3, 4 dc) in next shell, ch 5, picot in fifth ch of next ch-9 sp, ch 5, picot, (ch 5, picot) 7 times, ch 5, picot in fifth ch of next ch-9 sp, ch 5; repeat from * around, join. *(24 shells, 24 ch-3 sps, 96 dc, 264 ch-5 sps)*

Rnd 55: *(Shell, ch 1, shell) in next ch-3 sp, ch 7, skip next 2 ch sps, picot, (ch 5, picot) 6 times, ch 7, skip next 2 ch sps; repeat from * around, join. *(48 shells, 24 ch-1 sps, 144 ch-5 sps)*

Rnd 56: *Shell, ch 2, dc in next ch-1 sp, ch 2, shell, ch 7, skip next ch sp, picot, (ch 5, picot) 5 times, ch 7, skip next ch sp; repeat from * around, join. *(24 dc, 120 ch-5 sps)*

Rnd 57: *Shell, ch 2, dc in last dc of shell, ch 2, dc in next dc, ch 2, dc in first dc of next shell, ch 2, shell, ch 7, skip next ch sp, picot, (ch 5, picot) 4 times, ch 7, skip next ch sp; repeat from * around, join. *(72 dc, 96 ch-5 sps)*

Rnd 58: *Shell, ch 2, dc in last dc of shell, ch 2, dc in next dc, ch 2, 4 dc in next dc, ch 2, dc in next dc, ch 2, dc in first dc of next shell, ch 2, shell, ch 7, skip next ch sp, picot, (ch 5, picot) 3 times, ch 7, skip next ch sp; repeat from * around, join. *(192 dc, 72 ch-5 sps)*

Rnd 59: *Shell, ch 2, dc in last dc of shell, ch 2, dc in next dc, ch 2, skip next ch sp, block, ch 2, skip next 2 dc, block, ch 2, dc in next dc, ch 2, dc in first dc of next shell, ch 2, shell, ch 7, skip next ch sp, picot, (ch 5, picot) 2 times, ch 7, skip next ch sp; repeat from * around, join. *(96 dc, 48 blocks, 48 ch-5 sps)*

Rnd 60: (Shell, ch 2, dc in last dc of shell, ch 2, dc in next dc, ch 2, skip next ch sp, block, ch 7, sc in next ch-2 sp, ch 7, skip next 3 dc, block, ch 2, dc in next dc, ch 2, dc in first dc of next shell, ch 2, shell, ch 7, skip next ch sp, picot, ch 5, picot, ch 7, skip next ch sp) around, join. *(96 ch-7 sps, 24 ch-5 sps)*

Rnd 61: *Shell, ch 2, dc in last dc of shell, ch 2, dc in next dc, ch 2, skip next ch sp, block, ch 7, (sc in next ch sp, ch 7) 2 times, skip next 3 dc, block, ch 2, dc in next dc, ch 2, dc in first dc of next shell, ch 2, shell, ch 7, skip next ch sp, picot, ch 7, skip next ch sp; repeat from * round, join. *(120 ch-7 sps)*

Rnd 62: *Shell, ch 2, dc in last dc of shell, ch 2, dc in next dc, ch 2, skip next ch sp, block, ch 7, (sc in next ch sp, ch 7) 3 times, skip next 3 dc, block, ch 2, dc in next dc, ch 2, dc in first dc of next shell, ch 2, shell, ch 7, skip next 2 ch sps; repeat from * around, join.

Rnd 63: *Shell, ch 2, dc in last dc of shell, ch 2, dc in next dc, ch 2, skip next ch sp, block, ch 7, (sc in next ch sp, ch 7) 4 times, skip next 3 dc, block, ch 2, dc in next dc, ch 2, dc in first dc of next shell, ch 2, shell, ch 4, skip next ch sp; repeat from * around, join.

Rnd 64: *Shell, ch 2, dc in last dc of shell, ch 2, dc in next dc, ch 2, skip next ch sp, block, (ch 7, sc in next ch sp) 2 times, ch 3, 9 dc in next ch sp, ch 3, (sc in next ch sp, ch 7) 2 times, skip next 3 dc, block, ch 2, dc in next dc, ch 2, dc in first dc of next shell, ch 2, shell, ch 4, skip next ch sp; repeat from * around, join. *(312 dc, 96 ch-7 sps)*

Rnd 65: *Shell, ch 2, dc in last dc of shell, ch 2, dc in next dc, ch 2, skip next ch sp, block, (ch 7, sc in next ch sp) 2 times, ch 4, dc in next dc, (ch 1, dc in next dc) 8 times, ch 4, (sc in next ch sp, ch 7) 2 times, skip next 3 dc, block, ch 2, dc in next dc, ch 2, dc in first dc of next shell, ch 2, shell, ch 1, skip next ch sp; repeat from * around, join.

Rnd 66: Sl st across to first ch sp, ch 3, 3 dc in ch sp of first shell, ch 2, dc in last dc of same shell as last dc made, ch 2, dc in next dc, ch 2, skip next ch sp, block, (ch 7, sc in next ch sp) 2 times, ch 5, dc in next dc, (ch 2, dc in next dc) 8 times, ch 5, (sc in next ch sp, ch 7) 2 times, skip next 3 dc, block, ch 2, dc in next dc, ch 2, dc in first dc of next shell, ch 2, 4 dc in same shell as last dc made, *ch 3, skip next ch sp, 4 dc in ch sp of next shell, ch 2, dc in last dc of same shell as last dc made, ch 2, dc in next dc, ch 2, skip next ch sp, block, (ch 7, sc in next ch sp) 2 times, ch 5, dc in next dc, (ch 2, dc in next dc) 8 times, ch 5, (sc in next ch sp, ch 7) 2 times, skip next 3 dc, block, ch 2, dc in next dc, ch 2, dc in first dc of next shell, ch 2, 4 dc in same shell as last dc made; repeat from * around, join with dc in

Continued on page 24

9

Pineapple Passion

Pineapple Basket

Designed by Nancy Weddle

Finished Size: 8½" tall including Handle.

Materials:
- ❒ 200 yds. white size 10 crochet cotton thread
- ❒ Fabric stiffener
- ❒ Plastic wrap
- ❒ 1 yd. ⅜" ribbon
- ❒ Sewing needle and thread
- ❒ Rust-proof straight pins
- ❒ No. 8 steel hook or hook needed to obtain gauge

Gauge: 8 dc = 1"; 4 dc rnds = 1".

Basic Stitches: Ch, sl st, sc, dc, tr.

Special Stitches:
For **beginning dc shell (beg dc shell),** sl st in next st, (sl st, ch 3, dc, ch 3, 2 dc) in first ch sp.
For **dc shell,** (2 dc, ch 3, 2 dc) in next st or ch sp.
For **beginning double shell (beg dbl shell),** sl st in next st, (sl st, ch 3, dc, ch 3, 2 dc, ch 3, 2 dc) in first ch sp.

For **double shell (dbl shell),** (2 dc, ch 3, 2 dc, ch 3, 2 dc) in ch sp of next shell.

For **beginning treble shell (beg tr shell),** sl st in next st, (sl st, ch 4, tr, ch 3, 2 tr) in first ch sp.

For **treble shell (tr shell),** (2 tr, ch 3, 2 tr) in next ch sp.

BASKET

Rnd 1: Starting at bottom, ch 6, sl st in first ch to form ring, ch 3, 11 dc in ring, join with sl st in top of ch-3. *(12 dc made)*

Rnd 2: (Ch 3, dc) in first st, 2 dc in each st around, join. *(24)*

Rnd 3: Ch 3, 2 dc in next st, (dc in next st, 2 dc in next st) around, join. *(36)*

Rnd 4: Ch 3, dc in next st, 2 dc in next st, (dc in each of next 2 sts, 2 dc in next st) around, join. *(48)*

Rnd 5: Ch 3, dc in each of next 2 sts, 2 dc in next st, (dc in each of next 3 sts, 2 dc in next st) around, join. *(60)*

Rnd 6: Working this rnd in **back lps** *(see Stitch Guide),* ch 3, dc in each st around, join.

Rnd 7: (Ch 3, dc, ch 3, 2 dc) in first st *(first dc shell made),* ch 3, skip next 4 sts, (dc, ch 5, dc) in next st, ch 3, skip next 4 sts, ***dc shell** *(see Special Stitches)* in next st, ch 3, skip next 4 sts, (dc, ch 5, dc) in next st, ch 3, skip next 4 sts; repeat from * around, join. *(6 dc shells, 6 ch-5 sps)*

Rnd 8: Beg dc shell *(see Special Stitches),* ch 3, 11 tr in next ch-5 sp, ch 3, (dc shell in ch sp of next dc shell, ch 3, 11 tr in next ch-5 sp, ch 3) around, join. *(6 dc shells, 66 tr)*

Rnd 9: Beg dc shell, ch 3, dc in next st, (ch 1, dc in next st) 10 times, ch 3, *dc shell in ch sp of next dc shell, ch 3, dc in next st, (ch 1, dc in next st) 10 times, ch 3; repeat from * around, join. *(6 dc shells, 60 ch-1 sps)*

Rnd 10: Beg dc shell, ch 3, skip first ch-3 sp; to start first pineapple, (sc in next ch-1 sp, ch 3) 10 times, skip next ch-3 sp, *dc shell in ch sp of next dc shell, ch 3, skip next ch-3 sp; to start next pineapple, (sc in next ch-1 sp, ch 3) 10 times; skip next ch-3 sp; repeat from * around, join. *(6 dc shells, 6 pineapples)*

Rnd 11: Beg dc shell, ch 3, skip ch-3 sp, (sc in next ch-3 sp, ch 3) 9 times, skip next ch-3 sp, *dc shell in ch sp of next dc shell, ch 3, skip next ch-3 sp, (sc in next ch-3 sp, ch 3) 9 times, skip next ch-3 sp; repeat from * around, join.

Rnd 12: Beg dbl shell *(see Special Stitches),* ch 3, skip next ch-3 sp, (sc in next ch-3 sp, ch 3) 8 times, skip next ch-3 sp, ***dbl shell** *(see Special Stitches),* ch 3, skip next ch-3 sp, (sc in next ch-3 sp, ch 3) 8 times, skip next ch-3 sp; repeat from * around, join, **turn.** Fasten off.

Row 13: For **first point,** join with sl st in second ch sp of first dbl shell next to pineapple, ch 5, dc shell in same ch sp as sl st, ch 3, skip next ch-3 sp, (sc in next ch-3 sp, ch 3) 7 times, skip next ch-3 sp, dc shell in next ch sp of next dbl shell, turn.

Row 14: Ch 5, dc shell, ch 3, skip next ch-3 sp, (sc in next ch-3 sp, ch 3) 6 times, skip next ch-3 sp, dc shell, turn.

Row 15: Ch 5, dc shell, ch 3, skip next ch-3 sp, (sc in next ch-3 sp, ch 3) 5 times, skip next ch-3 sp, dc shell, turn.

Row 16: Ch 5, dc shell, ch 3, skip next ch-3 sp, (sc in next ch-3 sp, ch 3) 4 times, skip next ch-3 sp, dc shell, turn.

Row 17: Ch 5, dc shell, ch 3, skip next ch-3 sp, (sc in next ch-3 sp, ch 3) 3 times, skip next ch-3 sp, dc shell, turn.

Row 18: Ch 5, dc shell, ch 3, skip next ch-3 sp, (sc in next ch-3 sp, ch 3) 2 times, skip next ch-3 sp, dc shell, turn.

Row 19: Ch 5, dc shell, ch 3, skip next ch-3 sp, sc in next ch-3 sp, ch 3, 2 dc in ch sp of next dc shell, ch 1, sl st in ch sp of last dc shell made, ch 1, 2 dc in same ch sp as last dc made, ch 3, sl st in last dc of dc shell on row below. Fasten off.

Rows 13–19: For **remaining points,** repeat rows 13-19 of first point around, for a total of six points.

Rnd 20: For **Edging,** working in ch sps made on points, join with sc in ch sp on any row, ch 5, sc in same ch sp, ch 5, *(sc, ch 5, sc) in next ch sp, ch 5; repeat from * around, join with sl st in first sc. Fasten off.

BASE

Rnd 1: Join with sc in any **front lp** on rnd 5, ch 3, skip next st, (sc in next st, ch 3, skip next st) around, join with sl st in first sc. *(30 ch sps made)*

Rnd 2: (Sl st, ch 4, tr, ch 3, 2 tr) in first ch sp *(first tr shell made),* ch 3, sc in next ch sp, ch 3, ***tr shell** *(see Special Stitches),* ch 3, sc in next ch sp, ch 3; repeat from * around, join with sl st in top of ch-4. *(15 tr shells)*

Rnd 3: Beg tr shell *(see Special Stitches),* ch 4, (tr shell in ch sp of next tr shell, ch 4) around, join.

Rnd 4: Sl st in next st, (sc, ch 5, sc) in ch sp of first tr shell, ch 5, *(sc, ch 5, sc) in ch sp of next tr shell, ch 5; repeat from * around, join with sl st in first sc. Fasten off.

HANDLE

Row 1: Ch 8, sl st in first ch to form ring, ch 5, work 2 dc shells in ring, turn. *(2 dc shells, 1 ch-5 sp)*

Rows 2–34: Ch 5, dc shell in ch sp of next 2 dc shells, turn.

Row 35: Ch 5, 2 dc in ch sp of first dc shell, ch 3, 2 dc in ch sp of next dc shell, ch 3, sl st in top of ch 5 on last row. Fasten off.

FINISHING

Apply fabric stiffener to Basket and Handle according to manufacturer's instructions. Squeeze out excess liquid. Place plastic wrap and crochet Basket over bowls to form shape needed for Basket and Base. Place plastic wrap and crochet Handle on flat surface; pin to shape. Let items dry completely. Remove pins and plastic wrap.

Cut a 13" piece of ribbon. Weave ribbon through spaces between shells on Handle. With sewing needle and thread, sew ends of ribbon to each end on Handle.

Cut remaining ribbon in half.

Place one end of Handle to inside of Basket over shell on rnd 12 between two pineapples, insert ribbon between shell and pineapple on Basket, through ch-5 sp at end of row 1 on Handle and back through ch sp of shell on opposite end of row 1, and out between next shell and pineapple on Basket. Tie ends in bow. Repeat on opposite end of Handle. ❏❏

Pineapple Perfection

Pineapple Angel Designed by Delsie Rhoades
Table Topper Designed by Karon Brown

Pineapple Angel

Photo on page 13

Finished Size: 12¼" tall including Crown.

Materials:
- ❏ 400 yds. cream size 10 crochet cotton thread
- ❏ 3 medium satin ribbon roses
- ❏ 2 large satin ribbon roses
- ❏ 7" pearl 3-mm bead trim
- ❏ Pearl stamens
- ❏ 6" × 16" piece netting
- ❏ 3" of ¾"-wide lace
- ❏ 1 yd. of ⅛" satin ribbon
- ❏ 6" × 12" Styrofoam® cone *(if unable to find size needed, purchase a larger size and cut top to size needed)*
- ❏ 4" square of 1¼"-thick Styrofoam®
- ❏ Rust-proof straight pins
- ❏ Polyester fiberfill
- ❏ Plastic wrap
- ❏ 5 drinking straws
- ❏ Graph paper
- ❏ Fabric stiffener
- ❏ Glue gun
- ❏ Translucent pearl glaze spray
- ❏ No. 7 steel hook or hook needed to obtain gauge

Gauges: 9 sc = 1"; 9 sc rows = 1"; 1 shell, ch sp, 1 shell = 1"; 3 shell rows = 1".

Basic Stitches: Ch, sl st, sc, dc, tr.

Special Stitches:
For **shell**, (2 dc, ch 1, 2 dc) in st specified.
For **beginning shell (beg shell)**, sl st across to first ch sp, (sl st, ch 3, dc, ch 1, 2 dc) in first ch sp.
For **picot**, ch 3, sl st in third ch from hook.
For **double shell (dbl shell)**, (2 dc, ch 1, 2 dc, ch 1, 2 dc) in next ch sp.
For **V st**, (dc, ch 3, dc) in next ch sp.
For **beginning picot shell (beg picot shell)**, (sl st, ch 3, dc, picot, 2 dc) in first ch sp.
For **picot shell**, (2 dc, picot, 2 dc) in next ch sp.

HEAD & BODICE
Rnd 1: Starting at top of Head, ch 5, sl st in first ch to form ring, ch 1, 10 sc in ring, join with sl st in first sc. *(10 sc made)*

Rnd 2: Ch 1, 2 sc in each sc around, join. *(20 sc)*

Rnd 3: Ch 1, sc in first sc, 2 sc in next sc, (sc in next sc, 2 sc in next sc) around, join. *(30 sc)*

Rnds 4–12: Ch 1, sc in each sc around, join.

Rnd 13: Ch 1, sc in first sc, sc next 2 sc tog, (sc in next sc, sc next 2 sc tog) around, join. *(20 sc)*

Rnd 14: Ch 1, sc in each sc around, join.

Rnd 15: Ch 1, sc in each of first 3 sc, sc next 2 sc tog, (sc in each of next 3 sc, sc next 2 sc tog) around, join. *(16 sc)*

Rnd 16: Ch 1, sc in each sc around, join.

Rnd 17: For **Neck**, (ch 4, tr) in first sc, 2 tr in each sc around, join with sl st in top of ch-4. *(32 tr)*

Rnd 18: For **Bodice**, (ch 3, dc, ch 1, 2 dc) in first tr, ch 1, skip next 3 tr, *shell (see Special Stitches) in next tr, ch 1, skip next 3 tr; repeat from * around, join with sl st in top of ch-3. *(8 shells, 8 ch sps)*

Rnd 19: **Beg shell** *(see Special Stitches)* in ch sp of first shell, ch 2, skip next ch-1 sp, *V st *(see Special Stitches)* in ch sp of next shell, ch 2, shell in ch sp of next shell, ch 2, skip next ch-1 sp; repeat from * around, join. *(4 shells, 4 V sts)*

Rnd 20: Beg shell in ch sp of first shell, ch 2, skip next ch-2 sp, 5 dc in ch sp of next V st, ch 2, skip next ch-2 sp, (shell in ch sp of next shell, ch 2, skip next ch-2 sp; to start next pineapple, 5 dc in ch sp of next V st; ch 2, skip next ch-2 sp) around, join. *(4 shells, 4 pineapple groups)*

Rnd 21: Beg shell in first shell, ch 2, skip next ch-2 sp; working across pineapple, dc in next dc, (ch 1, dc in next dc) 4 times; ch 2, skip next ch-2 sp, *shell in next shell, ch 2, skip next ch-2 sp; working across pineapple, dc in next dc, (ch 1, dc in next dc) 4 times; ch 2, skip next ch-2 sp; repeat from * around, join. *(4 shells, 4 pineapple groups)*

Rnd 22: (Beg shell, ch 1, 2 dc) in first shell *(first dbl shell made)*, *[ch 2, skip next ch-2 sp; working across pineapple, (sc in next ch-1 sp, ch 3) 3 times, sc in next ch-1 sp, ch 2, skip next ch-2 sp], **dbl shell** *(see Special Stitches)* in next shell; repeat from * 2 more times; repeat between [ ], join. *(4 dbl shells, 4 pineapples)*

Rnd 23: Beg shell in ch sp of first dbl shell, *[shell in next ch-1 sp of same dbl shell, ch 2, skip next ch-2 sp; working across pineapple, (sc in next ch-3 sp, ch 3) 2 times, sc in next ch-3 sp, ch 2, skip next ch-2 sp], shell in ch sp of next dbl shell; repeat from * 2 more times; repeat between [ ], join. *(8 shells, 4 pineapples)*

Rnd 24: Beg shell in first shell, (*ch 1, shell in ch sp of next shell, ch 2, skip next ch-2 sp; working across pineapple, sc in next ch-3 sp, ch 3, sc in next ch-3 sp, ch 2, skip next ch-2 sp*, shell in next shell) 3 times; repeat between first *, join.

Rnd 25: Beg shell in first shell, (*shell in next ch-1 sp, shell in next shell, ch 3, skip next ch-2 sp; working across pineapple, sc in next ch-3 sp, ch 3, skip next ch-2 sp*, shell in next shell) 3 times; repeat between first *, join. *(12 shells, 4 pineapples)*

Rnd 26: Beg shell in first shell, (*ch 1, dbl shell in ch sp of next shell, ch 1, shell in next shell, ch 1, skip next ch-3 sp, tr in next sc, ch 1, skip next ch-3 sp*, shell in next shell) 3 times; repeat between first *, join.

Rnd 27: Beg shell in first shell, (*ch 1, skip next ch-1 sp, shell in ch-1 sp of next dbl shell, shell in ch-1 sp of same dbl shell, ch 1, skip next ch-1 sp, shell in next shell, ch 1, skip next ch-1 sp, next tr and next ch-1 sp*, shell in next shell) 3 times; repeat between first *, join. *(16 shells)*

Rnd 28: Sl st across to first ch sp, beg picot shell *(see Special Stitches)* in first shell, *[ch 2, skip next ch-1 sp, picot shell *(see Special Stitches)* in next shell, ch 2, picot shell in next shell, ch 2, skip next ch-1 sp, picot shell in next shell, ch 2, skip next ch-1 sp], picot shell in next shell; repeat from * 2 more times; repeat between [ ], join. Fasten off.

SKIRT
Rnd 1: Starting at top, ch 10, sl st in first ch to form

ring, ch 3, 11 dc in ring, join with sl st in top of ch-3. *(12 dc made)*

Rnd 2: (Ch 3, dc) in first dc, 2 dc in each dc around, join. *(24 dc)*

Rnd 3: (Ch 3, dc, ch 1, 2 dc) in first dc *(first shell made)*, (skip next 2 dc, shell in next dc) 7 times, skip last 2 sts, join. *(8 shells)*

Rnds 4–6: Beg shell in ch sp of first shell, shell in ch sp of each shell around, join.

Rnd 7: Beg shell in first shell, ch 1, V st in next shell, ch 1, (shell in next shell, ch 1, V st in next shell, ch 1) around, join. *(4 shells, 4 V sts)*

Rnd 8: Beg shell in first shell, (*ch 1, skip next ch-1 sp; to start next pineapple, 5 dc in ch sp of next V st; ch 1, skip next ch-1 sp*, shell in next shell) 3 times; repeat between first *, join. *(4 shells, 4 pineapples)*

Rnd 9: Beg shell in first shell, *[ch 1, skip next ch-1 sp; working across pineapple, dc in next dc, (ch 1, dc in next dc) 4 times, ch 1, skip next ch-1 sp], shell in next shell; repeat from * 2 more times; repeat between [ ], join. *(4 shell, 4 pineapples)*

Rnd 10: Beg shell in first shell, *[ch 2, skip next ch-1 sp; working across pineapple, (sc in next ch-1 sp, ch 3) 3 times, sc in next ch-1 sp, ch 2, skip next ch-1 sp], shell in next shell; repeat from * 2 more times; repeat between [ ], join.

Rnd 11: (Beg shell, ch 1, 2 dc) in first shell *(first dbl shell made)*, *[ch 2, skip next ch-2 sp; working across pineapple, (sc in next ch-3 sp, ch 3) 2 times, sc in next ch-3 sp, ch 2, skip next ch-2 sp], dbl shell in next shell; repeat from * 2 more times; repeat between [ ], join. *(4 dbl shells, 4 pineapples)*

Rnd 12: Beg shell in ch sp of first dbl shell, (*ch 1, shell in next ch sp of same dbl shell, ch 2, skip next ch-2 sp; working across pineapple, sc in next ch-3 sp, ch 3, sc in next ch-3 sp, ch 2, skip next ch-2 sp*, shell in ch sp of next dbl shell) 3 times; repeat between first *, join. *(8 shells, 4 pineapples)*

Rnd 13: Beg shell in first shell, (*ch 1, V st in next ch-1 sp, ch 1, shell in next shell, skip next ch-2 sp; working across pineapple, tr in next ch-3 sp, skip next ch-2 sp*, shell in next shell) 3 times; repeat between first *, join. *(8 shell, 4 V sts)*

Rnd 14: Sl st across to first ch sp, (sl st, ch 3, dc) in first shell, (*ch 2, skip next ch-1 sp; to start next pineapple, 7 dc in ch sp of next V st; ch 2, skip next ch-1 sp, 2 dc in next shell, ch 1, skip next tr*, 2 dc in next shell) 3 times; repeat between first *, join. *(eight 2-dc groups, 4 pineapples, 8 ch-2 sps, 4 ch-1 sps)*

Rnd 15: Sl st back into ch-1 sp, (ch 3, dc, ch 1, 2 dc) in same ch sp *(first shell made)*, ch 2, skip first 2 dc and next ch-2 sp; *[working across pineapple, dc in next dc, (ch 1, dc in next dc) 6 times, ch 2, skip next ch-2 sp and next 2 dc], shell in next ch-1 sp, ch 2, skip next 2 dc and next ch-2 sp; repeat from * 2 more times; repeat between [ ], join. *(4 shells, 4 pineapples)*

Rnd 16: Beg shell in first shell, *[ch 3, skip next ch-2 sp; working across pineapple, (sc in next ch-1 sp, ch 3) 6 times, skip next ch-2 sp], shell in next shell; repeat from * 2 more times; repeat between [ ], join.

Rnd 17: Beg shell in first shell, *[ch 3, skip next ch-3 sp; working across pineapple, (sc in next ch-3 sp, ch 3) 5 times, skip next ch-3 sp], shell in next shell; repeat from * 2 more times; repeat between [ ], join.

Rnd 18: Beg shell in first shell, *[ch 3, skip next ch-3 sp; working across pineapple, (sc in next ch-3 sp, ch 3) 4 times, skip next ch-3 sp], shell in next shell; repeat from * 2 more times; repeat between [ ], join.

Rnd 19: (Beg shell, ch 1, 2 dc) in first shell *(first dbl shell made)*, *[ch 3, skip next ch-3 sp; working across pineapple, (sc in next ch-3 sp, ch 3) 3 times, skip next ch-3 sp], dbl shell in next shell; repeat from * 2 more times; repeat between [ ], join.

Rnd 20: Beg shell in ch sp of first dbl shell, *[ch 1, shell in next ch sp of same dbl shell, ch 3, skip next ch-3 sp; working across pineapple, (sc in next ch-3 sp, ch 3) 2 times, ch 3, skip next ch-3 sp], shell in ch sp of next dbl shell; repeat from * 2 more times; repeat between [ ], join.

Rnd 21: Beg shell in first shell, *[ch 1, V st in next ch-1 sp, ch 1, shell in next shell, ch 3, skip next ch-3 sp; working across pineapple, sc in next ch-3 sp, ch 3, skip next ch-3 sp], shell in next shell; repeat from * 2 more times; repeat between [ ], join. *(8 shells, 4 V sts)*

Rnd 22: Beg shell in first shell, (*ch 2, skip next ch-1 sp; to start next pineapple, 7 dc in ch sp of next V st; ch 2, skip next ch-1 sp, shell in next shell, skip next ch-3 sp, tr in next sc, skip next ch-3 sp*, shell in next shell) 3 times; repeat between first *, join. *(8 shells, 4 pineapples)*

Rnd 23: Sl st across to first ch sp, (sl st, ch 3, dc) in ch sp of first shell, *[ch 2, skip next ch-2 sp; working across pineapple, dc in next dc, (ch 1, dc in next dc) 6 times, ch 2, skip next ch-2 sp, 2 dc in next shell, ch 1], 2 dc in next shell; repeat from * 2 more times; repeat between [ ], join, **turn.** *(eight 2-dc groups, 4 pineapples)*

Rnd 24: Sl st in last ch-1 sp, **turn,** (ch 3, dc, ch 1, 2 dc) in same ch sp *(first shell made)*, ch 3, skip first 2 dc and next ch-2 sp; *[working across pineapple, (sc in next ch-1 sp, ch 3) 6 times, skip next ch-2 sp and next 2 dc], shell in next ch-1 sp, ch 3, skip next 2 dc and next ch-2 sps; repeat from * 2 more times; repeat between [ ], join. *(4 shells, 4 pineapples)*

Rnd 25: Beg shell in first shell, *[ch 3, skip next ch-3 sp; working across pineapple, (sc in next ch-3 sp, ch 3) 5 times, skip next ch-3 sp], shell in next shell; repeat from * 2 more times; repeat between [ ], join.

Rnd 26: Beg shell in first shell, *[ch 3, skip next ch-3 sp; working across pineapple, (sc in next ch-3 sp, ch 3) 4 times, skip next ch-3 sp], shell in next shell; repeat from * 2 more times; repeat between [ ], join.

Rnd 27: (Beg shell, ch 1, 2 dc) in first shell, *[ch 4, skip next ch-3 sp; working across pineapple, (sc in next ch-3 sp, ch 3) 2 times, sc in next ch-3 sp, ch 4, skip next ch-3 sp], dbl shell in next shell; repeat from * 2 more times; repeat between [ ], join.

Rnd 28: Beg shell in ch sp of first dbl shell, (*ch 3, shell in next ch sp of same dbl shell, ch 4, skip next ch-4 sp; working across pineapple, sc in next ch-3 sp, ch 3, sc in next ch-3 sp, ch 4, skip next ch-4 sp*, shell in ch sp of next dbl shell) 3 times; repeat between first *, join. *(8 shells, 4 pineapples)*

Rnd 29: Beg shell in first shell, *[ch 2, tr in last dc of same shell, (ch 2, tr, ch 2, dc, ch 2, tr) in next ch-3 sp, ch 2, tr in first dc of next shell, ch 2, shell in ch sp of same shell, ch 4, skip next ch-4 sp; working across pineapple, sc in next ch-3 sp,

Continued on page 16

15

Pineapple Passion

ch 4, skip next ch-4 sp], shell in next shell; repeat from * 2 more times; repeat between [ ], join. *(8 shells, 16 tr, 4 dc, 4 sc)*

Rnd 30: Beg shell in first shell, *[ch 2, tr in last dc of same shell, (ch 2, skip next ch-2 sp, tr in next tr) 2 times, ch 2, skip next ch-2 sp, dc in next dc, (ch 2, skip next ch-2 sp, tr in next tr) 2 times, ch 2, tr in first dc of next shell, ch 2, shell in ch sp of same shell, skip next ch-4 sp, next sc and next ch-4 sp], shell in next shell; repeat from * 2 more times; repeat between [ ], join. *(8 shells, 24 tr, 4 dc)*

Rnd 31: Sl st across to first ch sp, (sl st, ch 3, dc) in ch sp of first shell, *[ch 2, tr in last dc of same shell, (ch 2, skip next ch-2 sp, tr in next tr) 3 times, ch 2, skip next ch-2 sp, dc in next dc, (ch 2, skip next ch-2 sp, tr in next tr) 3 times, ch 2, skip next ch-2 sp, tr in first dc of next shell, ch 2, 2 dc in ch sp of same shell, ch 1], 2 dc in ch sp of next shell; repeat from * 2 more times; repeat between [ ], join, **turn.**

Rnd 32: Sl st in last ch-1 sp, **turn,** (ch 3, dc, ch 1, 2 dc) in same ch sp *(first shell made),* ch 2, skip first dc, tr in next dc, *(ch 2, skip next ch-2 sp, tr in next tr) 4 times, ch 2, skip next ch-2 sp, dc in next dc, (ch 2, skip next ch-2 sp, tr in next tr) 4 times, ch 2, skip next ch-2 sp, tr in next dc, ch 2, skip next dc, shell in next ch-1 sp, ch 2, skip next dc, tr in next dc; repeat from * 2 more times, (ch 2, skip next ch-2 sp, tr in next tr) 4 times, ch 2, skip next ch-2 sp, dc in next dc, (ch 2, skip next ch-2 sp, tr in next tr) 4 times, ch 2, skip next ch-2 sp, tr in next dc, ch 2, skip last dc, join. *(4 shells, 48 ch sps)*

Rnd 33: For **Hem,** sl st across to first ch sp, beg picot shell in first shell, picot shell in each ch sp and in each shell around, join. Fasten off.

WING *(make 2)*

Row 1: Starting at top, ch 6, (dc, ch 1, 2 dc) in fourth ch from hook *(first shell made),* shell in each of next 2 chs, turn. *(3 shells made)*

Row 2: Beg shell in ch sp of first shell, (ch 2, shell in ch sp of next shell) 2 times, turn.

Row 3: Beg shell in first shell, ch 2, skip next ch-2 sp, dbl shell in next shell, ch 2, skip next ch-2 sp, shell in last shell, turn. *(2 shells, 1 dbl shell)*

Row 4: Beg shell in first shell, ch 2, skip next ch-2 sp, shell in ch sp of next dbl shell, ch 1, shell in next ch sp of same dbl shell, ch 2, skip next ch-2 sp, shell in last shell, turn. *(4 shells)*

Row 5: Beg shell in first shell, ch 2, skip next ch-2 sp, shell in next shell, ch 1, V st in next ch-1 sp, ch 1, shell in next shell, ch 2, shell in last shell, turn. *(4 shells, 1 V st)*

Row 6: Beg shell in first shell, ch 2, skip next ch-2 sp, shell in next shell, ch 1; to start next pineapple, 7 dc in ch sp of next V st; ch 1, shell in next shell, ch 2, shell in last shell, turn. *(4 shells, 1 pineapple)*

Row 7: Beg shell in first shell, ch 2, skip next ch-2 sp, shell in next shell, ch 1, skip next ch-1 sp; working across pineapple, (dc in next dc, ch 1) 7 times, skip next ch-1 sp, shell in next shell, ch 2, skip next ch-2 sp, shell in last shell, turn.

Row 8: Beg shell in first shell, ch 2, skip next ch-

2 sp, shell in next shell, ch 2, skip next ch-1 sp; working across pineapple, (sc in next ch-1 sp, ch 3) 5 times, sc in next ch-1 sp, ch 2, skip next ch-1 sp, shell in next shell, ch 2, skip next ch-2 sp, shell in last shell, turn.

Row 9: Beg shell in first shell, ch 2, skip next ch-2 sp, shell in next shell, ch 3, skip next ch-2 sp; working across pineapple, (sc in next ch-3 sp, ch 3) 5 times, skip next ch-2 sp, shell in next shell, ch 2, skip next ch-2 sp, shell in last shell, turn.

Row 10: Beg shell in first shell, ch 2, skip next ch-2 sp, shell in next shell, ch 3, skip next ch-3 sp; working across pineapple, (sc in next ch-3 sp, ch 3) 4 times, skip next ch-3 sp, shell in next shell, ch 2, skip next ch-2 sp, shell in last shell, turn.

Row 11: Beg shell in first shell, ch 2, skip next ch-2 sp, dbl shell in next shell, ch 3, skip next ch-3 sp; working across pineapple, (sc in next ch-3 sp, ch 3) 3 times, skip next ch-3 sp, dbl shell in next shell, ch 2, skip next ch-2 sp, shell in last shell, turn. *(2 shells, 2 dbl shells, 1 pineapple)*

Row 12: Beg shell in first shell, ch 2, skip next ch-2 sp, shell in ch sp of next dbl shell, ch 1, shell in next ch sp on same dbl shell, ch 3, skip next ch-3 sp; working across pineapple, (sc in next ch-3 sp, ch 3) 2 times, skip next ch-3 sp, shell in ch sp of next dbl shell, ch 1, shell in next ch sp on same dbl shell, ch 2, skip next ch-2 sp, shell in last shell, turn. *(6 shells, 1 pineapple)*

Row 13: Beg shell in first shell, ch 2, skip next ch-2 sp, shell in next shell, ch 2, skip next ch-1 sp, shell in next shell, ch 3, skip next ch-3 sp; working across pineapple, sc in next ch-3 sp, ch 3, skip next ch-3 sp, shell in next shell, ch 2, skip next ch-1 sp, shell in next shell, ch 2, skip next ch-2 sp, shell in last shell, turn.

Row 14: Beg shell in first shell, ch 2, skip next ch-2 sp, shell in next shell, ch 3, skip next ch-2 sp, 2 dc in next shell, ch 1, skip next ch-3 sp, next sc and next ch-3 sp, 2 dc in next shell, ch 3, skip next ch-2 sp, shell in next shell, ch 2, skip next ch-2 sp, shell in last shell, turn. *(4 shells, two 2-dc groups)*

Row 15: Beg shell in first shell, ch 2, skip next ch-2 sp, shell in next shell, ch 3, skip next ch-3 sp and next 2 dc, shell in next ch-1 sp, ch 3, skip next 2 dc and next ch-3 sp, shell in next shell, ch 2, skip next ch-2 sp, shell in last shell, turn. *(5 shells)*

Row 16: Beg shell in first shell, ch 2, skip next ch-2 sp, shell in next shell, ch 2, skip next ch-3 sp, dbl shell in next shell, ch 2, skip next ch-3 sp, shell in next shell, ch 2, skip next ch-2 sp, shell in last shell, turn. *(4 shells, 1 dbl shell)*

Row 17: Beg shell in first shell, ch 2, skip next ch-2 sp, shell in next shell, skip next ch-2 sp, shell in ch sp of next dbl shell, ch 1, shell in next ch sp of same dbl shell, skip next ch-2 sp, shell in next shell, skip next ch-2 sp, shell in last shell, turn. *(6 shells)*

Row 18: Beg shell in first shell, ch 2, skip next ch-2 sp, shell in next shell, 2 dc in next shell, ch 1, V st in next ch-1 sp, ch 1, 2 dc in next shell, shell in next shell, ch 2, skip next ch-2 sp, shell in last shell, turn. *(4 shells, two-2 dc groups, 1 V st)*

Row 19: Beg shell in first shell, ch 2, skip next ch-2 sp, shell in next shell, ch 1, skip next 2 dc and next ch-1 sp; to start next pineapple, 7 dc in ch sp of next V st; ch 1, skip next ch-1 sp and next 2 dc, shell in next shell, ch 2, shell in last shell, turn. *(4 shells, 1 pineapple)*

Rows 20–26: Repeat rows 7-13.

Row 27: Beg shell in first shell, ch 2, skip next ch-2 sp, shell in next shell, ch 3, skip next ch-2 sp, shell in next shell, skip next ch-3 sp, shell in next shell, ch 3, skip next ch-2 sp, shell in next shell, ch 2, skip next ch-2 sp, shell in last shell, turn.

Row 28: Beg shell in first shell, ch 2, skip next ch-2 sp, shell in next shell, ch 3, skip next ch-3 sp, 2 dc in next shell, ch 1, 2 dc in next shell, ch 3, skip next ch-3 sp, shell in next shell leaving last ch-2 sp and last shell unworked, turn. *(3 shell, two 2-dc groups)*

Row 29: Sl st across to first ch sp, (sl st, ch 3, dc) in first shell, ch 3, skip next ch-3 sp, shell in next ch-1 sp, ch 3, skip next ch-3 sp, shell in next shell, ch 2, shell in last shell, turn. *(3 shells, 2 dc)*

Row 30: Beg shell in first shell, ch 2, skip next ch-2 sp, shell in next shell, ch 3, skip next ch-3 sp, shell in next shell leaving last ch-3 and last 2 dc unworked, turn. *(3 shells)*

Row 31: Sl st across to first ch sp, (sl st, ch 3, dc) in first shell, ch 3, skip next ch-3 sp, shell in next shell, ch 2, skip next ch-2 sp, shell in last shell, turn. *(2 shells, 2 dc)*

Row 32: Beg shell in first shell, ch 2, skip next ch-2 sp, shell in last shell leaving last ch-3 sp and last 2 dc unworked, turn. *(2 shells)*

Row 33: Sl st across to first ch sp, (sl st, ch 3, dc) in first shell, ch 2, skip ch-2 sp, shell in last shell, turn. *(1 shell, 2 dc)*

Row 34: Beg shell in first shell, ch 5, skip next ch-2 sp and next dc, sl st in top of ch-3 on row 33, ch 1, work 2 dc in worked ch sp at beginning of row 33, ch 5, skip next unworked ch-3 sp and next sc on row 31, sl st in top of ch-3 at beginning of row 31, ch 1, work 2 dc in worked ch sp at beginning of row 31, ch 5, skip next ch-3 sp and next dc on row 29, sl st in top of ch-3 on row 29, ch 1, work 2 dc in worked ch sp at beginning of row 29, ch 5, skip next ch-2 sp on row 27, shell in unworked shell on row 27, turn. *(2 shells, 7 ch sps)*

Row 35: beg picot shell in first shell, picot shell in each ch sp and in each shell across. Fasten off.

FINISHING

1: Using crocheted Head & Bodice as pattern, trace and cut Bodice from graph paper; place graph paper over 4" square Styrofoam and cut to shape needed to fit inside of Bodice.

2: Stuff Head with fiberfill. Stiffen Head & Bodice with fabric stiffener according to manufacturer's directions, squeeze out excess liquid. Place Head & Bodice over shaped Styrofoam covered with plastic wrap; tie a separate piece of crochet thread around Neck. Shape and let dry completely. Remove crochet thread from Neck when dried.

3: Dampen Skirt with fabric stiffener, squeeze out any excess liquid. Place Skirt over Styrofoam cone covered with plastic wrap. Trim any excess Styrofoam off. Shape hem with wads of plastic wrap and let dry completely.

4: Place graph paper on a padded surface, cover paper and surface with plastic wrap. Dampen Wings with fabric stiffener, squeeze out any excess liquid. Using

lines on graph paper as a guide, pin and shape Wings. Let dry completely.

5: For **Hair,** cut 30 strands from crochet cotton, each 9" long. Separate strands into nine equal sections. Fold each section in half and tie a separate small length of crochet thread around fold of each section. Dip one section at a time into fabric stiffener, squeeze out excess liquid and wrap evenly around half of straw; if needed, pin strands in place with a bobby pin. Repeat with all sections. Let dry completely.

6: Remove Head & Bodice and Skirt from Styrofoam when dried. Fold netting in half, glue center of fold to inside of Neck. Center and glue both sides of Bodice to Skirt 1" from top *(see illustration)* with netting between.

7: Glue Wings on back side of Bodice and Skirt with top of Wings at Head *(see illustration)* for back.

8: Remove Hair from straws and gently separate strands using a crochet hook, pulling slightly to give Hair a bounce. Glue fold of each section of Hair to center top of Head leaving 1" uncovered for front of face.

9: For **Crown,** cut lace to fit snugly around Hair at top of Head. Glue ends of lace together. Dip into fabric stiffener. Shaping lace around a soft drink bottle lid. Let dry completely. Glue inside edge of Crown to top of Head.

10: Bring ends of netting together and glue to center front of Bodice for hands.

11: Make a figure eight out of bead trim *(see illustration),* glue over top of netting with center of beads over hands.

12: For **streamers,** cut two 5" pieces and one 6" piece from ribbon. Arrange 6" ribbon piece between the two 5" pieces, glue ribbon pieces to center of Skirt directly below Bodice under hands and pearls.

13: Make a six-loop bow with remaining ribbon, glue to center of pearls.

14: Cut stems off all ribbon roses. Cut stems off stamens leaving ¼" ends. Arrange and glue roses and stamens to bow *(see illustration).*

15: Optional: Place Angel over Styrofoam cone and spray with glaze. Let dry completely. ❑❑

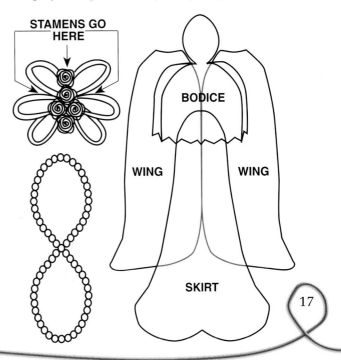

STAMENS GO HERE

BODICE

WING   WING

SKIRT

Table Topper

Photo on pages 12-13

Finished Size: 33" across.

Materials:
- ❑ 1,260 yds. jade size 10 crochet cotton thread
- ❑ No. 9 steel hook or hook needed to obtain gauge

Gauge: Rnds 1–3 = 2½" across.

Basic Stitches: Ch, sl st, sc, dc.

Special Stitches:

For **V st,** (dc, ch 2, dc) in next st or ch sp.

For **double V st (dbl V st),** (dc, ch 2, dc, ch 2, dc, ch 2, dc) in next ch sp.

For **beginning dc group (beg dc group),** (sl st, ch 3, 4 dc) in next dc.

For **dc group,** 5 dc in center dc of next dc group.

For **beginning dc decrease (beg dc dec),** sl st in next dc, ch 2, *yo, insert hook in same dc, yo, pull through dc, yo, pull through 2 lps on hook*, yo, insert hook in center dc of next dc group, yo, pull through dc, yo, pull through 2 lps on hook; repeat between first *, yo, pull through all 4 lps on hook.

For **dc decrease (dc dec),** (yo, insert hook in center dc of next dc group, yo, pull through dc, yo, pull through 2 lps on hook, yo, insert hook in same dc, yo, pull through dc, yo, pull through 2 lps on hook) 2 times, yo, pull through all 5 lps on hook.

For **dc cluster (dc cl),** yo, insert hook in ch sp specified in pattern, yo, pull through ch sp, yo, pull through 2 lps on hook, (yo, insert hook in same ch sp, yo, pull through ch sp, yo, pull through 2 lps on hook) 4 times, yo, pull through all 6 lps on hook.

For **beginning dc cluster (beg dc cl),** sl st in first ch sp, ch 2, (yo, insert hook in same ch sp, yo, pull through ch sp, yo, pull through 2 lps on hook) 4 times, yo, pull through all 5 lps on hook.

TABLE TOPPER

Rnd 1: Ch 10, sl st in first ch to form ring, ch 1, (sc in ring, ch 5) 10 times, join with sl st in first sc. *(10 sc, 10 ch sps made)*

Rnd 2: (Sl st, ch 1, 5 sc) in first ch sp, 5 sc in each ch sp around, join. *(50 sc)*

Rnd 3: Sl st in first 2 sc, (sl st, ch 5, dc) in next sc *(first V st made),* ch 5, *skip next 4 sc, **V st** (see Special Stitches) in next sc, ch 5; repeat from * 8 more times, join with sl st in third ch of ch-5. *(10 V sts, 10 ch sps)*

Rnd 4: (Sl st, ch 5, dc, ch 2, dc, ch 2, dc) in ch sp of first V st *(first dbl V st made),* ch 5, *skip next ch sp, sc in ch sp of next V st, ch 5, skip next ch sp, **dbl V st** (see Special Stitches) in ch sp of next V st, ch 5; repeat from * 3 more times, skip next ch sp, sc in ch sp of next V st, ch 5, skip last ch sp, join. *(5 dbl V sts, 10 ch sps)*

Rnd 5: (Sl st, ch 3, 4 dc) in first ch sp of first dbl V st, *[ch 3, V st in next ch sp of same dbl V st, ch 3, 5 dc in next ch sp of same dbl V st, (ch 5, sc in next ch sp) 2 times, ch 5], 5 dc in next ch sp of next dbl V st; repeat from * 3 more times; repeat between [ ], join with sl st in top of ch-3. *(10 dc groups, 5 V sts, 25 ch sps)*

Rnd 6: Sl st in first 2 dc, beg dc group, ch 3, skip first ch sp; *[to start next pineapple, 8 dc in ch sp of next V st; ch 3, skip next ch sp, dc group, ch 5, skip next ch sp, sc in next ch sp, ch 5, skip next ch sp], dc group, ch 3, skip next ch sp; repeat from * 3 more times; repeat between [ ], join. *(5 pineapples, 10 dc groups, 20 ch sps)*

Rnd 7: Sl st in first 2 dc, beg dc group, ch 3, skip first ch sp; *[working across pineapple, dc in next dc, (ch 1, dc in next dc) 7 times, ch 3, skip next ch sp, dc group, ch 5, (sc in next ch sp, ch 5) 2 times], dc group, ch 3, skip next ch sp; repeat from * 3 more times; repeat between [ ], join.

Rnd 8: Sl st in first 2 dc, beg dc group, ch 3, skip first ch sp; *[working across pineapple, (sc in next ch sp, ch 3) 7 times, skip next ch sp, dc group, ch 5, skip next ch sp, V st in next ch sp, ch 5, skip next ch sp], dc group, ch 3, skip next ch sp; repeat from * 3 more times; repeat between [ ], join.

Rnd 9: Sl st in first 2 dc, beg dc group, ch 3, skip first ch sp; *[working across pineapple, (sc in next ch sp, ch 3) 6 times, skip next ch sp, dc group, ch 5, skip next ch sp, V st in ch sp of next V st, ch 5, skip next ch sp], dc group, ch 3, skip next ch sp; repeat from * 3 more times; repeat between [ ], join.

Rnd 10: Sl st in first 2 dc, beg dc group, ch 3, skip first ch sp; *[working across pineapple, (sc in next ch sp, ch 3) 5 times, skip next ch sp, dc group, ch 5, skip next ch sp, dbl V st in next V st, ch 5, skip next ch sp], dc group, ch 3, skip next ch sp; repeat from * 3 more times; repeat between [ ], join.

Rnd 11: Sl st in first 2 dc, beg dc group, ch 3, skip first ch sp; working across pineapple, (sc in next ch sp, ch 3) 4 times, skip next ch sp, dc group, ch 5, skip next ch sp, 5 dc in first ch sp of first dbl V st, ch 3, V st in next ch sp of same dbl V st, ch 3, 5 dc in next ch sp of same dbl V st, *ch 5, skip next ch sp, dc group, ch 3, skip next ch sp; working across pineapple, (sc in next ch sp, ch 3) 4 times, skip next ch sp, dc group, ch 5, skip next ch sp, 5 dc in first ch sp of next dbl V st, ch 3, V st in next ch sp of same dbl V st, ch 3, 5 dc in next ch sp of same dbl V st; repeat from * 3 more times, ch 5, skip last ch sp, join.

Rnd 12: Sl st in first 2 dc, beg dc group, ch 3, skip first ch sp; *[working across pineapple, (sc in next ch sp, ch 3) 3 times, skip next ch sp, dc group, ch 5, skip next ch sp, dc group, ch 3, skip next ch sp; for next **pineapple,** 8 dc in next ch sp; ch 3, skip next ch sp, dc group, ch 5, skip next ch sp], dc group, ch 3, skip next ch sp; repeat from * 3 more times; repeat between [ ], join.

Rnd 13: Sl st in first 2 dc, beg dc group, ch 3, skip first ch sp; *[working across pineapple, (sc in next ch sp, ch 3) 2 times, skip next ch sp, dc group, ch 5, skip next ch sp, dc group, ch 3; working across next pineapple, dc in next dc, (ch 1, dc in next dc) 7 times, ch 3, skip next ch sp, dc group, ch 5, skip next ch sp], dc group, ch 3, skip next ch sp; repeat from * 3 more times; repeat between [ ], join.

Rnd 14: Sl st in first 2 dc, beg dc group, ch 3, skip first ch sp; *[working across pineapple, sc in next ch sp, ch 3, skip next ch sp, dc group, ch 5, skip next ch sp, dc group, ch 3, skip next ch sp;

working across next pineapple, (sc in next ch sp, ch 3) 7 times, skip next ch sp, dc group, ch 5, skip next ch sp], dc group, ch 3, skip next ch sp; repeat from * 3 more times; repeat between [ ], join.

Rnd 15: Sl st in first 2 dc, beg dc group, skip first 2 ch sps across pineapple, dc group, *[ch 5, skip next ch sp, dc group, ch 3, skip next ch sp; working across next pineapple, (sc in next ch sp, ch 3) 6 times, skip next ch sp, dc group, ch 5, skip next ch sp], dc group, skip next 2 ch sps across pineapple, dc group; repeat from * 3 more times; repeat between [ ], join.

Rnd 16: Sl st in first 2 dc, beg dc dec, *[ch 5, (dc, ch 5, dc) in next ch sp, ch 5, dc group, ch 3, skip next ch sp; working across pineapple, (sc in next ch sp, ch 3) 5 times, skip next ch sp, dc group, ch 5, (dc, ch 5, dc) in next ch sp, ch 5], dc dec; repeat from * 3 more times; repeat between [ ], join with sl st in top of beg dc dec.

Rnd 17: (Sl st, ch 1, sc) in first ch sp, ch 5, *[dc cl in next ch sp, (ch 3, dc cl in same ch sp) 4 times, ch 5, sc in next ch sp, ch 5, dc group, ch 3, skip next ch sp; working across pineapple, (sc in next ch sp, ch 3) 4 times, skip next ch sp, dc group, ch 5, sc in next ch sp, ch 5, dc cl in next ch sp, (ch 3, dc cl in same ch sp) 4 times, ch 5], (sc in next ch sp, ch 5) 2 times; repeat from * 3 more times; repeat between [ ], sc in last ch sp, ch 2, join with dc in first sc *(joining ch sp made)*.

Rnd 18: Ch 1, sc in joining ch sp, ch 5, sc in next ch sp, ch 5, *[dc cl in next ch sp, (ch 3, dc cl in next ch sp) 3 times, ch 5, (sc in next ch sp, ch 5) 2 times, dc group, ch 3, skip next ch sp; working across pineapple, (sc in next ch sp, ch 3) 3 times, skip next ch sp, dc group, ch 5, (sc in next ch sp, ch 5) 2 times, dc cl in next ch sp, (ch 3, dc cl in next ch sp) 3 times, ch 5], (sc in next ch sp, ch 5) 3 times; repeat from * 3 more times; repeat between [ ], sc in last ch sp, ch 2, join.

Rnd 19: Ch 1, sc in joining ch sp, ch 5, (sc in next ch sp, ch 5) 2 times, *[dc cl in next ch sp, (ch 3, dc cl in next ch sp) 2 times, ch 5, (sc in next ch sp, ch 5) 3 times, dc group, ch 3, skip next ch sp; working across pineapple, (sc in next ch sp, ch 3) 2 times, skip next ch sp, dc group, ch 5, (sc in next ch sp, ch 5) 3 times, dc cl in next ch sp, (ch 3, dc cl in next ch sp) 2 times], ch 5, (sc in next ch sp, ch 5) 4 times; repeat from * 3 more times; repeat between [ ], ch 5, sc in last ch sp, ch 5, join with sl st in first sc.

Rnd 20: Sl st in first 2 chs of first ch sp, (sl st, ch 6, dc) in same ch sp, *[ch 5, skip next ch sp, sc in next ch sp, ch 5, dc cl in next ch sp, ch 3, dc cl in next ch sp, ch 5, (sc in next ch sp, ch 5) 4 times, dc group, ch 3, skip next ch sp; working across pineapple, sc in next ch sp, ch 3, skip next ch sp, dc group, ch 5, (sc in next ch sp, ch 5) 4 times, dc cl in next ch sp, ch 3, dc cl in next ch sp, ch 5, sc in next ch sp, ch 5, skip next ch sp], (dc, ch 3, dc) in next ch sp; repeat from * 3 more times; repeat between [ ], join with sl st in third ch of ch-6.

Rnd 21: Beg dc cl in first ch sp, (ch 3, dc cl) 2 times in same ch sp, *[ch 5, skip next ch sp, sc in next ch sp, ch 5, dc cl in next ch sp, ch 5, (sc in next ch sp, ch 5) 5 times, dc dec, ch 5, (sc in next ch sp, ch 5) 5 times, dc cl in next ch sp, ch 5, sc in next ch sp, ch 5, skip next ch sp], dc cl in next ch sp, (ch

3, dc cl) 2 times in same ch sp; repeat from * 3 more times; repeat between [ ], join with sl st in top of beg dc cl.

Rnd 22: Beg dc cl in first ch sp, ch 3, dc cl in next ch sp, *ch 5, (sc in next ch sp, ch 5) 16 times, dc cl in next ch sp, ch 3, dc cl in next ch sp; repeat from * 3 more times, ch 5, (sc in next ch sp, ch 5) 16 times, join.

Rnd 23: Beg dc cl in first ch sp, *[ch 5, (sc in next ch sp, ch 5) 8 times, (dc, ch 5, dc) in next ch sp, ch 5, (sc in next ch sp, ch 5) 8 times], dc cl in next ch sp; repeat from * 3 more times; repeat between [ ], join.

Rnd 24: (Sl st, ch 1, sc) in first ch sp, ch 5, (sc in next ch sp, ch 5) 7 times, *[skip next ch sp; to start next fan, dc in next ch sp, (ch 2, dc) 5 times in same ch sp; ch 5, skip next ch sp], (sc in next ch sp, ch 5) 16 times; repeat from * 3 more times; repeat between [ ], (sc in next ch sp, ch 5) 7 times, sc in last ch sp, ch 2, join with dc in first sc *(joining ch sp made)*.

Rnd 25: Ch 1, sc in joining ch sp, ch 5, (sc in next ch sp, ch 5) 7 times, *[skip next ch sp, working across fan, V st in next dc, (ch 2, V st in next dc) 5 times, ch 5, skip next ch sp], (sc in next ch sp, ch 5) 15 times; repeat from * 3 more times; repeat between [ ], (sc in next ch sp, ch 5) 6 times, sc in last ch sp, ch 2, join.

Rnd 26: Ch 1, sc in joining ch sp, ch 5, (sc in next ch sp, ch 5) 8 times; *[working across fan, (sc in next ch sp, ch 5, skip next ch sp) 5 times, sc in next ch sp, ch 5], (sc in next ch sp, ch 5) 16 times; repeat from * 3 more times; repeat between [ ], (sc in next ch sp, ch 5) 7 times, join with sl st in first sc.

Rnd 27: (Sl st, ch 1, sc) in first ch sp, (ch 5, sc in next ch sp) around, ch 2, join with dc in first sc *(joining ch sp made)*.

Rnds 28–32: Ch 1, sc in joining ch sp, (ch 5, sc in next ch sp) around, ch 2, join.

Rnd 33: Ch 1, sc in joining ch sp, ch 5, (sc in next ch sp, ch 5) 2 times, *(dc, ch 5, dc) in next ch sp, ch 5, (sc in next ch sp, ch 5) 10 times; repeat from * 8 more times, (dc, ch 5, dc) in next ch sp, ch 5, (sc in next ch sp, ch 5) 6 times, sc in last ch sp, ch 2, join.

Rnd 34: Ch 1, sc in joining ch sp, ch 5, (sc in next ch sp, ch 5) 3 times, *[dbl V st in next ch sp, ch 5, (sc in next ch sp, ch 5) 5 times, (dc, ch 5, dc) in next ch sp, ch 5], (sc in next ch sp, ch 5) 5 times; repeat from * 8 more times; repeat between [ ], sc in last ch sp, ch 2, join.

Rnd 35: Ch 1, sc in joining ch sp, ch 5, (sc in next ch sp, ch 5) 3 times, *[skip next ch sp, 5 dc in first ch sp of next dbl V st, (ch 3, 5 dc in next ch sp of same dbl V st) 2 times, ch 5, skip next ch sp, (sc in next ch sp, ch 5) 4 times, skip next ch sp, dc cl in next ch sp, (ch 3, dc cl in same ch sp) 4 times, ch 5, skip next ch sp], (sc in next ch sp, ch 5) 4 times; repeat from * 8 more times; repeat between [ ], join with sl st in first sc.

Rnd 36: (Sl st, ch 1, sc) in first ch sp, *[ch 5, (dc, ch 5, dc) in next ch sp, ch 5, sc in next ch sp, ch 5, skip next ch sp, dc group, ch 3, skip next ch sp; to start next pineapple, dc in next dc, (ch 1, dc in next dc) 4 times; ch 3, skip next ch sp, dc group, ch 5, skip next ch sp, sc in next ch sp, ch 5, (dc,

Continued on page 23

Pineapple Passion

Finished Size: 13" long including waistband.

Materials:
- ❏ 850 yds. size 10 crochet cotton thread
- ❏ No. 9 steel hook or hook needed to obtain gauge

Gauge: 1 shell = ¾"; 2 tr rows = 1¼".

Basic Stitches: Ch, sl st, sc, tr.

Special Stitches:
For **cluster (cl)**, yo 2 times, insert hook in next ch sp, yo, pull through sp, (yo, pull through 2 lps on hook) 2 times, *yo 2 times, insert hook in same sp, yo, pull through sp, (yo, pull through 2 lps on hook) 2 times; repeat from *, yo, pull through all 4 lps on hook.

For **shell**, (3 tr, ch 3, 3 tr) in st or ch sp.

For **picot**, ch 4, sl st in top of last st made.

WAISTBAND & TIES

Row 1: Ch 24, tr in fifth ch from hook, tr in each of next 3 chs, ch 2, skip next 2 chs, tr in next ch, (ch 1, skip next ch, tr in next ch) 3 times, ch 2, skip next 2 chs, tr in next ch, tr in last 4 chs, turn. *(14 tr made)*

Row 2: Ch 4, tr in next 4 sts, ch 2, skip next ch sp, tr in next tr, (ch 1, skip next ch sp, tr in next st) 3 times, ch 2, skip next ch sp, tr in last 5 sts, turn.

Row 3: Ch 4, tr in next 4 sts, ch 2, skip next ch sp, tr in next st, ch 1, skip next ch sp, tr in next st; **cl** *(see Special Stitches)* in next ch sp, tr in next tr, ch 1, skip next ch sp, tr in next tr, ch 2, skip next ch sp, tr in last 5 sts, turn.

Row 4: Ch 4, tr in next 4 sts, ch 2, skip next ch sp, tr in next st, cl in next ch sp, tr in next st, ch 1, skip next cl, tr in next st, cl in next ch sp, tr in next st, ch 2, skip next ch sp, tr in last 5 sts, turn.

Row 5: Ch 4, tr in next 4 sts, ch 2, skip next ch sp, tr in next st, ch 1, skip next cl, tr in next st, cl in next ch sp, tr in next st, ch 1, skip next cl, tr in next st, ch 2, skip next ch sp, tr in last 5 sts, turn.

Row 6: Ch 4, tr in next 4 sts, ch 2, skip next ch sp, tr in next st, ch 1, skip next ch sp, tr in next st, ch 1, skip next cl, tr in next st, ch 1, skip next ch sp, tr in next st, ch 2, skip next ch sp, tr in last 5 sts, turn.

Rows 7–130: Repeat rows 3–6 consecutively.

Row 131: Repeat row 2. Fasten off.

SKIRT

Row 1: Working in ends of rows on Waistband, skip first 49 rows, join with sc in top of 50th row, (ch 5, sc in top of next row) 31 times leaving remaining rows unworked, turn. *(31 ch sps made)*

Row 2: Ch 4, **shell** *(see Special Stitches)* in third ch of next ch-5, (ch 2, sc in next ch sp, ch 2, shell in third ch of next ch-5) across, tr in last st, turn. *(16 shells)*

Row 3: Ch 5, shell in ch sp of next shell, (ch 5, sc in next sc, ch 5, shell in ch sp of next shell) across, **dtr** *(see Stitch Guide)* in last st, turn.

Row 4: Ch 5, shell in first shell, (ch 5, shell in next shell) across, dtr in top of ch-5, turn.

Row 5: Ch 8, (sc, ch 4, sc) in next shell, *ch 3, (tr, ch 3) 4 times in third ch of ch-5, (sc, ch 4, sc) in next shell; repeat from * across, ch 4, tr in top of ch-5, turn.

Row 6: Ch 8, *tr in next tr, (ch 2, cl in next ch sp, ch 2, tr in next tr) 3 times; repeat from * across, ch 4, tr in fourth ch of ch-8, turn.

Row 7: Ch 4, cl in next tr, ch 2, *[tr in next cl, ch 2, cl in next tr, ch 2, (tr, ch 3, tr) in next cl, ch 2, cl in next tr, ch 2, tr in next cl], (ch 4, sc in next tr) 2 times, ch 4; repeat from * 13 more times; repeat between [ ], ch 2, cl in next tr, tr in fourth ch of ch-8, turn.

Row 8: Ch 4, skip next cl, (*tr in next tr, ch 5, skip next cl, cl in next tr, ch 5, cl in next ch sp, ch 5, cl in next tr, ch 5, skip next cl, tr in next tr*, ch 1) 14 times; repeat between first *, tr in last st, turn.

Row 9: Ch 4, *[tr in next cl, ch 7, (tr, ch 5, tr) in next cl, ch 7, tr in next cl], ch 3, cl in next ch-1 sp, ch 3, tr in next cl, (ch 1, tr) 4 times in next ch sp, ch 1, tr in next cl, (ch 1, tr) 4 times in next ch sp, ch 1, tr in next cl, ch 3, cl in next ch-1 sp, ch 3; repeat from * 6 more times; repeat between [ ], tr in last st, turn.

Row 10: Ch 6, skip next ch sp, *[tr in next tr, ch 3, (cl, ch 3) 3 times in next ch sp, tr in next tr], ch 7, sc in next tr, ch 4, cl in next cl, ch 4, sc in next ch-1 sp, (ch 5, sc in next ch-1 sp) 9 times, ch 4, cl in next cl, ch 4, sc in next tr, ch 7; repeat from * 6 more times; repeat between [ ], ch 2, tr in last st, turn.

Row 11: Ch 4, *[cl in next cl, (ch 3, cl in next ch sp, ch 3, cl in next cl) 2 times], ch 3, cl in next tr, ch 3, cl in fourth ch of next ch-7, ch 5, sc in next cl, ch 5, skip next ch-4 sp, sc in next ch-5 sp, **picot** *(see Special Stitches)*, (ch 5, sc in next ch sp, picot) 8 times, ch 5, sc in next cl, ch 5, cl in fourth ch of next ch-7, ch 3, cl in next tr, ch 3; repeat from * 6 more times; repeat between [ ], tr in fourth ch of ch-6, turn.

Row 12: Ch 6, skip next cl, (tr in next cl, ch 3) 5 times, tr in next cl, *(ch 7, skip next 2 ch sps and next picot, sc in next ch sp, (ch 5, sc in next ch sp) 7 times, ch 7, tr in next cl], (ch 3, tr in next cl) 8 times; repeat from * 5 more times; repeat between [ ], ch 3, tr in next cl) 5 times, ch 2, skip last cl, tr in last st, turn.

Row 13: Ch 7, cl in next tr, (ch 4, sc in next tr, ch 4, cl in next tr) 2 times, *[ch 3, (cl, ch 4, cl) in next tr, ch 7, skip next ch sp, sc in next ch sp, picot, (ch 5, sc in next ch sp, picot) 6 times, ch 7, (cl, ch 4, cl) in next tr, ch 3, cl in next tr], (ch 4, sc in next tr, ch 4, cl in next tr) 3 times; repeat from * 5 more times; repeat between [ ], (ch 4, sc in next tr, ch 4, cl in next tr) 2 times, ch 3, tr in fourth ch of ch-6, turn.

Row 14: Ch 4, tr in first cl, (ch 9, sc in next cl) 2 times, *[ch 5, cl in next cl, ch 4, cl in next cl, ch 7, skip next ch sp and next picot, sc in next ch-5 sp, (ch 5, sc in next ch sp) 5 times, ch 7, cl in next cl, ch 4, cl in next cl, ch 5, cl in next cl], (ch 9, sc in next cl) 3 times; repeat from * 5 more times; repeat between [ ], ch 9, sc in next cl, ch 9, tr in next cl, tr in fourth ch of ch-7, turn.

Row 15: (Ch 9, sc in fifth ch of next ch-9) 2 times, *[ch 9, cl in next cl, ch 4, cl in next cl, ch 7, skip next ch sp, sc in next ch-5 sp, picot, (ch 5, sc in next ch sp, picot) 4 times, ch 7, cl in next cl, ch 4, cl in next cl], (ch 9, sc in fifth ch of next ch-9) 3 times; repeat from * 5 more times; repeat between [ ], (ch 9, sc in fifth ch of next ch-9) 2 times, ch 5, tr in last st, turn.

Row 16: Ch 13, skip first ch sp, sc in fifth ch of next ch-9, ch 9, sc in fifth ch of next ch-9, *[ch 9, cl in

Continued on page 22

Tea Apron

Designed by Lucille LaFlamme

Continued from page 20

next cl, ch 4, cl in next cl, ch 7, skip next ch sp and next picot, sc in next ch-5 sp, (ch 5, sc in next ch sp) 3 times, ch 7, cl in next cl, ch 4, cl in next cl], (ch 9, sc in fifth ch of next ch-9) 4 times; repeat from * 5 more times; repeat between [ ], (ch 9, sc in fifth ch of next ch-9) 2 times, ch 9, tr in fourth ch of ch-9, turn.

Row 17: (Ch 9, sc in fifth ch of next ch-9) 3 times, *[ch 9, cl in next cl, ch 4, cl in next cl, ch 7, skip next ch sp, sc in next ch-5 sp, picot, (ch 5, sc in next ch sp, picot) 2 times, ch 7, cl in next cl, ch 4, cl in next cl], (ch 9, sc in fifth ch of next ch-9) 5 times; repeat from * 5 more times; repeat between [ ], (ch 9, sc in fifth ch of next ch-9) 2 times, ch 9, skip next 4 chs, of ch-13, sc in next ch, ch 5, skip next 4 chs, tr in next ch, turn.

Row 18: Ch 13, skip first ch sp, sc in fifth ch of next ch-9, (ch 9, sc in fifth ch of next ch-9) 2 times, *[ch 9, cl in next cl, ch 4, cl in next cl, ch 7, skip next ch sp, sc in next ch-5 sp, ch 5, sc in next ch sp, ch 7, cl in next cl, ch 4, cl in next cl], (ch 9, sc in fifth ch of next ch-9) 6 times; repeat from * 5 more times; repeat between [ ], (ch 9, sc in fifth ch of next ch-9) 3 times, ch 9, tr in fourth ch of next ch-9, turn.

Row 19: (Ch 9, sc in fifth ch of next ch-9) 4 times, *[ch 9, cl in next cl, ch 4, cl in next cl, skip next ch-7 sp, tr in next ch-5 sp, cl in next cl, ch 4, cl in next cl, (ch 9, sc in fifth ch of next ch-9) 3 times], ch 1, (tr, ch 1) 9 times in next ch sp, sc in fifth ch of next ch-9, (ch 9, sc in fifth ch of next ch-9) 2 times; repeat from * 5 more times; repeat between [ ], ch 9, skip next 4 chs of ch-13, sc in next ch, ch 5, skip next 4 chs, tr in next ch, turn.

Row 20: Ch 13, skip first ch sp, sc in fifth ch of next ch-9, (ch 9, sc in fifth ch of next ch-9) 3 times, *ch 9, cl in next cl, skip next 2 cls, cl in next cl, (ch 9, sc in fifth ch of next ch-9) 2 times, ch 5, (cl, ch 4, cl) in fifth ch of next ch-9, ch 7, skip next ch-1 sp and next tr, sc in next ch sp, (ch 5, sc in next ch sp) 7 times, ch 7, (cl, ch 4, cl) in fifth ch of next ch-9, ch 5, sc in fifth ch of next ch-9, ch 9, sc in fifth ch of next ch-9; repeat from * 5 more times, cl in next cl, skip next 2 cls, cl in next cl, (ch 9, sc in fifth ch of next ch-9) 4 times, ch 9, tr in fourth ch of last ch-9, turn.

Row 21: (Ch 9, sc in fifth ch of next ch-9) 7 times, *ch 9, cl in next cl, ch 4, cl in next cl, ch 7, skip next ch sp, sc in next ch-5 sp, picot, (ch 5, sc in next ch sp, picot) 6 times, ch 7, cl in next cl, ch 4, cl in next cl, (ch 9, sc in fifth ch of next ch-9) 4 times; repeat from * 5 more times, (ch 9, sc in fifth ch of next ch-9) 2 times, ch 9, skip next 4 ch of ch 13, sc in next ch, ch 5, skip next 4 ch, tr in next ch, turn.

Row 22: Ch 13, skip first ch sp, sc in fifth ch of next ch-9, (ch 9, sc in fifth ch of next ch-9) 3 times, *ch 1, (tr, ch 1) 9 times in next ch sp, (sc in fifth ch of next ch-9, ch 9) 2 times, cl in next cl, ch 4, cl in next cl, ch 7, skip next ch sp and next picot, sc in next ch-5 sp, (ch 5, sc in next ch sp) 5 times, ch 7, cl in next cl, ch 4, cl in next cl, (ch 9, sc in fifth ch of next ch-9) 2 times; repeat from * 5 more times, ch 1, (tr, ch 1) 9 times in next ch sp, sc in fifth ch

of next ch-9, (ch 9, sc in fifth ch of next ch-9) 3 times, ch 9, tr in fourth ch of last ch-9, turn.

Row 23: (Ch 9, sc in fifth ch of next ch-9) 3 times, *[ch 5, (cl, ch 4, cl) in fifth ch of next ch-9, ch 5, cl in next tr, (ch 3, skip next tr, cl in next tr) 4 times, ch 5, (cl, ch 4, cl) in fifth ch of next ch-9, ch 5, cl in fifth ch of next ch-9], ch 9, cl in next cl, ch 4, cl in next cl, ch 7, skip next ch sp, sc in next ch-5 sp, picot, (ch 5, sc in next ch sp, picot) 4 times, ch 7, cl in next cl, ch 4, cl in next cl, ch 9, sc in fifth ch of next ch-9; repeat from * 5 more times; repeat between [ ], ch 9, sc in fifth ch of next ch-9, ch 9, skip next 4 chs of ch-13, sc in next ch, ch 5, skip next 4 chs, tr in next ch, turn.

Row 24: Ch 13, skip next ch sp, sc in fifth ch of next ch-9, ch 9, sc in fifth ch of next ch-9, *[ch 9, cl in next cl, ch 4, cl in next cl, ch 7, sc in next cl, (ch 6, sc in next cl) 4 times, ch 7, cl in next cl, ch 4, cl in next cl], ch 9, sc in fifth ch of next ch-9, ch 5, cl in next cl, ch 4, cl in next cl, ch 7, skip next ch sp and next picot, sc in next ch-5 sp, (ch 5, sc in next ch sp) 3 times, ch 7, cl in next cl, ch 4, cl in next cl, ch 5, sc in fifth ch of next ch-9; repeat from * 5 more times; repeat between [ ], (ch 9, sc in fifth ch of next ch-9) 2 times, ch 9, tr in fourth ch of last ch-9, turn.

Row 25: (Ch 9, sc in fifth ch of next ch-9) 3 times, *[ch 5, cl in next cl, ch 4, cl in next cl, ch 7, skip next ch sp, sc in next ch-6 sp, picot, (ch 6, sc in next ch sp, picot) 3 times, ch 7, cl in next cl, ch 4, cl in next cl, ch 5, sc in fifth ch of next ch-9], ch 9, cl in next cl, ch 4, cl in next cl, ch 7, skip next ch sp, sc in next ch-5 sp, picot, (ch 5, sc in next ch sp, picot) 2 times, ch 7, cl in next cl, ch 4, cl in next cl, ch 9, sc in fifth ch of next ch-9; repeat from * 5 more times; repeat between [ ], ch 9, sc in fifth ch of next ch-9, ch 9, skip next 4 chs of ch-13, sc in next ch, ch 5, skip next 4 chs, tr in next ch, turn.

Row 26: Ch 9, skip next ch sp, sc in fifth ch of next ch-9, ch 9, sc in fifth ch of next ch-9, *[ch 9, sc in third ch of next ch-5, ch 5, cl in next cl, ch 4, cl in next cl, ch 7, skip next ch sp and next picot, sc in next ch-6 sp, (ch 6, sc in next ch sp) 2 times, ch 7, cl in next cl, ch 4, cl in next cl, ch 5, sc in third ch of next ch-5], ch 9, sc in fifth ch of next ch-9, ch 5, cl in next cl, ch 4, cl in next cl, ch 7, skip next ch sp and next picot, sc in next ch-5 sp, ch 5, sc in next ch sp, ch 7, cl in next cl, ch 4, cl in next cl, ch 5, sc in fifth ch of next ch-9; repeat from * 5 more times; repeat between [ ], (ch 9, sc in fifth ch of next ch-9) 2 times, ch 9, sc in fourth ch of last ch-9, turn.

Row 27: (Ch 9, sc in fifth ch of next ch-9) 3 times, *[ch 9, cl in next cl, ch 4, cl in next cl, ch 7, skip next ch sp, sc in next ch-6 sp, ch 6, sc in next ch sp, ch 7, cl in next cl, ch 4, cl in next cl], ch 9, skip next ch sp, sc in fifth ch of next ch-9, ch 9, sc in third ch of next ch-5, ch 5, cl in next cl, ch 4, cl in next cl, ch 7, skip next ch sp, sc in next ch-5 sp, picot, ch 7, cl in next cl, ch 4, cl in next cl, ch 9, sc in third ch of next ch-5, ch 9, sc in fifth ch of next ch-9; repeat from * 5 more times; repeat between [ ], (ch 9, sc in fifth ch of next ch-9) 3 times, ch 5, tr in last tr on row 25, turn.

Row 28: Ch 9, skip next ch sp, sc in fifth ch of next ch-9, (ch 9, sc in fifth ch of next ch-9) 2 times, *[ch 9, cl in next cl, ch 4, cl in next cl, ch 7, skip next ch sp, sc in next ch-6 sp, picot, ch 7, cl in next cl, ch 4, cl in next cl, (ch 9, sc in fifth ch of next ch-9) 3 times], ch 9, cl in next cl, ch 4, cl in next cl, skip next picot, cl in next cl, ch 4, cl in next cl, ch 9, sc in third ch of next ch-5, (ch 9, sc in fifth ch of next ch-9) 2 times; repeat from * 5 more times; repeat between [ ], ch 9, sc in fourth ch of last ch-9, turn.

Row 29: (Ch 9, sc in fifth ch of next ch-9) 4 times, *[ch 9, cl in next cl, ch 4, cl in next cl, ch 2, tr in next picot, ch 2, cl in next cl, ch 4, cl in next cl, (ch 9, sc in fifth ch of next ch-9) 4 times], ch 5, cl in next cl, ch 1, skip next 2 cls, cl in next cl, ch 5, sc in fifth ch of next ch-9, (ch 9, sc in fifth ch of next ch-9) 3 times; repeat from * 5 more times; repeat between [ ], ch 5, tr in last tr on row 27, turn.

Row 30: Ch 9, skip first ch sp, sc in fifth ch of next ch-9, (ch 9, sc in fifth ch of next ch-9) 3 times, *[ch 5, cl in next cl, ch 1, tr in next tr, ch 1, skip next cl, cl in next cl, ch 5, sc in fifth ch of next ch-9, (ch 9, sc in fifth ch of next ch-9) 3 times], ch 9, sc in ch-1 sp between next 2 cls, ch 9, skip next ch sp, sc in fifth

ch of next ch-9, (ch 9, sc in fifth ch of next ch-9) 3 times; repeat from * 5 more times; repeat between [ ], ch 9, sc in fourth ch of last ch-9. Fasten off.

EDGING

Working in ends of rows and in sts around outer edge, join with sc in end of row 1 on right side of Skirt, *ch 3; for **picot shell, (3 tr, ch 5, sl st in fourth ch from hook, ch 2, 3 tr)** in top of next row, ch 3, sc in top of next row; repeat from * across, (ch 3, picot in fifth ch of next ch-9, ch 3, sc in next sc) 4 times, ch 3, picot shell in next tr, [ch 3, sc in next sc, (ch 3, picot shell in fifth ch of next ch-9, ch 3, sc in next sc) 8 times, ch 3, picot shell in next tr]; repeat between [ ] 5 more times, (ch 3, sc in next sc, ch 3, picot shell in fifth ch of next ch-9) 4 times, (ch 3, sc in top of next row, ch 3, picot shell in top of next row) across to row 1, ch 3, sc in row 1. Fasten off. ❐❐

Table Topper

Continued from page 19

Continued from page 19

ch 5, dc) in next ch sp, ch 5, sc in next ch sp, ch 5, skip next ch sp, dc cl in next ch sp, (ch 3, dc cl in next ch sp) 3 times, ch 5, skip next ch sp], sc in next ch sp; repeat from * 8 more times; repeat between [ ], join.

Rnd 37: (Sl st, ch 1, sc) in first ch sp, ch 5, *[dc cl in next ch sp, (ch 3, dc cl in same ch sp) 2 times, ch 5, (sc in next ch sp, ch 5) 2 times, dc group, ch 3, skip next ch sp; working across pineapple, (sc in next ch sp, ch 3) 4 times, skip next ch sp, dc group, ch 5, (sc in next ch sp, ch 5) 2 times, dc cl in next ch sp, (ch 3, dc cl in same ch sp) 2 times, ch 5, (sc in next ch sp, ch 5) 2 times, dc cl in next ch sp, (ch 3, dc cl in next ch sp) 2 times], ch 5, (sc in next ch sp, ch 5) 2 times; repeat from * 8 more times; repeat between [ ], ch 5, sc in last ch sp, ch 2, join with dc in first sc *(joining ch sp made).*

Rnd 38: Ch 1, sc in joining ch sp, ch 5, sc in next ch sp, ch 5, *[dc cl in next ch sp, ch 3, dc cl in next ch sp, ch 5, (sc in next ch sp, ch 5) 3 times, dc group, ch 3, skip next ch sp; working across pineapple, (sc in next ch sp, ch 3) 3 times, skip next ch sp, dc group, ch 5, (sc in next ch sp, ch 5) 3 times, dc cl in next ch sp, ch 3, dc cl in next ch sp, ch 5, (sc in next ch sp, ch 5) 3 times, dc cl in next ch sp, ch 3, dc cl in next ch sp, ch 5], (sc in next ch sp, ch 5) 3 times; repeat from * 8 more times; repeat between [ ], sc in last ch sp, ch 2, join.

Rnd 39: Ch 1, sc in joining ch sp, ch 5, (sc in next ch sp,

ch 5) 2 times, *[dc cl in next ch sp, ch 5, (sc in next ch sp, ch 5) 4 times, dc group, ch 3, skip next ch sp; working across pineapple, (sc in next ch sp, ch 3) 2 times, skip next ch sp, dc group, ch 5, (sc in next ch sp, ch 5) 4 times, dc cl in next ch sp, ch 5, (sc in next ch sp, ch 5) 4 times, dc cl in next ch sp, ch 5], (sc in next ch sp, ch 5) 4 times; repeat from * 8 more times; repeat between [ ], sc in last ch sp, ch 2, join.

Rnd 40: Ch 1, sc in joining ch sp, ch 5, (sc in next ch sp, ch 5) 8 times, *[dc group in next ch sp, ch 3, skip next ch sp; working across pineapple, sc in next ch sp, ch 3, skip next ch sp, dc group, ch 5], (sc in next ch sp, ch 5) 20 times; repeat from * 8 more times; repeat between [ ], (sc in next ch, ch 5) 10 times, sc in last ch sp, ch 2, join.

Rnd 41: Ch 1, sc in joining ch sp, ch 5, (sc in next ch sp, ch 5) 9 times, *dc dec, ch 5, (sc in next ch sp, ch 5) 21 times; repeat from * 8 more times; dc dec, ch 5, (sc in next ch sp, ch 5) 10 times, sc in last ch sp, ch 2, join.

Rnds 42-44: Ch 1, sc in joining ch sp, (ch 5, sc in next ch sp) around, ch 2, join.

Rnd 45: Ch 1, sc in joining ch sp, ch 3, 2 dc in next ch sp; for **picot,** ch 4, sl st in third ch from hook, ch 1 *(picot made),* 2 dc in same ch sp, ch 3, *sc in next ch sp, ch 3, (2 dc, picot, 2 dc) in next ch sp, ch 3; repeat from * around, join with sl st in first sc. Fasten off. ❐❐

top of ch-3. *(Joining dc counts as ch-3 sp—24 ch-3 sps, 504 dc, 96 ch-7 sps)*

Rnd 67: (Ch 3, 3 dc, ch 3, 4 dc) in joining ch-3 sp, *shell in next ch-3 sp, ch 2, skip next 3 dc, (dc in next dc, ch 2) 2 times, skip next ch sp, block, (ch 7, sc in next ch sp) 2 times, ch 5, dc in next dc, (ch 3, dc in next dc) 8 times, ch 5, (sc in next ch sp, ch 7) 2 times, skip next 3 dc, block, (ch 2, dc in next dc) 2 times, ch 2, skip next 3 dc; repeat from * around, join with sl st in top of ch-3. *(24 shells, 312 dc)*

NOTE: *In rnds 68–84, work beg shell for first shell of each rnd.*

Rnd 68: *Shell, ch 2, dc in last dc of shell, ch 2, dc in next dc, ch 2, skip next ch sp, block, (ch 7, sc in next ch sp) 2 times, ch 7, skip next ch sp, picot, (ch 5, picot) 7 times, ch 7, skip next ch sp, (sc in next ch sp, ch 7) 2 times, skip next 3 dc, block, ch 2, dc in next dc, ch 2, dc in first dc of next shell, ch 2; repeat from * around, join. *(96 dc, 144 ch-7 sps, 168 ch-5 sps)*

Rnd 69: *(Shell, ch 3, 4 dc) in next shell, ch 2, skip next ch sp, dc in next dc, ch 2, skip next ch sp, block, (ch 7, sc in next ch-7 sp) 2 times, ch 7, skip next ch sp, picot, (ch 5, picot) 6 times, ch 7, skip next ch sp, (sc in next ch-7 sp, ch 7) 2 times, skip next 3 dc, block, ch 2, dc in next dc, ch 2; repeat from * around, join. *(144 dc)*

Rnd 70: *Shell, ch 2, shell in next ch-3 sp, skip next ch sp, (dc in next dc, ch 2) 2 times, skip next 2 dc; work block across next 4 sts and chs, (ch 7, sc in next ch-7 sp) 2 times, ch 7, picot, (ch 5, picot) 5 times, ch 7, (sc in next ch-7 sp, ch 7) 2 times, skip first 4 chs of next ch-7, work block across next 3 chs and next dc, ch 2, skip next 2 dc, dc in next dc, ch 2, dc in next dc; repeat from * around, join. *(48 shells, 96 dc, 120 ch-5 sps)*

Rnd 71: *Shell, ch 4, dc in next ch sp, ch 4, shell, skip next dc, (dc in next dc, ch 2) 2 times, skip next 2 dc, work block across next 4 sts and chs, (ch 7, sc in next ch-7 sp) 2 times, ch 7, picot, (ch 5, picot) 4 times, ch 7, (sc in next ch-7 sp, ch 7) 2 times, skip first 4 chs of next ch-7, work block across next 3 chs and next dc, ch 2, skip next 2 dc, dc in next dc, ch 2, dc in next dc, skip next dc; repeat from * around, join. *(120 dc, 96 ch-5 sps, 48 ch-4 sps)*

Rnds 72–74: *Shell, ch 4, (dc in next ch sp, ch 4) across to next shell, shell, skip next dc, (dc in next dc, ch 2) 2 times, skip next 2 dc, work block across next 4 sts and chs, (ch 7, sc in next ch-7 sp) 2 times, ch 7, picot, (ch 5, picot) across to next ch-7 sp, ch 7, (sc in next ch-7 sp, ch 7) 2 times, skip first 4 chs of next ch-7, work block across next 3 chs and next dc, ch 2, skip next 2 dc, dc in next dc, ch 2, dc in next dc, skip next dc; repeat from * around, join. *(At end of last rnd, 192 dc, 24 ch-5 sps, 120 ch-4 sps.)*

Rnd 75: *Shell, ch 4, (dc in next ch sp, ch 4) across to next shell, shell, skip next dc, (dc in next dc, ch 2) 2 times, skip next 2 dc, work block across next 4 sts and chs, (ch 7, sc in next ch-7 sp) 2 times, ch 7, picot, ch 7, (sc in next ch-7 sp, ch 7) 2 times, skip first 4 chs of next ch-7, work block across next 3 chs and next dc, ch 2, skip next 2 dc, dc in next

dc, ch 2, dc in next dc, skip next dc; repeat from * around, join. *(216 dc, 144 ch-4 sps)*

Rnds 76–78: *Shell, ch 4, (dc in next ch sp, ch 4) across to next shell, shell, skip next dc, (dc in next dc, ch 2) 2 times, skip next 2 dc, work block across next 4 sts and chs, ch 7, (sc in next ch-7 sp, ch 7) across to last ch-7 sp before next block, skip first 4 chs of next ch-7, work block across next 3 chs and next dc, ch 2, skip next 2 dc, dc in next dc, ch 2, dc in next dc, skip next dc; repeat from * around, join. *(At end of last rnd, 288 dc, 216 ch-4 sps, 72 ch-7 sps.)*

Rnd 79: *Shell, ch 4, (dc in next ch sp, ch 4) across to next shell, shell, skip next dc, (dc in next dc, ch 2) 2 times, skip next 2 dc, work block across next 4 sts and chs, ch 7, sc in next ch-7 sp, ch 7, skip first 4 chs of next ch-7, work block across next 3 chs and next dc, ch 2, skip next 2 dc, dc in next dc, ch 2, dc in next dc, skip next dc; repeat from * around, join. *(312 dc, 240 ch-4 sps, 48 ch-7 sps)*

Rnd 80: *Shell, ch 5, (dc in next ch sp, ch 5) across to next shell, shell, skip next dc, (dc in next dc, ch 2) 2 times, skip next 2 dc, work block across next 4 sts and chs, ch 7, skip first 4 chs of next ch-7, work block across next 3 chs and next dc, ch 2, skip next 2 dc, dc in next dc, ch 2, dc in next dc, skip next dc; repeat from * around, join. *(336 dc, 264 ch-5 sps, 24 ch-7 sps)*

Rnd 81: *Shell, ch 5, (dc in next ch sp, ch 5) across to next shell, shell, skip next dc, (dc in next dc, ch 2) 2 times, skip next 2 dc, work block across next 4 sts and chs, ch 2, skip next ch, work block across next 3 chs and next dc, ch 2, skip next 2 dc, dc in next dc, ch 2, dc in next dc, skip next dc; repeat from * around, join. *(360 dc, 288 ch-5 sps)*

Rnd 82: *Shell, ch 5, (dc in next ch sp, ch 4) across to next shell, shell, skip next dc, (dc in next dc, ch 2) 2 times, skip next 2 dc, work block across next 4 sts and chs, ch 2, skip next 2 dc, dc in next dc, ch 2, dc in next dc, skip next dc; repeat from * around, join. *(384 dc, 312 ch-5 sps)*

Rnd 83: *Shell, ch 5, (dc in next ch sp, ch 5) across to next shell, shell, skip next dc, (dc in next dc, ch 2) 2 times, skip next 2 dc, dc in next dc, ch 2, dc in next dc, skip next dc; repeat from * around, join. *(408 dc, 336 ch-5 sps)*

Rnd 84: *Shell, ch 5, (dc in next ch sp, ch 5) across to next shell, shell, skip next dc, dc in next dc, ch 2, dc in next dc, skip next dc; repeat from * around, join. *(384 dc, 360 ch-5 sps)*

Rnd 85: Sl st across next 3 dc of first shell, (sl st, ch 3, 3 dc) in next ch sp, ch 5, (dc in next ch sp, ch 5) across to next shell, 4 dc in ch sp of next shell, *ch 3, skip next 2 dc, 4 dc in ch sp of next shell, ch 4, (dc in next ch sp, ch 4) across to next shell, 4 dc in ch sp of next shell; repeat from * around, join with dc in top of first ch-3. *(Joining dc counts as ch-3 sp—24 ch-3 sps, 552 dc, 384 ch-5 sps)*

Rnd 86: Working beg shell for first shell of rnd, *shell in next ch-3 sp, ch 5, skip next 4 dc worked in shell, (dc in next ch sp, ch 5) across to next 4 dc worked in shell; repeat from * around, join with sl st in top of ch-3. *(384 dc, 408 ch-5 sps, 24 shells)*

Rnd 87: Sl st in next 3 dc, ch 1, *picot in center ch of next ch sp, ch 3, (2 tr, ch 3, sc in third ch from hook, 2 tr) in center ch of next ch sp, ch 3; repeat from * around, join with sl st in first sc. Fasten off. ❏❏

Christmas Creations

The
bountiful spirit of
Christmas is synonymous
with giving, not just in the
tantalizing form of fresh-baked
pastries or the engaging mystery
of gaily wrapped boxes heaped under
the tree, but in the warming simplicity
of gifts handmade and offered with
a generous heart.
Threading through the jolly festivity is
the pristine beauty of the crocheter's art.
Delicate, glittering, decked with
ribbons, these are snowflakes,
ornaments and doilies Santa
himself will admire.

Satin Balls

Designed by Carol Allen

Finished Sizes: Fits 9"-diameter satin ball.

Materials For One:
❏ 15 yds. size 30 crochet cotton thread
❏ No. 11 steel hook

Basic Stitches: Ch, sl st, sc, hdc, dc, tr.

GENERAL INSTRUCTIONS

Each pattern contains written instructions for the crochet piece only. After working first few rounds lay piece over satin ball to check that it will lay smoothly.

To attach crochet piece to satin ball, use pearl- or gold-head straight pins inserted through the piece and into the ball in desired arrangement.

Decorate each satin ball as desired *(see photo)* using ribbon roses, lace, bead trim and ribbon. Decorated head straight pins or craft glue can be used to secure.

For **hanger,** use metallic thread by forming a loop and tacking the ends to the center of the crochet piece with sewing thread and needle or craft glue.

ORNAMENT NO. 1 *(shown at top right in photo)*

Rnd 1: Ch 10, sl st in first ch to form ring, ch 4, 23 tr in ring, join with sl st in top of ch-4. *(24 tr made)*

Rnd 2: Working in **back lps** *(see Stitch Guide),* (ch 3, dc) in first st, dc in next st, (2 dc in next st, dc in next st) around, join with sl st in top of ch 3. *(36 dc)*

Rnd 3: Working in **back lps,** (ch 2, hdc) in first st, hdc in next st, (2 hdc in next st, hdc in next st) around, join with sl st in top of ch 2. *(54 hdc)*

Rnd 4: Working in **back lps,** ch 1, sc in each st around, join with sl st in first sc. *(54 sc)*

Rnd 5: Working in **back lps,** ch 3, skip next 2 sts, (sc in next st, ch 3, skip next 2 sts) around, join with sl st in first ch of first ch-3. *(18 ch sps)*

Rnd 6: Sl st in first ch sp, ch 4, (sc in next ch sp, ch 4) around, join with sl st in first ch of first ch-4.

Rnd 7: Sl st in first ch sp, ch 5, (sc in next ch sp, ch 5) around, join with sl st in first ch of first ch-5.

Rnd 8: Sl st in first ch sp, ch 1, (2 sc, ch 3, 2 sc) in each ch sp around, join with sl st in first sc.

Rnd 9: Sl st in next st and in next ch sp, (ch 3, 2 dc, ch 3, 3 dc) in same ch sp, (ch 3, sc in next ch sp) 2 times, ch 3, *(3 dc, ch 3, 3 dc) in next ch sp, (ch 3, sc in next ch sp) 2 times, ch 3; repeat from * around, join with sl st in top of ch-3.

Rnd 10: Sl st in each of next 2 sts and in next ch sp, (ch 3, 3 dc, ch 4, 4 dc) in same ch sp, ch 4, skip next ch sp, (sc, hdc, dc, tr, dc, hdc, sc) in next ch sp, ch 4, skip next ch sp, *(4 dc, ch 4, 4 dc) in next ch sp, ch 4, skip next ch sp, (sc, hdc, dc, tr, dc, hdc, sc) in next ch sp, ch 4, skip next ch sp; repeat from * around, join.

Rnd 11: Sl st in each of next 3 sts and in next ch sp, (ch 3, 4 dc, ch 5, 5 dc) in same ch sp, ch 5, sc in next tr, ch 5, skip next ch sp, *(5 dc, ch 5, 5 dc) in next ch sp, ch 5, sc in next tr, ch 5, skip next ch sp; repeat from * around, join.

Rnd 12: Sl st in next 4 sts and in next ch sp, (ch 3, 5 dc, ch 6, 6 dc) in same ch sp, ch 6, sc in next sc, ch 6, skip next ch sp, *(6 dc, ch 6, 6 dc) in next ch sp, ch 6, sc in next sc, ch 6, skip next ch sp; repeat from * around, join. Fasten off.

Finish according to General Instructions on this page.

ORNAMENT NO. 2 *(shown at bottom right in photo)*

Rnd 1: Ch 10, sl st in first ch to form ring, ch 4, 23 tr in ring, join with sl st in top of ch-4. *(24 tr made)*

Rnd 2: Working in **back lps** *(see Stitch Guide),* (ch 3, dc) in first st, dc in next st, (2 dc in next st, dc in next st) around, join with sl st in top of ch-3. *(36 dc)*

Rnd 3: Working in **back lps,** (ch 2, hdc) in first st, hdc in next st, (2 hdc in next st, hdc in next st) around, join with sl st in top of ch-2. *(54 hdc)*

Rnd 4: Working in **back lps,** ch 1, sc in each st around, join with sl st in first sc. *(54 sc)*

Rnd 5: Working in **back lps,** ch 5, skip next 2 sts, (sc in next st, ch 5, skip next 2 sts) around, join with sl st in first ch of ch 5. *(18 ch sps)*

Rnd 6: (Sl st, ch 3, 2 dc, ch 4, 3 dc) in first ch sp, ch 1, sc in next ch sp, ch 1, *(3 dc, ch 4, 3 dc) in next ch sp, ch 1, sc in next ch sp, ch 1; repeat from * around, join with sl st in top of ch-3.

Rnd 7: Sl st in each of next 2 sts and in next ch sp, (ch 3, 4 dc, ch 5, 5 dc) in same ch sp, ch 3, sc in next sc, ch 3, skip next ch-1 sp, *(5 dc, ch 5, 5 dc) in next ch sp, ch 3, sc in next sc, ch 3, skip next ch-1 sp; repeat from * around, join.

Rnd 8: Sl st in next 4 sts and in next ch sp, (ch 3, 6 dc, ch 7, 7 dc) in same ch sp, ch 5, sc in next sc, ch 5, skip next ch sp, *(7 dc, ch 7, 7 dc) in next ch sp, ch 5, sc in next sc, ch 5, skip next ch sp; repeat from * around, join.

Rnd 9: Sl st in next 6 sts and in next ch sp, (ch 3, 8 dc, ch 3, 9 dc) in same ch sp, ch 7, sc in next sc, ch 7, skip next ch sp, *(9 dc, ch 3, 9 dc) in next ch sp, ch 7, sc in next sc, ch 7, skip next ch sp; repeat from * around, join. Fasten off.

Finish according to General Instructions on this page.

ORNAMENT NO. 3 *(shown at top center in photo)*

Rnd 1: Ch 10, sl st in first ch to form ring, ch 4, 23 tr in ring, join with sl st in top of ch-4. *(24 tr made)*

Rnd 2: Working in **back lps** *(see Stitch Guide),* (ch 3, dc) in first st, dc in next st, (2 dc in next st, dc in next st) around, join with sl st in top of ch-3. *(36 dc)*

Rnd 3: Working in **back lps,** (ch 2, hdc) in first st, hdc in next st, (2 hdc in next st, hdc in next st) around, join with sl st in top of ch-2. *(54 hdc)*

Rnd 4: Working in **back lps,** ch 1, sc in each st around, join with sl st in first sc. *(54 sc)*

Rnd 5: Working in **back lps,** ch 6, skip next st, (tr in next st, ch 2, skip next st) around, join with sl st in fourth ch of ch-6. *(27 tr)*

Rnd 6: Working in **back lps,** ch 1, sc in first st, ch 3, (sc in next st, ch 3) around, join with sl st in first sc. *(27 ch sps)*

Rnd 7: (Sl st, ch 3, dc, ch 2, 2 dc) in first ch sp, (2 dc, ch 2, 2 dc) in each ch sp around, join with sl st in top of ch-3.

Rnd 8: Sl st in next st and in next ch sp, ch 1, sc in same ch sp, ch 3, (sc in next ch sp, ch 3) around, join with sl st in first sc.

Rnd 9: Sc in first ch sp, ch 4, (sc in next ch sp, ch 4) around, join.

Rnd 10: (Sl st, ch 3, 2 dc, ch 3, 3 dc) in first ch sp, (3 dc, ch 3, 3 dc) in each ch sp around, join.

Rnd 11: Sl st in each of next 2 sts and in next ch sp, (ch 3, 2 dc, ch 3, 3 dc) in same ch sp, (3 dc,

Continued on page 31

Christmas Creations

Fantasy Trees

Designed by Dolores Coyle

SMALL FANTASY TREE
Finished Size: 7½" tall.

Materials:
- ❑ 165 yds. white size 10 crochet cotton thread
- ❑ Plastic wrap
- ❑ Fabric stiffener
- ❑ 9"-tall Styrofoam® cone
- ❑ No. 7 steel hook

Basic Stitches: Ch, sl st, sc, dc, tr.

TREE
Rnd 1: Starting at tip, ch 4, sl st in first ch to form ring, ch 3, 9 dc in ring, join with sl st in top of ch-3. *(10 dc made)*

Rnd 2: Ch 4, tr in each dc around, join with sl st in top of ch-4.

Rnd 3: (Ch 4, tr) in first tr, 2 tr in each tr around, join. *(20 tr)*

Rnd 4: Ch 4, tr in each of next 3 tr, (2 tr in next tr, tr in next 4 tr) around to last tr, 2 tr in last tr, join. *(24)*

Rnd 5: Ch 4, tr in each tr around, join.

Rnd 6: Ch 4, tr in next 4 tr, (2 tr in next tr, tr in next 5 tr) around to last tr, 2 tr in last tr, join. *(28)*

Rnd 7: Ch 6 *(counts as tr and ch 2)*, (skip next tr, tr in next tr, ch 2) around skipping last tr, join with sl st in fourth ch of ch-6. *(14 tr, 14 ch sps)*

Rnd 8: Ch 4, (tr in next ch sp, tr in next tr, 2 tr in next ch sp, tr in next tr, 2 tr in next ch sp, tr in next tr) around to last 2 ch sps, tr in next ch sp, tr in last tr, tr in last ch sp, join. *(36 tr)*

Rnd 9: Ch 1, sc in each tr around, join with sl st in first sc.

Rnd 10: Ch 6, (skip next sc, tr in next sc, ch 2) around skipping last sc, join with sl st in fourth ch of ch-6. *(18)*

Rnd 11: Ch 4, (tr in next ch sp, tr in next tr, 2 tr in next ch sp, tr in next tr) around to last 2 ch sps, tr in next ch sp, tr in last tr, tr in last ch sp, join with sl st in top of ch-4. *(44)*

Rnd 12: Ch 1, sc in each tr around, join with sl st in first sc.

Rnd 13: Ch 6, skip next sc, tr in next sc, (ch 2, skip next sc, tr in next sc) around, ch 2, join with sl st in fourth ch of ch-6. *(22 tr, 22 ch sps)*

Rnd 14: Ch 4, (tr in next ch sp, tr in next tr) 2 times, *2 tr in next ch sp, (tr in next tr, tr in next ch sp) 2 times, tr in next st; repeat from * 4 more times, (2 tr in next ch sp, tr in next tr, tr in next ch sp, tr in next st) 2 times, 2 tr in last ch sp, join with sl st in top of ch-4. *(52 tr)*

Rnd 15: Ch 1, sc in each st around, join with sl st in first sc.

Rnds 16–17: Ch 4, tr in each tr around, join with sl st in top of ch-4.

Rnd 18: Ch 1, sc in each tr around, join with sl st in first sc. Fasten off.

First Ruffle
Rnd 1: Join with **sc front post** *(fp—see Stitch Guide)* around any tr on rnd 2, (ch 3, sc fp around next tr) around, ch 3, join with sl st in first sc. *(10 ch sps made)*

Rnd 2: Sl st in first ch-3 sp, (ch 3, 2 dc, ch 2, 3 dc) in same ch sp *(first shell made)*, sc in next ch sp, *(3 dc, ch 2, 3 dc) in next ch sp *(next shell made)*, sc in next ch sp; repeat from * around, join with sl st in top of ch-3. *(5 shells, 5 sc)*

Rnd 3: Sl st across each dc and into first ch-2 sp, (ch 4, 3 tr, ch 2, 4 tr) in same ch sp, ch 3, *(4 tr, ch 2, 4 tr) in next ch sp, ch 3; repeat from * around, join with sl st in top of ch-4. *(5 shells, 5 ch sps)*

Rnd 4: Ch 1, sc in first tr, *[(ch 3, sc in next tr) 3 times, (sc, ch 5, sc) in next ch-2 sp, (sc in next tr, ch 3) 3 times, sc in next tr, 3 sc in next ch-3 sp], sc in next tr; repeat from * around to last shell and last ch sp; repeat between [ ], join with sl st in first sc. Fasten off.

Second Ruffle
Rnd 1: Join with sc fp around any tr on rnd 4, (ch 3, skip next tr, sc fp around next tr) around, ch 3, skip last tr, join with sl st in first sc. *(24 ch sps made)*

Rnd 2: Sl st in first ch-3 sp, (ch 3, 2 dc, ch 2, 3 dc) in same ch sp *(first shell made)*, sc in next ch sp, *(3 dc, ch 2, 3 dc) in next ch sp *(next shell made)*, sc in next ch sp; repeat from * around, join with sl st in top of ch-3. *(5 shells, 5 sc)*

Rnd 3: Sl st across each dc and into first ch-2 sp, (ch 4, 3 tr, ch 2, 4 tr) in same ch sp, ch 3, *(4 tr, ch 2, 4 tr) in next ch sp, ch 3; repeat from * around, join with sl st in top of ch-4. *(5 shells, 5 ch sps)*

Rnd 4: Ch 1, sc in first tr, *[(ch 3, sc in next tr) 3 times, (sc, ch 5, sc) in next ch-2 sp, (sc in next tr, ch 3) 3 times, sc in next tr, 3 sc in next ch-3 sp], sc in next tr; repeat from * around to last shell and last ch sp; repeat between [ ], join with sl st in first sc. Fasten off.

Remaining Ruffles
For each Ruffle, repeat Second Ruffle on rnd 6, rnd 8, rnd 11 and rnd 14.

FINISHING
Dampen Tree with undiluted fabric stiffener according to manufacturer's directions, squeeze out excess liquid. Cover Styrofoam cone with plastic wrap. Place Tree on cone; shape as it dries.

Decorate Tree as desired.

LARGE FANTASY TREE
Finished Size: 8½" tall.

Materials:
- ❑ 185 yds. white size 10 crochet cotton thread
- ❑ Plastic wrap
- ❑ Fabric stiffener
- ❑ 9"-tall Styrofoam® cone
- ❑ No. 7 steel hook

Basic Stitches: Ch, sl st, sc, dc, tr.

TREE
Rnd 1: Starting at tip, ch 4, sl st in first ch to form ring, ch 3, 7 dc in ring, join with sl st in top of ch-3. *(8 dc made)*

Rnd 2: Ch 4, tr in same dc, 2 tr in each dc around, join with sl st in top of ch-4. *(16 tr)*

Rnd 3: Ch 4, tr in each tr around, join.

Rnd 4: Ch 6 *(counts as tr and ch 2)*, (skip next tr,

Continued on page 30

tr in next tr, ch 2) around to last tr, skip last tr, join with sl st in fourth ch of ch-6. *(8 tr, 8 ch sps)*

Rnd 5: Ch 4, (2 tr in next ch sp, tr in next tr) around to last ch sp, 2 tr in last ch sp, join with sl st in top of ch-4. *(24 tr)*

Rnd 6: Ch 4, tr in each tr around, join.

Rnd 7: Ch 6, skip next tr, tr in next tr, (ch 2, skip next tr, tr in next tr) around to last tr, ch 2, skip last tr, join with sl st in fourth ch of ch-6. *(12 tr)*

Rnd 8: Ch 4, *tr in next ch sp, tr in next tr, 2 tr in next ch sp, tr in next tr, 2 tr in next ch sp, tr in next tr; repeat from * around to last 3 ch sps, tr in next ch sp, tr in next tr, 2 tr in next ch sp, tr in next tr, 2 tr in last ch sp, join with sl st in top of ch-4. *(32 tr)*

Rnd 9: Ch 1, sc in each tr around, join with sl st in first sc.

Rnd 10: Ch 4, tr in each sc around, join with sl st in top of ch-4.

Rnd 11: Ch 6, (skip next tr, tr in next tr, ch 2) around to last tr, skip last tr, join with sl st in fourth ch of ch-6. *(16 tr)*

Rnd 12: Ch 4, (tr in next ch sp, tr in next tr, 2 tr in next ch sp, tr in next tr) 7 times, tr in next ch sp, tr in next tr, 2 tr in last ch sp, join with sl st in top of ch-4. *(40 tr)*

Rnd 13: Ch 1, sc in each tr around, join with sl st in first sc.

Rnd 14: Ch 4, tr in each sc around, join with sl st in top of ch-4.

Rnd 15: Ch 6, (skip 1 tr, tr in next tr, ch 2) around to last tr, skip last tr, join with sl st in fourth ch of ch-6. *(20 tr)*

Rnd 16: Ch 4, *tr in next ch sp, tr in next tr, 2 tr in next ch sp, tr in next tr; repeat from * around to last 4 ch sps, tr in next ch sp, (tr in next tr, tr in next ch sp) 3 times, join with sl st in top of ch-4. *(48 tr)*

Rnd 17: Ch 4, tr in each tr around, join with sl st in top of ch-4.

Rnd 18: Ch 1, sc in each tr around, join with sl st in first sc.

Rnd 19: Ch 4, tr in each sc around, join with sl st in top of ch-4.

Rnd 20: Ch 4, tr in next 4 tr, (2 tr in next tr, tr in next 5 tr) around to last tr, 2 tr in last tr, join. *(56 tr)*

Rnd 21: Ch 1, sc in each tr around, join with sl st in first sc. Fasten off.

First Ruffle

Rnd 1: Join with sc fp around any tr on rnd 3, (ch 3, skip next tr, sc fp around next tr) around to last tr, ch 3, skip last tr, join with sl st in first sc. *(16 ch sps made)*

Rnd 2: Sl st in first ch-3 sp, (ch 3, 2 dc, ch 2, 3 dc) in same ch sp *(first shell made)*, sc in next ch sp, *(3 dc, ch 2, 3 dc) in next ch sp (next shell made)*, sc in next ch sp*; repeat from * around, join with sl st in top of ch-3. *(8 shells, 8 sc)*

Rnd 3: Sl st across each dc and into first ch-2 sp, (ch 4, 3 tr, ch 2, 4 tr) in same ch sp, ch 2, *(4 tr, ch 2, 4 tr) in next ch sp, ch 2; repeat from * around, join with sl st in top of ch-4. *(8 shells, 8 ch sps)*

Rnd 4: Sl st across each tr and into first ch-2 sp, (ch 4, 3 tr, ch 2, 4 tr) in same ch sp, ch 3, sc in next ch sp, ch 3, *(4 tr, ch 2, 4 tr) in next ch sp, ch 3, sc in next ch sp, ch 3; repeat from * around, join. *(8 shells, 16 ch sps)*

Rnd 5: Ch 1, sc in first tr, *[(ch 3, sc in next tr) 3 times, sc in next ch-2 sp, ch 5, sc in same ch sp, (sc in next tr, ch 3) 3 times, sc in next tr, 3 sc in each of next 2 ch-3 sps], sc in next tr*; repeat from * around to last shell and last 2 ch sps; repeat between [ ], join with sl st in first sc. Fasten off.

Second Ruffle

Rnd 1: Join with sc fp around any tr on rnd 6, (ch 3, skip next tr, sc fp around next tr) around to last tr, ch 3, skip last tr, join with sl st in first sc. *(24 ch sps made)*

Rnd 2: Sl st in first ch-3 sp, (ch 3, 2 dc, ch 2, 3 dc) in same ch sp *(first shell made)*, sc in next ch sp, *(3 dc, ch 2, 3 dc) in next ch sp (next shell made)*, sc in next ch sp*; repeat from * around, join with sl st in top of ch-3. *(8 shells, 8 sc)*

Rnd 3: Sl st across each dc and into first ch-2 sp, (ch 4, 3 tr, ch 2, 4 tr) in same ch sp, ch 2, *(4 tr, ch 2, 4 tr) in next ch sp, ch 2; repeat from * around, join with sl st in top of ch-4. *(8 shells, 8 ch sps)*

Rnd 4: Sl st across each tr and into first ch-2 sp, (ch 4, 3 tr, ch 2, 4 tr) in same ch sp, ch 3, sc in next ch sp, ch 3, *(4 tr, ch 2, 4 tr) in next ch sp, ch 3, sc in next ch sp, ch 3; repeat from * around, join. *(8 shells, 16 ch sps)*

Rnd 5: Ch 1, sc in first tr, *[(ch 3, sc in next tr) 3 times, sc in next ch-2 sp, ch 5, sc in same ch sp, (sc in next tr, ch 3) 3 times, sc in next tr, 3 sc in each of next 2 ch-3 sps], sc in next tr*; repeat from * around to last shell and last 2 ch sps; repeat between [ ], join with sl st in first sc. Fasten off.

Remaining Ruffles

For each Ruffle, repeat Second Ruffle on rnd 10, rnd 14 and rnd 17.

FINISHING

Dampen Tree with undiluted fabric stiffener according to manufacturer's directions, squeeze out excess liquid. Cover Styrofoam cone with plastic wrap. Place Tree on cone; shape as it dries.

Decorate Tree as desired. ❏❏

ch 3, 3 dc) in each ch sp around, join. Fasten off. Finish according to General Instructions on page 27.

ORNAMENT NO. 4 (shown at bottom left in photo)
Rnd 1: Ch 10, sl st in first ch to form ring, ch 4, 23 tr in ring, join with sl st in top of ch-4. *(24 tr made)*

Rnd 2: Working in **back lps** (see Stitch Guide), (ch 3, dc) in first st, dc in next st, (2 dc in next st, dc in next st) around, join with sl st in top of ch-3. *(36 dc)*

Rnd 3: Working in **back lps,** (ch 2, hdc) in first st, hdc in next st, (2 hdc in next st, hdc in next st) around, join with sl st in top of ch-2. *(54 hdc)*

Rnd 4: Working in **back lps,** ch 1, sc in each st around, join with sl st in first sc. *(54 sc)*

Rnd 5: Working in **back lps,** ch 4, skip next st, (dc in next st, ch 1, skip next st) around, join with sl st in third ch of ch-4. *(27 ch sps)*

Rnd 6: Sl st in first ch sp, ch 5, (dc in next ch sp, ch 2) around, join with sl st in third ch of ch-5.

Rnd 7: Sl st in first ch sp, ch 6, (dc in next ch sp, ch 3) around, join with sl st in third ch of ch-6.

Rnd 8: (Sl st, ch 3, 2 dc, ch 3, 3 dc) in first ch sp, 3 sc in each of next 2 ch sps, *(3 dc, ch 3, 3 dc) in next ch sp, 3 sc in each of next 2 ch sps; repeat from * around, join with sl st in top of first ch-3.

Rnd 9: Sl st in each of next 2 sts and in next ch sp, (ch 3, 4 dc, ch 5, 5 dc) in same ch sp, ch 2, skip next sc, sc in next 4 sc, ch 2, skip next sc, *(5 dc, ch 5, 5 dc) in next ch sp, ch 2, skip next sc, sc in next 4 sc, ch 2, skip next sc; repeat from * around, join.

Rnd 10: Sl st in next 4 sts and in next ch sp, (ch 3, 6 dc, ch 7, 7 dc) in same ch sp, ch 5, skip next sc, sc in next sc, ch 5, skip next 2 sc and next ch sp, *(7 dc, ch 7, 7 dc) in next ch sp, ch 5, skip next sc, sc in next sc, ch 5, skip next 2 sc and next ch sp; repeat from * around, join.

Rnd 11: Sl st in next 6 sts and in next ch sp, (sc, hdc, dc, tr, **dtr**—see Stitch Guide, tr, dc, hdc, sc) in same ch sp, ch 5, sc in next ch sp, ch 3, sc in next ch sp, ch 5, *(sc, hdc, dc, tr, dtr, tr, dc, hdc, sc) in next ch sp, ch 5, sc in next ch sp, ch 3, sc in next ch sp, ch 5; repeat from * around, join with sl st in first sc. Fasten off.
Finish according to General Instructions on page 27.

ORNAMENT NO. 5 (shown at bottom center in photo)
Rnd 1: Ch 10, sl st in first ch to form ring, ch 4, 19 tr in ring, join with sl st in top of ch-4. *(20 tr made)*

Rnds 2–3: Working in **back lps** (see Stitch Guide), (ch 3, dc) in first st, 2 dc in each st around, join with sl st in top of ch-3. *(40 dc, 80 dc)*

Rnd 4: Working in **back lps,** ch 1, sc in each st around, join with sl st in first sc. *(80 sc)*

Rnd 5: Working in **back lps,** ch 10, skip next 9 sts, (sc in next st, ch 9, skip next 9 sts) around, join with sl st in first ch of ch-10. *(8 ch sps)*

Rnd 6: (Sl st, 5 sc, ch 5, 5 sc) in first ch sp, 10 sc in next ch sp, *(5 sc, ch 5, 5 sc) in next ch sp, 10 sc in next ch sp; repeat from * around, join with sl st in first sc.

NOTE: *Work remaining rnds in* **back lps.**

Rnd 7: Sl st in next 4 sts and in next ch sp, (ch 3, 3 dc, ch 4, 4 dc) in same ch sp, ch 4, skip next 6 sc, sc in next 8 sc, skip next 6 sc, ch 4, *(4 dc, ch 4, 4 dc) in next ch sp, ch 4, skip next 6 sc, sc in next 8 sc, ch 4, skip next 6 sc; repeat from * around, join with sl st in top of ch-3.

Rnd 8: Sl st in each of next 3 sts and in next ch sp, (ch 3, 4 dc, ch 5, 5 dc) in same ch sp, ch 5, skip next sc, sc in next 6 sc, skip next sc and next ch sp, ch 5, *(5 dc, ch 5, 5 dc) in next ch sp, ch 5, skip next sc, sc in next 6 sc, ch 5, skip next sc and next ch sp; repeat from * around, join.

Rnd 9: Sl st in next 4 sts and in next ch sp, (ch 3, 5 dc, ch 6, 6 dc) in same ch sp, ch 9, skip next sc, sc in next 4 sc, ch 9, skip next sc and next ch sp, *(6 dc, ch 6, 6 dc) in next ch sp, ch 9, skip next sc, sc in next 4 sc, ch 9, skip next sc and next ch sp; repeat from * around, join.

Rnd 10: Sl st in next 5 sts and in next ch sp, (ch 3, 6 dc, ch 3, 7 dc) in same ch sp, ch 11, skip next sc, sc in each of next 2 sc, ch 11, skip next sc and next ch sp, *(7 dc, ch 3, 7 dc) in next ch sp, ch 11, skip next sc, sc in each of next 2 sc, ch 11, skip next sc and next ch sp; repeat from * around, join. Fasten off.
Finish according to General Instructions on page 27.

ORNAMENT NO. 6 (shown at top left in photo)
Rnd 1: Ch 10, sl st in first ch to form ring, ch 4, 19 tr in ring, join with sl st in top of ch-4. *(20 tr made)*

Rnds 2–3: Working in **back lps** (see Stitch Guide), (ch 3, dc) in first st, 2 dc in each st around, join. *(40 dc, 80 dc)*

Rnd 4: Working in **back lps,** ch 1, sc in each st around, join with sl st in first sc. *(80 sc)*

Rnd 5: Working in **back lps,** ch 5, skip next 4 sts, (sc in next st, ch 5, skip next 4 sts) around, join with sl st in first ch of first ch-5. *(16 ch sps)*

Rnd 6: (Sl st, sc, hdc, dc, tr, dc, hdc, sc) in first ch sp, sc in next sc, *(sc, hdc, dc, tr, dc, hdc, sc) in next ch sp, sc in next sc; repeat from * around, join with sl st in first sc.

Rnd 7: Sl st in each of next 3 sts, (ch 6, dc) in same st, ch 7, sc in next tr, ch 7, *(dc, ch 3, dc) in next tr, ch 7, sc in next tr, ch 7; repeat from * around, join with sl st in third ch of ch-6.

Rnd 8: (Sl st, ch 4, 2 tr, ch 3, 3 tr) in first ch sp, ch 5, sc in next sc, ch 5, skip next ch sp, *(3 tr, ch 3, 3 tr) in next ch sp, ch 5, sc in next sc, ch 5, skip next ch sp; repeat from * around, join with sl st in top of ch-4.

Rnd 9: Sl st in each of next 2 sts and in next ch sp, (ch 4, 3 tr, ch 4, 4 tr) in same ch sp, ch 3, (sc in next ch sp, ch 3) 2 times, *(4 tr, ch 4, 4 tr) in next ch sp, ch 3, (sc in next ch sp, ch 3) 2 times; repeat from * around, join. Fasten off.
Finish according to General Instructions on page 27. ❏❏

Poinsettias & Lace

Designed by Donna Jones

Finished Sizes: Centerpiece is about 29½" across. Doily is about 14¾" across.

Materials:
- ❒ Size 10 crochet cotton thread for Centerpiece:
    - 360 yds. white
    - 120 yds. green
    - 110 yds. red
    - 10 yds. yellow
- ❒ Size 10 crochet cotton thread for Doily:
    - 250 yds. white
    - 36 yds. green
    - 33 yds. red
    - 3 yds. yellow
- ❒ No. 6 and No. 7 steel hooks or hooks needed to obtain gauges

Gauges:
For **Centerpiece: No. 7 hook,** 2 shells and 2 ch sps = 2"; 6 shell rows = 2".
For **Doily: No. 7 hook,** rnds 1–3 = 2" across. Poinsettia is 4" across.

Basic Stitches: Ch, sl st, sc, hdc, dc, tr.

Special Stitches:
For **beginning shell (beg shell),** (sl st, ch 5, 2 dc) in first ch sp.
For **shell,** (2 dc, ch 2, 2 dc) in ch sp of next shell or inc shell.
For **beginning increase shell (beg inc shell),** (sl st, ch 5, 2 dc, ch 2, 2 dc) in ch sp of next shell. *(Counts as 2 shells.)*
For **increase shell (inc shell),** (2 dc, ch 2, 2 dc, ch 2, 2 dc) in ch sp of next shell. *(Counts as 2 shells.)*
For **lacet,** ch 2, sc in next ch sp, ch 2.

Notes:
Use No. 7 hook for Centerpiece or Doily and No. 6 hook for Poinsettia.
Use the above instructions for working Special Stitches throughout.

CENTERPIECE
Row 1: With white, ch 109, dc in ninth ch from hook, (ch 3, skip next 3 chs, dc in next ch) 24 times, ch 6, skip next 3 chs, sl st in last ch, **do not turn.** *(26 ch sps made)*

Continued on page 34

Rnd 2: Working in remaining lps on opposite side of starting ch, (ch 5, 2 dc) in same ch as last sl st made *(half of first shell made)*, *ch 4, skip next 7 chs, (2 dc, ch 2, 2 dc) in next ch *(next shell made)*; repeat from * 11 more times, ch 4, skip next 6 chs, (2 dc, ch 2, 2 dc) in next ch, ch 4, skip next 2 chs, (2 dc, ch 2, 2 dc) in next ch; now working across top of row 1, ◊ch 4, skip next ch sp, next dc and next ch sp, (2 dc, ch 2, 2 dc) in next dc; repeat from ◊ 11 more times, ch 4, skip next ch sp, next dc and next 3 chs, (2 dc, ch 2, 2 dc) in next ch, ch 4, dc in first ch sp *(first shell completed)*, join with sl st in third ch of ch-5. *(28 shells)*

Rnd 3: Beg inc shell, lacet, (shell, lacet) 12 times, (inc shell, lacet) 2 times, (shell, lacet) 12 times, inc shell, lacet, dc in first ch sp, join.

Rnd 4: Beg shell, ch 1, *(shell, ch 4) 13 times, shell, ch 1, shell, ch 4*, shell, ch 1; repeat between first *, dc in first ch sp, join.

Rnd 5: Beg inc shell, *ch 2, inc shell, lacet, (shell, lacet) 12 times, inc shell, ch 2, inc shell, lacet*, inc shell; repeat between first *, dc in first ch sp, join.

Rnd 6: Beg shell, ch 1, shell, ch 4, shell, ch 1, shell, ch 4, (shell, ch 4) 12 times, (shell, ch 1, shell, ch 4) 4 times, (shell, ch 4) 12 times, (shell, ch 1, shell, ch 4) 2 times, dc in first ch sp, join.

Rnd 7: Beg shell, lacet, (shell, lacet) around, dc in first ch sp, join.

Rnd 8: Beg shell, ch 4, (shell, ch 4) around, dc in first ch sp, join.

Rnd 9: Beg shell, lacet, inc shell, lacet, (shell, lacet) 16 times, inc shell, lacet, (shell, lacet) 2 times, inc shell, lacet, (shell, lacet) 16 times, inc shell, lacet, shell, lacet, dc in first ch sp, join.

Rnd 10: Beg shell, ch 4, *shell, ch 1, (shell, ch 4) 17 times, shell, ch 1*, (shell, ch 4) 3 times; repeat between first *, (shell, ch 4) 2 times, dc in first ch sp, join.

Rnd 11: Beg shell, lacet, (shell, lacet) around, dc in first ch sp, join.

Rnd 12: Beg shell, ch 4, shell, ch 4, *inc shell, ch 4, (shell, ch 4) 16 times, inc shell, ch 4*, (shell, ch 4) 4 times; repeat between first *, (shell, ch 4) 2 times, dc in first ch sp, join.

Rnd 13: Beg shell, lacet, shell, lacet, *shell, ch 1, (shell, lacet) 17 times, shell, ch 1*, (shell, lacet) 5 times; repeat between first *, (shell, lacet) 3 times, dc in first ch sp, join.

Rnd 14: Beg inc shell, ch 4; skipping ch-1 sps, (shell, ch 4) 22 times, (inc shell, ch 4) 2 times, (shell, ch 4) 22 times, inc shell, ch 4, dc in first ch sp, join.

Rnd 15: Beg shell, ch 1, (shell, lacet) 23 times, (shell, ch 1, shell, lacet) 2 times, (shell, lacet) 22 times, shell, ch 1, shell, lacet, dc in first ch sp, join.

Rnd 16: Beg shell, ch 4, (shell, ch 4) around, dc in first ch sp, join.

Rnd 17: (Ch 3, 4 dc; for **picot, ch 3, sl st in top of last dc made;** 5 dc) in first ch-2 sp, ch 1, sc in next ch-4 sp, ch 1, *(5 dc, picot, 5 dc) in next ch-2 sp, ch 1, sc in next ch-4 sp, ch 1; repeat from * around, join. Fasten off.

Make 10 Poinsettias using the following instructions and attach to Centerpiece.

POINSETTIA
Rnd 1: Starting at center, with yellow, ch 2, (dc, ch 1, sl st) in second ch from hook, (ch 1, dc, ch 1, sl st) 4 times in same ch. Fasten off. *(5 sl sts made)*

Rnd 2: For **Small Petals,** join red with sl st in any sl st, *(ch 10, sc in second ch from hook, hdc in next ch, dc in next ch, tr in each of next 3 chs, dc in next ch, hdc in next ch, sc in next ch, sl st in same sl st on rnd 1 as last sl st), ch 2, sl st in next sl st on rnd 1; repeat from * 3 more times; repeat between ( ), ch 1, join with sc in first sl st *(joining sc forms joining ch sp—5 Small Petals)*

Rnd 3: For **Large Petals,** working behind rnd 2, (ch 13, sc in second ch from hook, hdc in next ch, dc in next ch, tr in next 6 chs, dc in next ch, hdc in next ch, sc in last ch, sl st in same ch sp on rnd 2, ch 2, sl st in next ch sp) around, join with sl st in first ch of first ch-13. Fasten off.

NOTE: Mark desired locations on crochet piece for joining Poinsettias. Choose one of the following options to attach Poinsettias:

Option 1: To **join tip of Leaf on Poinsettia to crochet piece or to another Poinsettia as you work,** *change last ch at tip of Leaf to a sl st in desired location on Centerpiece or to tip of Leaf on another Poinsettia and complete Leaf instructions as stated on rnd 4.*

Option 2: *Complete Poinsettia as stated in rnd 4. Position on Centerpiece and tack in place.*

Rnd 4: For **Leaves,** working behind rnd 3, join green with sl st in ch sp behind any Small Petal, *ch 6, sl st in **back strands** of sc (see Stitch Guide) at tip of corresponding Small Petal, ch 6, sc in second ch from hook, hdc in next ch, dc in next ch, tr in next 2 chs, tr in **back bar** (see Stitch Guide) of next sl st, tr in each of next 3 chs, dc in next ch, hdc in next ch, sc in last ch, sl st in same ch sp on rnd 3, ch 10, sl st in back strands of sc at tip of next Large Petal, ch 2, sc in second ch from hook, hdc in back bar of next sl st, dc in next ch, tr in next 6 chs, dc in next ch, hdc in next ch, sc in next ch, ch 1, sl st in next ch sp on last rnd; repeat from * around with last sl st of last repeat in joining sl st. Fasten off.

DOILY
Rnd 1: With white, ch 4, sl st in first ch to form ring, ch 3, dc in ring, ch 1, (2 dc in ring, ch 1) 5 times, join with sl st in top of ch-3. *(6 ch sps made)*

Rnd 2: Beg shell, ch 1, (shell, ch 1) around, dc in first ch sp, join with sl st in third ch of ch-5.

Rnd 3: Beg shell, lacet, (shell, lacet) around, dc in first ch sp, join.

Rnd 4: Beg inc shell, ch 3, skip lacets, (inc shell, ch 3) around, dc in first ch sp, join.

Rnd 5: Beg shell, shell, lacet, (shell 2 times, lacet) around, dc in first ch sp, join.

Rnd 6: Beg shell, ch 3, (shell, ch 3) around, dc in first ch sp, join.

Rnd 7: Beg inc shell, lacet, (inc shell, lacet) around, dc in first ch sp, join.

Rnd 8: Beg shell, ch 1, shell, ch 2, (shell, ch 1, shell, ch 2) around, dc in first ch sp, join.

Rnd 9: Beg shell, lacet, (shell, lacet) around, dc in first ch sp, join.

Rnd 10: Beg shell, ch 2, (shell, ch 2) around, dc in first ch sp, join.

Rnd 11: Beg shell, lacet, (shell, lacet) around, dc in first ch sp, join.

Rnd 12: Beg shell, ch 3, (shell, ch 3) around, dc in first ch sp, join.

Rnd 13: Beg inc shell, lacet, (shell, lacet, inc shell, lacet) 11 times, shell, lacet, dc in first ch sp, join.

Rnd 14: Beg shell, ch 1, *(shell, ch 2) 2 times, shell, ch 1; repeat from * 10 more times, (shell, ch 2) 2 times, dc in first ch sp, join.

Rnd 15: Beg shell, lacet, (shell, lacet) around, dc in first ch sp, join.

Rnd 16: Beg shell, ch 3, (shell, ch 3) around, dc in first ch sp, join.

Rnd 17: Beg shell, lacet, (shell, lacet) around, dc in first ch sp, join.

Rnd 18: Beg shell, ch 4, (shell, ch 4) around, dc in first ch sp, join.

Rnd 19: (Ch 3, 4 dc, picot, 5 dc) in first ch-2 sp, sc in next ch-4 sp, *(5 dc, picot, 5 dc) in next ch-2 sp, sc in next ch-4 sp; repeat from * around, join with sl st in top of ch-3. Fasten off.

Make three Poinsettias and attach to Doily. ❏❏

*W*hat flower is more synonymous with the spirit of Christmas than the showy scarlet poinsettia? Whether a single large bloom bedecked with ribbon adorning a table or mantel, or a floral array of pots lining a walk or stairwell, no flower makes more of a seasonal impact than this colorful native of tropical Mexico.

Legend has it that the poinsettia was a wayside weed of nondescript green before it was changed by the tenderhearted act of a poor little Mexican girl. Desperate for a gift to offer the baby Jesus, she presented Him with an armload of poinsettia branches she had lovingly picked. Once in His Holy presence, the uppermost leaves spontaneously turned a vivid red.

History tells us the poinsettia first became a mainstay of the holidays after it was introduced into the United States by Joel Robert Poinsett, the American Minister to Mexico in the 1920s. He was so taken with the plant's striking appeal that he brought some back with him when he returned to his native state of South Carolina.

As a result, their popularity grew so fast that Mexican producers could scarcely keep up with the demand. In appreciation for this sudden new industry, the growers named the plant poinsettia for the diplomat who had become their benefactor.

The bright flowers of the poinsettia are not blossoms at all, but bracts, or colored leafy growth, that surround the plant's small yellow flowers.

Millions of the plants are displayed and sold every year during the poinsettia's peak blooming months of November and December. Although the traditional red remains the most popular choice, newer varieties of poinsettias include white, pink, peach, yellow and mottled colors.

A less common member of the same plant family, also known for its wintertime green foliage and contrasting crimson blooms, is the Crown of Thorns. Sometimes seen displayed alongside poinsettias, together the two ornamentals capture the spectacular celebration and solemn symbolism that is the commemoration of our Saviour's birth.

BASIC INSTRUCTIONS

Finished Sizes: Snowflakes and Sachets range in size from 4½" across to 5¾" across.

Basic Materials:
- ❏ Size 10 white crochet cotton thread *(amount and color listed in individual pattern)*
- ❏ Two satin fabric circles of desired color *(size listed in individual pattern)*
- ❏ Polyester fiberfill
- ❏ Fabric stiffener *(for Snowflake only)*
- ❏ Potpourri oil
- ❏ Sewing thread and needle
- ❏ No. 7 steel hook or hook needed to obtain gauge

Basic Stitches: Ch, sl st, sc, hdc, dc, tr.

SNOWFLAKE

For **Snowflake,** make one Front piece of desired Sachet. Dampen Snowflake thoroughly with fabric stiffener. Shape Snowflake *(see General Instructions on page 159).* Let dry completely.

SACHET PILLOW

Allowing ¼" for seam, sew satin circles right sides together, leaving opening for turning. Clip and trim edge. Turn. Place potpourri oil between 2 layers of fiberfill, insert in opening; finish stuffing around fiberfill layers, shaping Pillow. Sew opening closed.

HANGER

For Hanger, use desired length of ribbon to match color of satin fabric. Insert one end of ribbon through desired point on last rnd of Sachet or Snowflake and tie ends in knot or bow, forming a loop.

SACHET NO. 1

Materials:
- ❏ 40 yds. white size 10 crochet cotton thread
- ❏ Two 2¾" circles of desired color satin fabric

Gauge: Rnds 1–3 = 2½" across.

PILLOW

Make one according to Sachet Pillow in Basic Instructions on this page.

BACK

Rnd 1: Ch 6, sl st in first ch to form ring, ch 1, sc in ring, (ch 15, sc in ring) 11 times, ch 8, **triple treble** *(ttr—see Stitch Guide)* in ring *(ch 8 and ttr count as a ch sp),* **do not join.** *(12 ch sps made)*

Rnd 2: Ch 1, sc in first ch sp, ch 5, (sc in next ch sp, ch 5) around, join with sl st in first sc. *(12 sc, 12 ch sps)*

Rnd 3: Ch 1, sc in first st, 5 sc in next ch sp, (sc in next st, 5 sc in next ch sp) around, join. Fasten off. *(72 sc)*

FRONT

Rnds 1–3: Repeat rnds 1–3 of Back. At end of last rnd, **do not fasten off.**

Rnd 4: Place Front and Back wrong sides together; working through both thicknesses in **back lps** *(see Stitch Guide),* ch 1, sc in each st

around, inserting Pillow before completing rnd, join.

Rnd 5: Ch 1, sc in first st, *(for **picot, ch 6, sl st in fifth ch from hook)** 6 times, [ch 1, sl st in base of second picot from hook, ch 5, sl st in same st, ch 1, dc in base of next picot, ch 5, sl st in top of dc just made, ch 1, tr in base of next picot, ch 5, sl st in top of tr just made, ch 1, ttr in base of next picot, ch 5, sl st in top of ttr just made, ch 1, ttr in base of next picot, ch 5, sl st in top of ttr just made, ch 1, skip next 7 sts on rnd 4, sc in next st, ch 4, skip next st, tr in next st, (ch 5, sl st in fifth ch from hook) 3 times, sl st in top of last tr made, ch 4, skip next st], sc in next st; repeat from * 4 more times, picot 6 times; repeat between [ ], join. Fasten off.

SACHET NO. 2

Materials:
- ❏ 50 yds. white size 10 crochet cotton thread
- ❏ Two 3¼" circles of desired color satin fabric

Gauge: Rnds 1–2 = 2¾" across.

PILLOW

Make one according to Sachet Pillow in Basic Instructions on this page.

BACK

Rnd 1: Ch 5, sl st in first ch to form ring, ch 1, (sc in ring, ch 15) 6 times, join with sl st in first sc. *(6 sc, 6 ch-15 sps made)*

Rnd 2: Ch 1, sc in first st; for **petal, (3 sc, hdc, 4 dc, 2 tr, ch 3, 2 tr, 4 dc, hdc, 3 sc) in next ch sp;** (sc in next st, petal) around, join with sl st in first sc. Fasten off. *(6 petals)*

FRONT

Rnds 1–2: Repeat rnds 1–2 of Back.

Rnd 3: Place Front and Back wrong sides together; working through both thicknesses, join with sc in ch-3 sp of any petal, ch 11, (sc in ch-3 sp of next petal, ch 11) around, inserting Pillow before completing rnd, join.

Rnd 4: Ch 1, sc in first st, 13 sc in next ch-11 sp, (sc in next st, 13 sc in next ch-11 sp) around, join. *(84 sc)*

Rnd 5: Ch 1, sc in first st, ch 9, skip next 6 sts, (sc in next st, ch 9, skip next 6 sts) around, join. *(12 ch-9 sps)*

Rnd 6: Ch 1, sc in first st; for **picot, ch 4, sl st in top of sc just made;** *(4 sc, picot, 7 sc) in next ch-9 sp, (sc, picot) in next st, [7 sc in next ch-9 sp, ch 11, **turn;** skip next picot, sl st in same st as next picot, **turn;** (4 sc, picot, 3 sc) in ch-11 sp, (ch 4, sl st in fourth ch from hook) 3 times, sl st in last sc made, (3 sc, picot, 4 sc) in same ch-11 sp, (sc, picot, 3 sc) in same ch-9 sp on rnd 5], (sc, picot) in next st, (4 sc, picot, 7 sc) in next ch-9 sp, (sc, picot) in next st; repeat from * 4 more times; repeat between [ ], join. Fasten off.

SACHET NO. 3

Materials:
- ❏ 45 yds. white size 10 crochet cotton thread
- ❏ Two 2¾" circles of desired color satin fabric

Continued on page 38

Snowflake Sachets

Designed by Lucille LaFlamme

Snowflake Sachets

Continued from page 36

Gauge: Rnds 1–2 = 1" across.

PILLOW
Make one according to Sachet Pillow in Basic Instructions on page 36.

BACK
Rnd 1: Ch 6, sl st in first ch to form ring, ch 1, 12 sc in ring, join with sl st in first sc. *(12 sc made)*

Rnd 2: Ch 1, sc in first st, ch 5, skip next st, (sc in next st, ch 5, skip next st) around, join. *(6 ch-5 sps)*

Rnd 3: Ch 1, sc in first st; for **petal, (hdc, 2 dc, 3 tr, 2 dc, hdc) in next ch sp;** (sc in next st, petal) around, join. *(6 petals)*

Rnd 4: Working behind petals, ch 6, (sl st in next sc between petals, ch 6) around, join with sl st in first ch of first ch-6.

Rnd 5: For **petals,** (sc, hdc, 2 dc, 3 tr, 2 dc, hdc, sc) in each ch sp around, join. Fasten off.

FRONT
Rnds 1–5: Repeat rnds 1–5 of Back.

Rnd 6: Place Front and Back wrong sides together; working through both thicknesses, join with sc in center tr of any petal, ch 4, sc in same tr, ch 9, *(sc, ch 4, sc) in center tr of next petal, ch 9; repeat from * around, inserting Pillow before completing rnd, join.

Rnd 7: Sl st in next ch-4 sp, ch 5, (tr, ch 1, tr) in same sp; for **picot, ch 5, sl st in fourth ch hook;** (ch 4, sl st in fourth ch from hook) 2 times, sl st in base of picot, ch 2, (tr, ch 1) 2 times in same ch-4 sp, tr in same ch-4 sp, ch 3, (sc, picot) in next ch-9 sp, ch 3, *(tr, ch 1) 2 times in next ch-4 sp, tr in same ch-4 sp, picot, (ch 4, sl st in fourth ch from hook) 2 times, sl st in base of picot, ch 2, (tr, ch 1) 2 times in same ch-4 sp, tr in same ch-4 sp, ch 3, (sc, picot) in next ch-9 sp, ch 3; repeat from * around, join with sl st in fourth ch of first ch-5. Fasten off.

SACHET NO. 4

Materials:
❏ 25 yds. white size 10 crochet cotton thread
❏ Two 2½" circles of desired color satin fabric

Gauge: Rnds 1–2 = 1¾" across.

PILLOW
Make one according to Sachet Pillow in Basic Instructions on page 36.

BACK
Rnd 1: Ch 7, sl st in first ch to form ring, ch 6, (dc in ring, ch 3) 17 times, join with sl st in third ch of ch 66. *(18 ch sps made)*

Rnd 2: (Sl st, ch 1, sc) in next ch sp, (ch 5, sc in next ch sp) 17 times, ch 2, join with dc in first sc *(joining ch sp made)*.

Rnd 3: Ch 1, sc in joining ch sp, (ch 5, sc in next ch sp) 17 times, ch 2, join with dc in first sc. Fasten off.

Continued on page 42

Finished Sizes: Snowflakes range in size from 3" to 4" across.

Materials:
❏ 44 yds. white size 10 crochet cotton thread
❏ 2½ yds. of 1½" satin ribbon
❏ 5½ yds. of 1½" foil ribbon
❏ Large spray of baby's breath
❏ Fabric stiffener
❏ Hot glue or craft glue
❏ Plastic wrap
❏ 11½" Styrofoam® wreath
❏ Small piece florist wire
❏ 6"-square cardboard
❏ 8¾"-tall cardboard box
❏ Rust-proof straight pins
❏ No. 5 steel hook

Basic Stitches: Ch, sl st, sc, dc.

FIRST SNOWFLAKE
Side (make 4)
Rnd 1: Ch 6, sl st in first ch to form ring, ch 1, 12 sc in ring, join with sl st in first sc. *(12 sc made)*

Rnd 2: Ch 1, sc in first st, (ch 3, sc in next st, ch 5, sc in next st) 5 times, ch 3, sc in next st, ch 5, join. *(6 ch-3 sps, 6 ch-5 sps)*

Rnd 3: (Sl st, ch 1, sc) in first ch-3 sp, *[ch 3, 2 dc in next ch-5 sp, ch 6, sl st in fifth ch from hook, (ch 5, sl st in fifth ch from hook) 2 times, sl st in first ch of ch-6, 2 dc in same ch sp as last 2 dc made, ch 3], sc in next ch-3 sp; repeat from * 4 more times; repeat between [ ], join. Fasten off.

SECOND SNOWFLAKE
Side (make 2)
Ch 8, sl st in first ch to form ring, ch 3, dc in ring; for **picot, ch 5, sl st in fifth ch from hook;** (*2 dc in ring, ch 10, sl st in seventh ch from hook, ch 8, sl st in fifth ch from hook, picot 2 times, sl st in each of next 3 chs on last ch-8, ch 7, sl st in seventh ch from hook, sl st in each of next 3 chs of ch-10*, 2 dc in ring, picot) 5 times; repeat between first *, join with sl st in top of first ch-3. Fasten off.

SNOWFLAKE FINISHING
Wrap box in plastic wrap.

To stiffen, apply undiluted fabric stiffener to Side. Place right side of one Side centered over edge of box. Pin to shape. Let dry completely. Repeat for each Side.

With wrong sides together, glue center fold of two matching Snowflake Sides together. Repeat with remaining Snowflakes.

WREATH ASSEMBLY
Wrap satin ribbon around Wreath, covering completely. Secure ends with straight pins on back.

Cut 2½ yds. foil ribbon. Wrap around Wreath, secure ends with straight pins.

For bow, with remaining foil ribbon leaving 2" and 4" ends, wrap around cardboard, slide loops off cardboard, wrap wire around center of all loops. Glue baby's breath spray over half of Wreath *(see photo)*, glue bow centered over baby's breath. Glue Snowflakes around Wreath. ❏❏

Snowflake Wreath

Designed by Dot Drake

Globe & Bells

Designed by Wilma Bonner

GENERAL INSTRUCTIONS

Finished Sizes: Globe is 4" in diameter. Bells are 5" high without decoration.

Materials:
- ❒ Size 10 crochet cotton thread *(amount and color listed in individual pattern)*
- ❒ Clear glitter paint
- ❒ Small paintbrush
- ❒ Fabric stiffener
- ❒ Small covered plastic container
- ❒ Glue gun and glue stick
- ❒ Plastic wrap
- ❒ No. 8 steel hook or hook needed to obtain gauge

Basic Stitches: Ch, sl st, sc, hdc, dc, tr.

Special Stitches:
For **beginning V st (beg V st),** (ch 5, dc) in st or ch sp indicated.
For **V st,** (dc, ch 2, dc) in st or ch sp indicated.
For **beginning shell (beg shell),** (sl st, ch 3, dc, ch 2, 2 dc) in st or ch sp indicated.
For **shell,** (2 dc, ch 2, 2 dc) in st or ch sp indicated.
For **picot,** (sc, ch 3, sc) in st or ch sp indicated.

PORCELAIN-LOOK ROSE

1: To make bread dough roses with a porcelain look, remove crusts from three slices of white bread; mix bread with two tablespoons craft glue and a small amount of desired-color acrylic paint.

2: Knead dough mixture; it will be sticky at first, but continue kneading until it pulls away from your fingers; then pinch off a small amount and shape into a tiny ½" petal *(see illustration).*

3: Continue making petals, pressing base of each petal lightly over previous petals to form a rose, making each layer of petals slightly larger than the previous layer.

4: Let Rose dry for about two days until hard.

BASIC FINISHING

1: Using balloon or Styrofoam bell, undiluted fabric stiffener and plastic wrap, stiffen and shape crocheted piece according to Starching Instructions in General Instructions on page 159. Keep Handle on Bells in an upright position as they dry.

2: Paint the stiffened piece with glitter paint and allow to dry.

GLOBE

Materials:
- ❒ 50 yds. white size 10 crochet cotton thread
- ❒ Two 1⅛" plastic rings
- ❒ 7" of gold metallic cord
- ❒ 9" round white balloon
- ❒ 2 yds. of ³⁄₁₆" ribbon
- ❒ One "porcelain-look" rose *(see General Instructions on this page)* or artificial flower *(about 1" across)*
- ❒ Three satin rose leaves
- ❒ 12" × 16" piece of colored tulle

Gauge: 14 sts = 1".

FIRST HALF

Rnd 1: Join crochet thread with sc in ring *(see Stitch Guide)*, work 47 more sc in ring, join with sl st in first sc. *(48 sc made)*

Rnd 2: Ch 1, sc in first st, ch 5, skip next 7 sc, (sc in next sc, ch 5, skip next 7 sc) 5 times, join. *(6 sc, 6 ch sps)*

Rnd 3: Ch 1, sc in first st, (sc, 2 hdc, dc, tr, dc, 2 hdc, sc) in next ch sp *(petal made),* *sc in next sc, (sc, 2 hdc, dc, tr, dc, 2 hdc, sc) in next ch sp *(petal made);* repeat from * 4 more times, join. *(6 petals, 6 sc)*

Rnd 4: Ch 1, sc in first st, ch 5, skip next petal, (sc in next sc between petals, ch 5, skip next petal) 5 times, join. *(6 sc, 6 ch sps)*

Rnd 5: Ch 1, sc in first st, (sc, 2 hdc, 2 dc, 2 tr, **ttr—** *see Stitch Guide,* 2 tr, 2 dc, 2 hdc, sc) in next ch sp, *sc in next sc, (sc, 2 hdc, 2 dc, 2 tr, ttr, 2 tr, 2 dc, 2 hdc, sc) in next ch sp; repeat from * 4 more times, join. *(6 petals)*

Rnd 6: Sl st in next 7 sts, ch 1, sc in next st, (ch 11, sc in ttr at center of next petal) 5 times, ch 11, skip sl sts, join. *(6 ch sps)*

Rnd 7: **Beg V st** *(see Special Stitches)* in first st, skip next 3 chs, (**V st**–*see Special Stitches*–in next ch, skip next 3 chs) 2 times, *V st in next st, skip next 3 chs, (V st in next ch, skip next 3 chs) 2 times; repeat from * 4 more times, join. *(18 V sts)*

Rnd 8: Ch 3, 3 dc in next ch sp, skip next dc, (dc in next dc, 3 dc in next ch sp, skip next dc) 17 times, join. *(72 dc)*

Rnd 9: Ch 1, sc in first st, ch 3, skip next dc, (sc in next dc, ch 3, skip next dc) 35 times, join. *(36 ch sps)*

Rnds 10–11: Sl st in next 2 chs, ch 1, sc in ch sp, ch 3, (sc in next ch sp, ch 3) 35 times, skip sl sts, join. At end of last rnd, fasten off.

SECOND HALF

Rnds 1–10: Repeat rnds 1–10 of First Half.

Rnd 11: For **joining rnd,** sl st in next 2 chs, sc in ch sp, ch 2; matching wrong sides, sc in any ch sp on First Half, ch 2, (sc in next ch sp on Second Half, ch 2, sc in next ch sp on First Half, ch 2) around, join. Fasten off.

FINISHING

1: Work Basic Finishing in General Instructions on this page.

2: Insert tulle into Globe through center of one plastic ring.

3: With ribbon, make a multi-loop bow and glue to the Globe covering rnd 10 of both Halves.

4: For **Hanger,** fold 7" gold metallic cord in half, glue ends to center of bow.

5: Glue Rose and satin leaves over ends of Hanger at center of bow.

BELLS

Materials For One:
- ❒ 80 yds. white size 10 crochet cotton thread
- ❒ Styrofoam® bell form 3¾" high × 3½"-diameter base
- ❒ Two yds. of ⅛" ribbon
- ❒ Two "Porcelain-look" Roses *(see General Instructions on this page)* or artificial flower *(about 1" across)*
- ❒ Six satin rose leaves
- ❒ Rust-proof straight pins

Gauge: Rnd 1 = ¾" across.

Continued on page 42

BELL NO. 1

Rnd 1: Ch 10, join with sl st in first ch to form ring, ch 3, 23 dc in ring, join with sl st in top of ch-3. *(24 sc made)*

Rnd 2: Beg V st *(see Special Stitches on page 41)* in first st, ch 1, skip next 3 sts, (**V st**—*see Special Stitches*—in next st, ch 1, skip next 3 sts) 5 times, join with sl st in third ch of ch-5. *(6 V sts)*

Rnd 3: Ch 3, 5 dc in next ch-2 sp, dc in next dc, skip next ch-1 sp, (dc in next dc, 5 dc in next ch-2 sp, dc in next dc, skip next ch-1 sp) 5 times, join. *(42 dc, 6 ch sps)*

Rnd 4: Beg V st in first st, skip next 2 dc, (V st in next dc, skip next 2 dc) 13 times, join. *(14 V sts)*

Rnd 5: Ch 3, 3 dc in next ch-2 sp, skip next dc, (dc in next dc, 3 dc in next ch-2 sp, skip next dc) 13 times, join. *(56 dc)*

Rnd 6: Beg V st in first st, skip next 3 dc, (V st in next dc, skip next 3 dc) 13 times, join. *(14 V sts)*

Rnd 7: Ch 3, 3 dc in next ch-2 sp, skip next dc, (dc in next dc, 3 dc in next ch-2 sp, skip next dc) 13 times, join. *(56 dc)*

Rnd 8: Ch 23, sc in first st, sc in next dc, **picot** *(see Special Stitches)* in next dc, sc in next dc, (sc in next dc, ch 23, sc in same dc as last sc, sc in next dc, picot in next dc, sc in next dc) 13 times, join with sl st at base of first ch-23. Fasten off.

Rnd 9: Join with sl st in any ch-23 sp, ch 3, 8 dc in same sp, (9 dc in next ch-23 sp) 13 times, skip sl st, join.

Rnd 10: Ch 1, picot in first st, sc in each of next 3 dc, picot in next dc, sc in each of next 3 dc, picot in next dc, *(picot in next dc, sc in each of next 3 dc) 2 times, picot in next dc; repeat from * 12 more times, join with sl st in first sc. Fasten off.

HANDLE

Join crochet thread with sl st in sp between any 2 dc on rnd 1, ch 18, sl st in sp between 2 dc on opposite side of edge from where thread was joined, ch 1, (9 sc, 7 hdc, 9 sc) in ch-18 sp, sl st in same sp as first sl st. Fasten off.

FINISHING

1: Work Basic Finishing in General Instructions on page 41.

2: For **Hanger,** cut a 12"–16" length of ribbon and run through Handle, tie ends together.

3: With remaining ribbon, make two multi-loop bows and glue one to each side of Bell next to Handle.

4: Glue one Rose and three Leaves over center of each bow.

BELL NO. 2

Rnd 1: Ch 4, dc in fourth ch from hook, ch 2, (2 dc, ch 2) 5 times same ch as first dc, join with sl st in top of ch-4. *(12 dc, 6 ch sps made)*

Rnd 2: Beg shell *(see Special Stitches on page 41)* in first ch sp, ch 1, skip next 2 dc, (**shell**—*see Special Stitches*—in next ch sp, ch 1, skip next 2 dc) 5 times, join with sl st in top of ch-3. *(6 shells, 6 ch-1 sps)*

Rnd 3: Ch 3, dc in next dc, shell in next ch-2 sp, dc in next 2 dc, ch 1, skip next ch-1 sp, (dc in next 2 dc, shell in next ch-2 sp, dc in next 2 dc, ch 1, skip next ch-1 sp) 5 times, join. *(48 dc—including dc of shells)*

Rnd 4: Ch 3, dc in each of next 3 dc, shell in next ch-2 sp, dc in next 4 dc, ch 1, skip ch-1 sp, (dc in next 4 dc, shell in next ch-2 sp, dc in next 4 dc, ch 1, skip ch-1 sp) 5 times, join. *(72 dc)*

Rnd 5: Ch 3, dc in next 5 dc, (dc, ch 10, dc) in next ch-2 sp, dc in next 6 dc, ch 10, skip ch-1 sp, *dc in next 6 dc, (dc, ch 10, dc) in next ch-2 sp, dc in next 6 dc, ch 10, skip ch-1 sp; repeat from * 4 more times, join, **turn.** *(12 ch-10 sps)*

Rnd 6: Sl st in next 4 chs of first ch-10, (ch 3, 2 dc, ch 3, 3 dc) in same ch-10 sp, (3 dc, ch 3, 3 dc) in each ch-10 sp around, skip sl sts, join. *(72 dc, 12 ch sps)*

Rnd 7: Sl st across to next ch-3 sp, ch 13, dc in same ch-3 sp, (dc in next ch-3 sp, ch 10, dc in same ch-3 sp) 11 times, skip sl sts, join with sl st in third ch of ch-13. *(12 ch-10 sps)*

Rnd 8: Sl st in next 4 chs of first ch-10, (ch 3, 2 dc, ch 3, 3 dc) in same ch-10 sp, (3 dc, ch 3, 3 dc) in each ch-10 sp around, skip sl sts, join. *(72 dc, 12 ch sps)*

Rnd 9: Ch 1, sc in first st, **picot** *(see Special Stitches)* in next dc, sc in next dc, picot in next ch-3 sp, sc in next dc, picot in next dc, sc in next dc, (sc in next dc, picot in next dc, sc in next dc, picot in next ch-3 sp, sc in next dc, picot in next dc, sc in next dc) 11 times, join. Fasten off.

HANDLE

Work Handle for Bell No. 1.

FINISHING

Work Finishing for Bell No. 1. ❏❏

Snowflake Sachets
Continued from page 38

FRONT

Rnds 1–3: Repeat rnds 1–3 of Back. At end of last rnd, **do not fasten off.**

Rnd 4: Place Front and Back wrong sides together; working through both thicknesses, ch 1, sc in first sp, *(3 dc, ch 3, 3 dc) in next ch sp, sc in next ch sp, ch 5, sc in next ch sp; repeat from * 4 more times, insert Pillow, (3 dc, ch 3, 3 dc) in next ch sp, sc in next ch sp, ch 2, join with dc in first sc.

Rnd 5: Ch 1, sc in first sp; *[for **picot, ch 4, sl st in top of st just made;** ch 2, (dc, picot) in next st, dc in next st, (dc, picot) in next st, 2 dc in next ch sp, (ch 4, sl st in fourth ch from hook) 5 times, sl st in top of last dc made, ch 1, 2 dc in same ch sp, (dc, picot) in next st, dc in next st, (dc, picot) in next st, ch 2], sc in next ch sp; repeat from * 4 more times; repeat between [ ], join with sl st in first sc. Fasten off. ❏❏

Wedding Wonders

In
times past, no
betrothed young woman
would be wed without first
preparing her trousseau, a
trunkful of romantic clothing and
lovingly stitched household linens.
Though pre-ceremony wedding showers
have supplanted this quaint custom,
even a modern bride would embrace
the age-old lace and grace of
thread crochet.
Following is a trove of sentiment, all
rosettes and curlicues, fashioned
into exquisite accessories that
befit the joy of two
becoming one.

Bride's Headdress

Designed by Dot Drake

Finished Size: Make to fit.

Materials:
- ❏ 225 yds. white size 10 crochet cotton thread
- ❏ Three ¾" fabric flowers with stamens
- ❏ Two 1"-long fabric leaves
- ❏ Two pearl loop sprays with 3 strands each
- ❏ One spray of pearl strands
- ❏ Spray starch or fabric stiffener
- ❏ Hot glue gun
- ❏ White sewing thread
- ❏ Sewing needle
- ❏ No. 8 steel hook or hook needed to obtain gauge

Gauge: 5 sc = ½"; 7 sc **back sp** rows = 1".

HEADBAND

Row 1: Ch 7, sc in second ch from hook and in each ch across, ch 1, turn. *(6 sc)*

Row 2: Working in **back lps** only *(see Stitch Guide),* sc in each sc across, ch 1, turn.

Rows 3–132: Or to double the desired length; Repeat row 2, ending with an even numbered row divisible by 2; fold in half matching first and last rows together; working through both thicknesses, sl st in each st across, forming a seam. **Do not fasten off.**

Edging

Rnd 1: Ch 5 in seam, (skip next row, dc in end of next row, ch 2) around, join with sl st in third ch of ch-5. *(68 ch sps)*

Rnd 2: Sl st in first ch sp, (ch 2, 2 dc, ch 1; for **picot, ch 4, sl st in fourth ch from hook;** ch 1, 3 dc) in same ch sp, ch 2, sc in next ch sp, ch 2, *(3 dc, ch 1, picot, ch 1, 3 dc) in next ch sp, ch 2, sc in next ch sp, ch 2; repeat from * around, join with sl st in top of ch-2. Fasten off.

Joining with sl st in seam. repeat rnds 1 and 2 on opposite edge of Headband.

Shape and stiffen *(see General Instructions on page 159)* Edging only.

FIRST FLORET

Rnd 1: Ch 6, sl st in first ch to form ring, ch 6, (dc in ring, ch 3) 5 times, join with sl st in third ch of ch-6. *(6 sc, 6 ch sps)*

Rnd 2: For **petals,** sl st into ch sp, *[ch 2, 5 dc in same ch sp, work (4 dc, hdc, sc) around next dc so that petal is continuous but curving toward center], ch 2, sc in next ch sp; repeat from * 4 more times; repeat between [ ], ch 2, join with sl st in first st of first petal. Fasten off.

SECOND FLORET

Rnd 1: Ch 6, sl st in first ch to form ring, ch 6, (dc in

ring, ch 3) 5 times, join with sl st in third ch of ch-6. *(6 sc, 6 ch sps)*

Rnd 2: For **petals,** sl st in first ch sp, ch 2, 5 dc in same ch sp, ch 1, sl st in fifth dc on any petal of First Floret, ch 1, work (4 dc, hdc, sc) around next dc *(see Stitch Guide)* on this Floret, ch 2, sc in next ch sp, *[ch 2, 5 dc in same ch sp as sc, work (4 dc, hdc, sc) around next dc], ch 2, sc in next ch sp; repeat from * 3 more times; repeat between [ ], ch 2, join with sl st in first st of first petal. Fasten off.

THIRD FLORET

Rnd 1: Ch 6, sl st in first ch to form ring, ch 6, (dc in ring, ch 3) 5 times, join with sl st in third ch of ch-6. *(6 sc, 6 ch sps)*

Rnd 2: For **petals,** sl st in first ch sp, ch 2, 5 dc in same ch sp, ch 1, sl st in fifth dc of petal on second Floret according to dot on Joining Diagram, ch 1, work (4 dc, hdc, sc) around next dc on this Floret, ch 2, sc in next ch sp, *[ch 2, 5 dc in same ch sp, work (4 dc, hdc, sc) around next dc], ch 2, sc in next ch sp*, 5 dc in same ch sp, ch 1, sl st in fifth dc of marked petal on First Floret, ch 1, work (4 dc, hdc, sc) around next dc on this Floret, ch 2, sc in next ch sp; repeat between first * 2 times; repeat between [ ], ch 2, join with sl st in first st of first petal. Fasten off.

Glue a fabric flower to center of each Floret.

PICOT CHAIN WITH LEAVES

For **leaf,** ch 2, (hdc, dc, 2 tr) in second ch from hook, ch 2, **turn;** sc in first sc, sc in each of next 2 tr, sc in next dc, sc in next hdc, sl st in next ch; for picot chain, *ch 3, sc in third ch from hook; repeat from * until chain measures 36" long; for **leaf,** ch 2, (hdc, dc, 2 tr) in second ch from hook, ch 2, **turn;** sc in first sc, sc in each of next 2 tr, sc in next dc, sc in next hdc, sl st in next ch. Fasten off.

Shape Picot Chain into a loop; with white sewing thread, sew looped Picot Chain to back of the Florets so that you have several loops on top and 3 on the bottom, leaving 4" and 5" of leaf ends hanging.

Sew Florets with Picot Chain to Headband. Then glue one leaf to each side of Florets on Headband. Glue pearl loops on top and spray on bottom at back of Headband. ❏❏

JOINING DIAGRAM

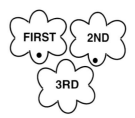

Finished Size: Fits a tall stemmed glass *(model shown is 8" tall).*

Materials For One:
- ❏ 57 yds. of desired color embroidery floss or size 20 crochet cotton thread
- ❏ 110 yds. metallic blending filament to match floss
- ❏ ½ yd. 3-mm bead trim
- ❏ 1½ yds. of ³⁄₁₆" ribbon
- ❏ Tall stemmed glass
- ❏ Craft glue
- ❏ Hot glue
- ❏ Size 24 tapestry needle
- ❏ No. 10 steel hook or hook needed to obtain gauge

Gauge: 5 dc = ½"; 2 dc rows = ½".

Basic Stitches: Ch, sl st, sc, hdc, dc, tr.

Special Stitches:
For **shell,** (2 dc, ch 2, 2 dc) in next ch sp or next st.
For **V st,** (dc, ch 3, dc) in next ch sp or next st.
For **dc next 3 sts tog,** (yo, insert hook in next st, yo, pull through st, yo, pull through 2 sps on hook) 3 times, yo, pull through all 4 sps on hook.
For **3 treble crochet cluster, (3-tr cl),** yo 2 times, insert hook in fifth ch from hook, yo, pull through ch, (yo, pull through 2 sps on hook) 2 times, *yo 2 times, insert hook in same ch, yo, pull through ch, (yo, pull through 2 sps on hook) 2 times; repeat from *, yo, pull through all 4 sps on hook.

Note: Use three strands of floss and one strand of metallic filament held together as one throughout or use one strand of crochet cotton thread and one strand of metallic filament held together as one throughout.

FAN *(make 2)*
Row 1: Starting at bottom, ch 4, (dc, ch 3, 2 dc) in fourth ch from hook, turn. *(4 dc, 1 ch-3 sp made)*
Row 2: Ch 3, dc in next st, ch 2, (2 dc, ch 3, 2 dc) in next ch-3 sp, ch 2, dc in last 2 sts, turn. *(8 dc, 2 ch-2 sps, 1 ch-3 sp)*
Row 3: Ch 3, dc in next st, ch 2, skip next ch-2 sp and next 2 sts, (2 dc, ch 2, 3 dc, ch 2, 2 dc) in next ch-3 sp, ch 2, skip next 2 sts and last ch-2 sp, dc in last 2 sts, turn. *(11 dc, 4 ch-2 sps)*
Row 4: Ch 3, dc in next st, ch 2, skip next ch-2 sp and next 2 sts, **shell** *(see Special Stitches)* in next ch-2 sp, ch 3, skip next 3 sts, shell in next ch-2 sp, ch 2, skip next 2 sts and last ch-2 sp, dc in last 2 sts, turn. *(2 shells, 4 dc, 2 ch-2 sps, 1 ch-3 sp)*
Row 5: Ch 3, dc in next st, ch 3, skip next ch-2 sp and next st, dc in next st, 2 dc in ch sp of next shell, dc in next 2 sts, 3 dc in next ch-3 sp, dc in next 2 sts, 2 dc in ch sp of next shell, dc in next st, ch 3, skip next st and last ch-2 sp, dc in last 2 sts, turn. *(17 dc, 2 ch-3 sps)*
Row 6: Ch 3, dc in next st, ch 3, skip next ch-3 sp, **V st** *(see Special Stitches)* in next st, (ch 2, skip next 2 sts, V st in next st) 4 times, ch 3, skip last ch-3 sp, dc in last 2 sts, turn. *(5 V sts, 4 dc, 4 ch-2 sps, 2 ch-3 sps)*
Row 7: Ch 3, dc in next st, ch 3, skip next ch-3 sp, tr in ch sp of next V st, ch 3, dc in center

strand of tr *(see illustration),* (ch 2, skip next ch-2 sp, tr in ch sp of next V st, ch 3, dc in center strand of tr) 4 times, ch 3, skip last ch-3 sp, dc in last 2 sts, turn. *(4 dc, 4 ch-2 sps, 7 ch-3 sps)*

Row 8: Ch 3, dc in next st, ch 3, skip next ch-3 sp, 5 dc in next ch-3 sp, (ch 2, skip next ch-2 sp, 5 dc in next ch-3 sp) 4 times, ch 3, skip last ch-3 sp, dc in last 2 sts, turn. *(29 dc, 4 ch-2 sps, 2 ch-3 sps)*
Row 9: Ch 3, dc in next st, ch 4, skip next ch-3 sp and next st, **dc next 3 sts tog** *(see Special Stitches),* (ch 7, skip next st, next ch-2 sp and next st, dc next 3 sts tog) 4 times, ch 4, skip next st and last ch-3 sp, dc in each of last 2 sts, turn. *(9 dc, 4 ch-7 sps, 2 ch-4 sps)*
Row 10: Ch 1, sc in each of first 2 sts, ch 9, skip next ch-4 sp and next st, sc in next ch-7 sp, (ch 9, skip next st, sc in next ch-7 sp) 3 times, ch 9, skip last ch-4 sp, sc in each of last 2 sts, **do not turn or fasten off.** *(8 sc, 5 ch-9 sps)*
Rnd 11: Now working in rnds, 3 sc in end of next 9 dc rows; working in remaining lps on opposite side of starting ch on row 1, 2 sc in ch; 3 sc in end of next 9 rows, sc in next 2 sc on row 10, 12 sc in next 5 ch-9 sps, sc in each of last 2 sc, join with sl st in first sc. Fasten off.

ROSE *(make 2)*
Rnd 1: Ch 2, sc in second ch from hook, (ch 3, sc in same ch as last sc made) 2 times, ch 3, join with sl st in first sc. *(3 ch-3 sps made)*
Rnd 2: For **petals,** (sc, hdc, 4 dc, hdc, sc) in each ch-3 sp around, **do not join.** *(3 petals)*
Rnd 3: Working behind petals, sl st in **back strands** *(see Stitch Guide)* of first sc on row 2, (ch 3, sc in back strands of next sc on rnd 1) 3 times, ch 3, **do not join.** *(4 ch-3 sps)*
Rnd 4: For **petals,** (sc, 8 dc, sc) in each ch-3 sp around. *(4 petals)*
Rnd 5: Ch 2, working in rnd 3 behind sts of rnd 4, sc between *(see illustration)* center 2 sts on next petal, (ch 4, sc between center 2 sts on next petal) 3 times, ch 4, skip first ch-2, join with sl st in first sc.

Rnd 6: For **petals,** (11 dc, sc) in each ch sp around, join with sl st in joining sl st. Fasten off. *(4 petals)*

LEAF SPRAY *(make 6)*
Starting at bottom of stem, ch 10, for **first Leaf, *3-tr cl** (see Special Stitches)* in fifth ch from hook; for **tip,** ch 3, sl st in top of 3-tr cl; ch 4, sl st in same ch as last 3-tr cl was made*; for **second Leaf,** ch 7; repeat between first *, sl st in next 2 chs on ch-7 of second Leaf; for **third Leaf,** ch 5; repeat between first *, sl st in last 5 chs of ch-10. Fasten off.

ROSE BUD *(make 3)*
Row 1: Ch 9, sc in fifth ch from hook, (ch 3, skip next ch, sc in next ch) 2 times, turn. *(3 sc, 3 ch-3 sps made)*
Row 2: (Sl st, ch 4, 4 tr) in first ch-3 sp, (ch 4, sl st in next sc, ch 4, 4 tr in next ch-3 sp) 2 times, ch 4, sl st in same ch-3 sp as last tr made. Fasten off.
Roll ends together, tack to secure.

Continued on page 51

Glass Sleeves

Designed by Bettie Dowler

Album Cover

Designed by
Lucille LaFlamme

Finished Size: Fits a 9" × 11" album.

Materials:
- ❏ 675 yds. white size 10 crochet cotton thread
- ❏ 9" × 11" wedding album
- ❏ 1 yd. of ¼" white ribbon
- ❏ 2 yds. thread elastic
- ❏ White sewing thread
- ❏ Plastic wrap
- ❏ 2½"-square cardboard
- ❏ Fabric stiffener
- ❏ Embroidery needle
- ❏ No. 6 steel hook or hook needed to obtain gauge

Gauges: 10 cl = 3"; 9 pattern rows = 2".

Basic Stitches:
Ch, sl st, sc, hdc, dc, tr.

Special Stitches:
For **double crochet cluster (dc cl)**, *yo, insert hook in st, yo, pull lp through, yo, pull through 2 lps on hook leaving last lps on hook; working in same st, repeat from * number of times needed for number of dc in cluster, yo and pull through all lps on hook.

For **double cluster (dbl cl)**, yo, insert hook in next st, (yo, pull through st, yo, pull through 2 lps on hook, yo insert hook in same st, yo, pull through st, yo, pull through 2 lps on hook, yo, pull through all 3 lps on hook—*first half of dbl cl made)*, ch 3, sl st in same st, ch 3, yo, insert hook in same st as last sl st; repeat between ( ) *(second half of dbl cl made)*.

For **shell**, 5 dc in next st.

For **double V st (dbl V st)**, (dc, ch 2, dc, ch 2, dc) in st or ch sp.

COVER

Row 1: Ch 230, dc in fourth ch from hook, dc in each ch across, turn. *(Front of row 1 is right side of work— 228 dc made)*

Row 2: Ch 1, sc in first st, ch 3, **2-dc cl** *(see Special Stitches)* in same st as last sc, *skip next 5 sts, **dbl cl** *(see Special Stitches)* in next st; repeat from * 36 more times, skip next 4 sts, (2-dc cl, ch 3, sl st) in last st, turn. *(37 dbl cl, 2 cl, 1 sc)*

Row 3: Ch 4, (skip first 2-dc cl, dbl cl in next cl, skip next cl, dbl cl in next cl) 37 times, tr in last sc, turn. *(38 dbl cl, 2 tr)*

Row 4: Ch 1, sc in first st, ch 5, skip next 2 cls, (sc in next cl, ch 5 skip next cl) 37 times, sc in last tr, turn. *(39 sc, 38 ch sps)*

Row 5: Ch 3, **shell** *(see Special Stitches)* in center ch of next ch-5, (3-dc cl—*see Special Stitches*—in next sc, shell in center ch of next ch-5) 37 times, dc in last st, turn. *(38 shells, 37 3-dc cl, 2 dc)*

Row 6: (Ch 5, dc) in first st, dbl V st *(see Special Stitches)* in each 3-dc cl across to last st, (dc, ch 2, dc) in last st, turn. *(37 dbl V st, 2 V sts)*

Row 7: (Ch 5, dc) in first st, dbl V st in center dc of each dbl V st across to last st, (dc, ch 2, dc) in last st, turn.

Row 8: Ch 4, (dc in next st, ch 1, dc in next st, 3-dc cl in next st) 37 times, (dc in next st, ch 1) 2 times, dc in third ch of ch-5, turn. *(78 dc, 37 3-dc cl, 39 ch sps)*

Row 9: Ch 3, skip first ch sp, (shell in next ch sp, 3-dc cl in next 3-dc cl) 37 times, shell in next ch sp,

skip last ch sp, dc in last st, turn. *(38 shells, 37 3-dc cl, 2 dc)*

Rows 10–45: Repeat rows 6–9 consecutively.

Row 46: (Ch 1, sc, ch 3, 2-dc cl) in first st, (skip next shell, dbl cl in next 3-dc cl) 37 times, skip last shell, (2-dc cl, ch 3, sl st) in last st, turn. *(37 dbl cl, 2 2-dc cl)*

Row 47: Ch 4, dbl cl in first 2-dc cl, (skip next cl, dbl cl in next cl) 37 times, skip last 2-dc cl, tr in last sc, turn. *(38 dbl cl, 2 tr)*

Row 48: Ch 1, sc in first st, (ch 5, skip next cl, sc in next cl) 37 times, ch 5, skip last 2 cls, sc in last st, turn. *(39 sc, 38 ch sps)*

Row 49: Ch 3, (5 dc in next ch sp, dc in next st) across. Fasten off. *(229 dc)*

Lay Cover wrong side up and place opened Album over Cover.

To form flap, turn short ends on Cover over each short edge of Album stretching to fit snugly. Working through both thicknesses, matching sts, with needle and crochet thread, sew top edge of flap together and bottom edge of flap together. Repeat on second side of Cover.

For fitted Cover, with needle and thread elastic, run double elastic through stitches around outer edges at top and bottom and flaps, tie ends together.

If needed, run thread elastic through center stitch at top edge of Cover between pages of Album, tie to center stitch at bottom edge of Cover.

ROSETTE (make 3)

Rnd 1: Ch 6, sl st in first ch to form ring, ch 3, 3 dc in ring, drop sp from hook insert hook in top of ch 3, pull dropped sp through ch *(first popcorn made)*, ch 4; *4 dc in ring, drop lp from hook insert hook in top of first dc in group, pull dropped lp through st *(next popcorn made)*, ch 4; repeat from * 2 more times, join with sl st in top of first popcorn. *(4 popcorns, 4 ch sps made)*

Rnd 2: Sl st in first ch sp, ch 1; for **petals**, (sc, hdc, 2 dc, hdc, sc) in each ch sp around, join with sl st in first sc. *(4 petals)*

Rnd 3: Working behind petals, ch 4, *sc bottom back strand of 2 dc sts *(see illustration)* on next petal tog, ch 4, sc back strand of next 2 sc tog, ch 4; repeat from * 2 more times, sc bottom back strand of next 2 dc sts on next petal tog, ch 4, join with sl st in first ch. *(8 ch sps)*

Rnd 4: Sl st in first ch sp; for **petals**, (sc, hdc, 3 dc, hdc, sc) in each ch sp around, join with sl st in first sc. Fasten off. *(8 petals)*

OPEN LACE FLOWER (make 3)

Rnd 1: Ch 7, sl st in first ch to form ring, ch 1, (sc in ring, ch 11) 6 times, join with sl st in first sc. *(6 sc, 6 ch sps made)*

Rnd 2: Sl st in first ch sp, ch 1, 18 sc in each ch sp around, join. Fasten off.

PETAL FLOWER (make 2)

Rnd 1: Ch 5, sl st in first ch to form ring, ch 1, 8 sc in ring, join with sl st in first sc. *(8 sc made)*

Rnd 2: For **petals**, *ch 4, (2 tr, ch 3, sl st in top of

Continued on page 50

Wedding Wonders

last tr made, 2 tr) in next st, ch 4, sl st in next st; repeat from * 2 more times, (2 tr, ch 3, sl st in top of last tr made, 2 tr) in next st, ch 4, join with sl st in first ch of ch-4. Fasten off. *(4 petals)*

BUD CLUSTER (make 3)

For Bud, (ch 4, 13 dc in fourth ch from hook, ch 3, sl st in same ch) 3 times. Fasten off. *(3 buds made)*

Fold one edge on one Bud to center, fold second edge over first edge, tack to secure. Repeat on each Bud.

CURLICUE (make 3)

Ch 16, 4 dc in fourth ch from hook, 4 dc in each ch across. Fasten off.

IRISH LEAF (make 2)

Row 1: Ch 16, sc in second ch from hook, sc in next 13 chs, 3 sc in last ch; working in remaining lps on opposite side of starting ch, sc in next 12 chs, leaving last 2 chs unworked, turn. *(29 sc)*

Rows 2–5: Working in **back lps** *(see Stitch Guide),* (ch 2, sc) in first st, sc in next 12 sts, 3 sc in next st, sc in next 12 sts, turn. At end of last row, fasten off.

OPEN LACE LEAF (make 2)

Row 1: Ch 15, sc in second ch from hook, (ch 1, skip next ch, dc in next ch) 6 times, ch 1, 3 sc in last ch; working in remaining lps on opposite side of starting ch, ch 1, (dc in next ch, ch 1, skip next ch) 6 times, sc in last ch, **do not turn.** *(17 sts made)*

Rnd 2: Ch 3, sc in first st, (ch 3, sc in next st) 15 times, ch 3, sl st in last st. Fasten off.

BELL (make 2)

Rnd 1: Starting at top, ch 6, sl st in first ch to form ring, ch 1, 12 sc in ring, join with sl st in first sc. *(12 sc made)*

Rnd 2: Ch 1, sc in first st, ch 3, skip next st, (sc in next st, ch 3, skip next st) around, join. *(6 sc, 6 ch sps)*

Rnd 3: Sl st in first ch, ch 1, sc in same ch sp, ch 4, (sc in next ch sp, ch 4) around, join.

Rnd 4: Sl st in first 2 chs, ch 1, sc in same ch sp, ch 4, (sc in next ch sp, ch 4) around, join.

Rnd 5: Sl st in first 2 chs, ch 1, sc in same ch sp, ch 5, (sc in next ch sp, ch 5) around, join.

Rnd 6: Sl st in first 3 chs, ch 1, sc in same ch sp, ch 5, (sc in next ch sp, ch 5) around, join.

Rnd 7: Sl st in first 3 chs, ch 1, sc in same ch sp, ch 6, (sc in next ch sp, ch 6) around, join.

Rnd 8: Sl st in first 3 chs, ch 1, sc in same ch sp, ch 7, (sc in next ch sp, ch 7) around, join.

Rnd 9: Ch 1, (4 sc, ch 3, sl st in last sc made, 4 sc) in first ch sp, *(4 sc, ch 3, sl st in last st made, 4 sc) in next ch sp; repeat from * around, join. Fasten off. *(48 sc)*

Soak Bell in fabric stiffener. Stuff plastic wrap inside Bell to form shape. Let dry. Remove plastic wrap when dry.

FINISHING

Arrange Rosettes, Open Lace Flowers, Petal Flowers, Bud Clusters, Curlicues, Irish Leaves, Open Lace Leaves and Bells on front of Cover according to placement illustration. With needle and thread, tack all pieces in place.

Tack one Bud Cluster to center top of Bells. For **Bow,** cut a 25" piece from ribbon. Wrap ribbon around a 2½" piece of cardboard five times.

Cut a 3" piece of ribbon. Slide bow off cardboard, wrap 3" piece of ribbon around center of Bow, tie in knot to secure. Sew bow above Bud Cluster directly above Bells. ❑❑

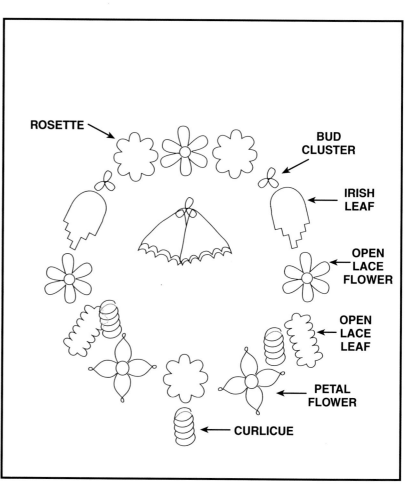

Glass Sleeves

Continued from page 46

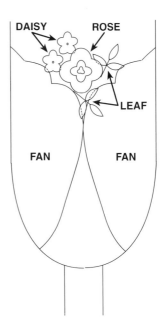

DAISY *(make 4)*
Make **slip ring** *(see Stitch Guide)*, (ch 3, dc in ring, ch 3, sl st in ring) 5 times; for **picot**, ch 3, sl st in third ch from hook, pull end of slip ring tightly to close. Leaving 6" for sewing, fasten off. Sew picot to center of ring.

ASSEMBLY
Glue top and sides of each Fan over glass with bottom of Fans touching at top of stem. Glue one Rose, two Leaves and two Daisies between each side of Fan *(see illustration)*.

Cut three pieces of ribbon 18" long.

Weave one piece of ribbon through row 1 on each Fan, tie in bow.

Tie remaining ribbons in a bow. Glue each bow to center of first bow.

Glue Rose Buds to center of bow and one Leaf Spray at top of Buds toward top of glass and one Leaf Spray at bottom of Buds toward bottom of glass.

Cut three strands of bead trim, each 3" long; glue one end of each strand behind bows. □⌐

F or the guests, a wedding celebration turns from observation to participation at the moment of the traditional toast. The requisite tribute to the newlyweds is a joyous communal blessing to the couple's married life together as all present lift their glasses in unison.

The toast, typically performed with wine or champagne, precedes the cutting of the cake and serving of refreshments, and is sometimes followed by the marriage cup toast, where the bride and groom drink from the same bowl-like cup with two handles, called a "coupe de mariage."

The act of drinking to one's welfare, known as "drinking a health," did not become known as a "toast" until sometime in the early 1700s in England, a reference to the then popular practice of floating pieces of spiced toast in one's wine.

An old German custom called for a Kostenbidder (or wedding inviter), to personally deliver wedding invitations to guests. He then acted as the "toastmaster" at the reception, calling each guest forward to propose a toast and present a gift to the newly-wedded couple.

Remnants of these rituals remain today. In England, for example, the best man calls for numerous toasts by family and friends and shares personal anecdotes about the couple, as well as reading aloud written congratulations they have received.

In Brittany, members of the wedding party drink from a glass of brandy poured over a piece of white bread. The bridal couple get the last sip and the bread for good luck.

Finished Sizes: 13", 14" or 15" neck.

Materials:
- ❏ 1,100 yds. white size 10 crochet cotton thread
- ❏ 280 yds. white size 5 crochet cotton
- ❏ Fabric glue
- ❏ Three white ⅜" pearl buttons
- ❏ White and contrasting color sewing thread
- ❏ Sewing and embroidery needles
- ❏ *For optional Lining*—tracing paper and ½ yd. flesh-color lining fabric
- ❏ *For optional Yoke Insert*—disappearing ink pen and plain-bodice dress or blouse with back opening
- ❏ No. 1 and No. 7 steel hooks or hooks needed to obtain gauges

Gauge: **No. 1 hook and size 5 crochet cotton,** corded trim = ¼" wide. **No. 7 hook and size 10 crochet cotton,** 9 chs = 1"; 23 yoke rows = 8"; 15 sc = 2". Rose is 1½" across, Violet is ¾" across.

Basic Stitches: Ch, sl st, sc, hdc, dc.

Special Stitches:
For **sc picot (scp),** sc in next ch sp, ch 4, sl st in **front lp and left bar** *(see Stitch Guide)* of last sc made sc in same ch sp.

Note: Instructions are for 13" neck; changes for 14" and 15" are in [ ].

YOKE

Row 1: Beginning at bottom center front, with No. 7 hook and size 10 crochet cotton, ch 6, **dtr** *(see Stitch Guide)* in sixth ch from hook, ch 9, 2 dtr in same ch, turn. *(4 dtr, 1 ch sp made)*

Row 2: Ch 5, dtr in next st, ch 9; **scp** *(see Special Stitches),* ch 9, dtr in each of last 2 sts, turn. *(4 dtr, 2 ch sps)*

Rows 3–4: Ch 5, dtr in next st, (ch 9, scp) across to last 2 sts, ch 9, dtr in each of last 2 sts, turn. At end of last row *(4 dtr, 4 ch sps).*

Row 5: Ch 5, dtr in next st, ch 5, (scp, ch 9) across to last 2 sts, dtr in each of last 2 sts, turn. *(4 dtr, 5 ch sps)*

Row 6: Ch 5, dtr in next st, (ch 9, scp) across to last ch sp, ch 9, skip last ch sp, sc in each of last 2 sts, turn. *(2 dtr, 5 ch sps, 2 sc)*

Row 7: Ch 5, dtr in next st, (ch 9, scp) across to last 2 sts, ch 5, dtr in each of last 2 sts, turn. *(4 dtr, 6 ch sps)*

Row 8: Ch 1, sc in each of first 2 sts, ch 9, skip first ch sp, (scp, ch 9) across to last 2 sts, dtr in each of last 2 sts, turn. *(2 sc, 6 ch sps, 2 dtr)*

Rows 9–23: Repeat rows 5–8 consecutively, ending with row 7. *(4 dtr, 14 ch sps)*

Row 24: For **first back,** ch 1, sc in each of first 2 sts, ch 9, skip first ch sp, (scp, ch 9) 4 times, scp, ch 5, dtr in next ch sp leaving last 7 sps unworked, turn. *(2 sc, 6 ch sps, 1 dtr)*

Row 25: Ch 9, skip first ch sp, (scp, ch 9) across to last ch sp, scp, ch 5, dtr in each of last 2 sts, turn. *(6 ch sps, 2 dtr)*

Row 26: Ch 1, sc in each of first 2 sts, ch 9, skip first ch sp, scp, (ch 9, scp) across to last ch sp, ch 5, dtr in last ch sp, turn. *(2 sc, 5 ch sps, 1 dtr)*

Row 27: Ch 9, skip first ch sp, (scp, ch 9) across to last ch sp, scp, ch 5, dtr in each of last 2 sts, turn. *(5 ch sps, 2 dtr)*

Row 28: Ch 1, sc in each of first 2 sts, ch 9, skip first ch sp, (scp, ch 9) across to last ch sp, sc in last ch sp, turn. *(3 sc, 4 ch sps)*

Row 29: Ch 13, scp, (ch 9, scp) across to last 2 sts, ch 5, dtr in each of last 2 sts, turn. *(5 ch sps, 2 dtr)*

Rows 30–35: Repeat rows 28 and 29 alternately.

Row 36: Ch 1, sc in each of first 2 sts, ch 9, skip first ch sp, (scp, ch 9) across to last ch sp, (sc, ch 5, dtr) in last ch sp, turn. Mark row 36 at neck edge. *(5 ch sps)*

Row 37: Ch 13, skip first ch-5, (scp, ch 9) across to last ch sp, scp, ch 5, dtr in each of last 2 sts, turn. *(5 ch sps)*

Rows 38–40: Repeat rows 26 and 27 alternately, ending with row 26. *(3 ch sps)*

Row 41: Ch 13, skip first ch sp, scp, ch 9, scp, ch 5, dtr in each of last 2 sts, turn.

Row 42: Ch 1, sc in each of first 2 sts, ch 9, skip first ch sp, scp, ch 5, dtr in last ch sp, turn. *(2 ch sps)*

Row 43: Ch 9, skip first ch sp, sc in last ch sp, **do not turn.** Fasten off.

Row 24: For **second back,** join with sl st in top of ch 5 at beginning of row 23, ch 5, dtr in next st, (ch 9, scp) 5 times, ch 5, dtr in next ch sp leaving center ch sp unworked, turn. *(3 dtr, 6 ch sps)*

Rows 25–43: Repeat rows 25–43 of first back.

CORDED TRIM

With No. 1 hook and size 5 crochet cotton, ch 2, sc in second ch from hook; turn last st made to left *(so back of the sc is facing you);* sc in strand on left side of st *(see illustration 1);* *turn last st made to left; sc in parallel strands on left side of st *(see illustration 2);* repeat from * until trim piece measures 8 ft. long. Fasten off.

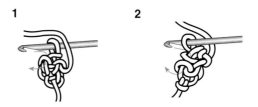

1   2

Make second piece of Corded Trim to measure 21". Lay aside.

Basting Trim in place with contrasting color sewing thread as you work, place beginning end of 8 ft.-long Corded Trim over row 37 at neck edge on first back; covering ends of rows with trim, make first 1¼" loop at end of row 43 according to assembly diagram, evenly space three more 1¼" loops across to row 4 on front, make 1¼" loop at top of row 4, make 2½" loop at tip of row 1 at center front; working across other side, make 1¼" loop in top of row 5, evenly space three more 1¼" loops across to row 43 on second back, make 1¼" loop at end of row 43, cover ends of rows across to row 36. Unravel any excess trim not used and fasten off.

With white sewing thread, sew trim in place, remove basting thread.

Continued on page 54

Wedding Collar

Wedding Collar

Continued from page 52

NECKBAND

Row 1: Working in ch sps across neck edge of Yoke, with No. 7 hook, join size 10 crochet cotton with sc in marked row 36, 4 sc in same ch sp, 5 sc in next ch sp, *4 [5, 6] sc in next ch sp, 5 sc in each of next 2 ch sps; repeat from * 5 more times, 5 sc in other marked row 36, turn. *(99 sc made) [105 sc, 111 sc made]*

NOTE: *For **optional lining pattern**, trace Yoke onto tracing paper, allowing ½" on all sides for seams. Fold pattern in half at center front and cut out pattern so both sides are the same. Lay aside.*

Row 2: Ch 4, skip next st, dc in next st, (ch 1, skip next st, dc in next st, across, turn. *(50 dc, 49 ch) [53 dc, 52 ch; 56 dc, 55 ch]*

Row 3: Ch 3, dc in first ch sp, ch 4, skip next ch sp, (scp in next ch sp, ch 8, skip 2 ch sps) 15 [16, 17] times, scp in next ch sp, ch 4, skip next ch sp, 2 dc in third ch of ch-4, turn. *(17 ch sps) [18 ch sps, 19 ch sps]*

Row 4: Ch 1, sc in each of first 2 sts, ch 9, skip first ch sp, (scp, ch 9) across to last ch sp, skip last ch sp, sc in each of last 2 sts, turn. *(16 ch sps) [17 ch sps, 18 ch sps]*

Row 5: Ch 5, dtr in next st, ch 5, scp, (ch 9, scp) across to last 2 sts, ch 5, dtr in each of last 2 sts, turn.

Row 6: Ch 1, sc in each of first 2 sts, ch 9, skip first ch sp, (scp, ch 9) across to last ch sp, skip last ch sp, sc in each of last 2 sts, turn.

Row 7: Ch 4, skip next st, (dc, ch 1) 3 times in each ch sp across, skip next st, dc in last st, turn. *(49 ch sps) [52 ch sps, 55 ch sps]*

Row 8: Ch 1, sc in first ch-1 sp, ch 6, **turn;** sl st in sixth ch from hook, ch 1, **turn;** 8 sc in ch-6 sp, sl st in **front lp and left bar** of sc worked in ch-1 sp, *2 sc in each of next 3 ch-1 sps, ch 6, **turn;** sl st in sixth ch from hook, ch 1, **turn;** 4 sc in ch-6 sp, ch 5, **turn;** sc in fifth sc worked in last ch-6 sp, **turn;** (4 sc, ch 4, sl st in **front lp and left bar** of last sc made, 4 sc) in ch-5 sp, 4 sc in remainder of ch-6 sp, sl st in **front lp and left bar** of last sc worked in ch-1 sp; repeat from * across. Fasten off.

ROSE (make 17)

Rnd 1: With No. 7 hook and size 10 crochet cotton; make **slip ring** *(see Stitch Guide)*, ch 3, 9 sc in ring, pull 4" end tightly to close ring, join with sl st in top of ch-3. *(10 dc made)*

Rnd 2: Ch 1, sc in same st, sc in each dc around, join with sl st in first sc.

Rnd 3: Ch 3, skip next st, (sc in next st, ch 2, skip next st) around, sc in joining sl st of rnd 2. *(5 ch sps)*

Rnd 4: For **petals,** (sl st, ch 2, 4 dc, ch 2, sl st) in each ch sp around. *(5 petals)*

Rnd 5: Working behind petals, ch 1, (sc in back lp of next skipped sc on rnd 2, ch 4) around, join with sl st in first sc. *(5 sps)*

Rnd 6: For **petals,** (sl st, ch 2, 7 dc, ch 2, sl st) in each ch sp around. *(5 petals)*

Rnd 7: Working behind petals, ch 2, *sc around ch between center 2 dc on next petal *(see illustra

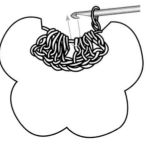

tion)*, ch 5; repeat from * around, join with sl st in first sc. *(5 ch sps)*

Rnd 8: (Sl st, ch 2, 10 dc, ch 2, sl st) in each ch sp around. Fasten off.

LEAF SPRAY (make 13)

Row 1: Beginning at bottom of stem, with No. 7 hook and size 10 crochet cotton, ch 31; for **first leaf,** 6 tr in fifth ch from hook, turn. *(7 tr made)*

Row 2: Ch 3, (dc next 2 sts tog) 2 times, dc in next st leaving last st unworked, turn. *(4 dc)*

Row 3: Ch 1, skip first st, sc next 2 sts tog leaving last st unworked, **do not turn;** for **tip of leaf,** ch 3, sc in third ch from hook; working down side of leaf, ch 1, sl st in top of st at end of row 2, ch 2, sl st in top of st at end of row 1, ch 4, sl st in same ch as 6 tr of row 1. **Do not turn or fasten off.**

For **second leaf,** ch 9, repeat rows 1–3 of first leaf; sc in next 4 ch below second leaf. **Do not fasten off.**

For **third leaf,** repeat rows 1–3 of first leaf; sc in each ch across stem. Fasten off.

VIOLET (make 28)

Rnd 1: With No. 7 hook and size 10 crochet cotton, ch 2, 5 sc in second ch from hook. *(5 sc made)*

Rnd 2: (Sl st, ch 2, 2 dc, ch 2, sl st) in each st around. Fasten off.

COLLAR FINISHING

1: Mark exact center of 21" Corded Trim; make 2¼" loop at center, sew top of loop at point where trim crosses to row 2 at center front of neckband *(see assembly diagram on next page)*. Make 1¼" loop 2" on each side of center front loop and sew top of these loops to row 2. Sew remaining cord in place, leaving loops unsewn.

2: Glue flowers and leaves to right side of Yoke and neckband according to placement diagrams; allow to dry. Working on wrong side, sew each piece in place.

3: Sew buttons to ends of rows 1, 4 and 7 on right end of neckband.

4: For **button loop,** join with sl st in st at left end of row 1 on neckband, ch 10, sl st in tenth ch from hook. Fasten off. Repeat on rows 4 and 7.

OPTIONAL FABRIC LINING

1: From fabric, using paper pattern made earlier for neckband, cut 2 lining pieces.

2: Holding pieces right sides tog, sew ½" seam around all edges, leaving 5" opening for turning. Trim seams and clip corners. Turn right side out. Sew 5" opening closed. Press.

3: Matching edges, sew lining to wrong side of crocheted Yoke.

OPTIONAL YOKE INSERT

1: Fold bodice in half, press center front and center back lines; unfold.

2: Place crocheted Yoke over bodice, matching center fronts; match center back edges to back opening. Taking care that edges are the same distance from center front or back on each side, pin all outer edges of crocheted Yoke to bodice.

3: For cutting line, working between sts and ch sps 1" from edge of crocheted Yoke, with disappearing ink pen, carefully mark every ½" across front and back of bodice; remove pins and crocheted Yoke.

4: Fold bodice in half at center front and back so both sides are the same; match and pin tog at neck edges, armholes, side seams and close to cutting line. Cut along cutting line. *(If back opening has zipper, open*

zipper, cut ends leaving 1" extended above marks, remove 2" of stitching on each side.)

5: For hem, clipping ⅓" slashes as needed for edges to lay flat, press raw edges under ¼", press under again ½". Sew hem in place. *(Fold zipper ends under even with edge of hem, sew in place.)*

6: Place edges of crocheted Yoke over hem, sew in place, leaving Corded Trim loops unsewn. ❑❑

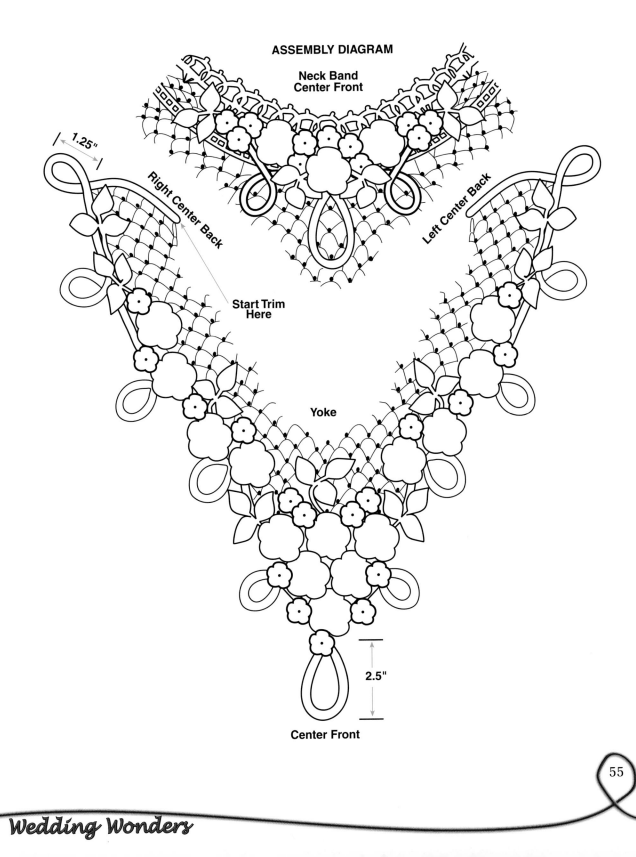

ASSEMBLY DIAGRAM

Neck Band
Center Front

1.25"

Right Center Back

Left Center Back

Start Trim
Here

Yoke

2.5"

Center Front

Wedding Wonders

Nosegay Doily

Finished Size: 16½" across.

Materials:
- ❑ 132 yds. white size 10 crochet cotton thread or bedspread cotton
- ❑ 1 yd. of ⅜" satin ribbon
- ❑ No. 7 steel hook or hook needed to obtain gauge

Gauge: 8 dc = 1"; 4 dc rows = 1".

Special Stitches:
For **treble cluster (tr cluster)**, *yo 2 times, insert hook in st, yo, pull lp through, (yo, pull through 2 lps on hook) 2 times leaving last lps on hook; working in same st, repeat from * for each tr of cluster, yo and pull through all lps on hook.

For **double treble cluster (dtr cluster)**, yo 3 times, insert hook in st, yo, pull lp through, (yo, pull through 2 lps on hook) 3 times leaving last lps on hook; working in same st, repeat from *, yo and pull through all lps on hook.

DOILY

Rnd 1: Ch 108, sl st in first ch to form ring, ch 6, skip next 2 ch, (dc in next ch, ch 3, skip next 2 ch) around, join with sl st in third ch of ch-6. *(36 dc, 36 ch sps)*

Rnd 2: Sl st across to middle of next ch sp, sc in same ch sp, (*ch 2, dc in next ch sp, ch 4, **3-tr cluster**—*see Special Stitches*—in same ch sp, ch 5, 3-tr cluster in next ch sp, ch 4, dc in same ch sp, ch 2*, sc in next ch sp) 11 times; repeat between first *, ending with sl st in first sc.

Rnd 3: Ch 4, skip first ch sp, dc in next ch sp, *ch 3, (3-tr cluster, ch 5) 3 times in next ch sp, 3-tr cluster in same ch sp, ch 3; holding last lp of next 3 sts on hook, dc in next ch-4 sp, tr in next sc, dc in next ch-4 sp, yo and pull through all lps on hook; repeat from * around, ending with sl st in top of ch-4.

Rnd 4: Sl st across ch-3, tip of tr cluster and 2 chs of next ch sp, (ch 7, tr in next ch sp, ch 7, tr in same ch sp, ch 7, sc in next ch sp, ch 8, skip next 2 ch-3 sps, sc in next ch sp) around, ending with sl st at base of first ch-7.

Rnd 5: Sl st across to middle of ch-7, ch 10, *(**dtr cluster**—*see Special Stitches*, ch 7) 3 times in next ch sp, dtr cluster in same ch sp, ch 5, tr in each of next 3 ch sps, ch 5; repeat from * around, ending with sl st in fifth ch of ch-10.

Rnd 6: Sl st in 2 sts of remaining ch, *(ch 5, sc in next ch sp, ch 5, sc in same ch sp) 3 times, ch 5, sc in next ch sp, dc in center tr, sc in next ch sp; repeat from * around, ending with sl st at base of first ch-5.

Rnd 7: Sl st across to middle of next ch ch sp, *(ch 6, sc in next ch sp) 6 times, dc in next dc, sc in next ch sp; repeat from * around, ending with sl st at base of first ch-6. 7, sc in next ch sp) 5

Continued on page 60

Wedding Ornaments

Designed by Carol Allen

Finished Size: Cover fits 3" satin ball.

Materials For One:
❏ 30 yds. size 30 crochet cotton thread
❏ Pearl-head straight pins
❏ 3" satin ball
❏ No. 11 steel crochet hook or hook needed to obtain gauge

Gauge: Rnds 1–4 = 2" across *(piece will be cupped).*

Basic Stitches: Ch, sl st, sc, hdc, dc, tr.

GENERAL INSTRUCTIONS
Pattern instructions are for the **crochet pieces** only. After working the first few rnds of an Ornament, lay the piece over the satin ball to be sure it will lay smooth.

To attach Cover, place the Cover over the satin ball with the center opening on Cover at the top of the ball; pulling the ch sps which form points snug so the cover will lay smooth, secure each point with a pearl-head straight pin. Add additional pearl-head straight pins as needed for shaping of Cover.

For **Hanger,** form a loop with crochet cotton thread or narrow ribbon pinned to the top of the satin ball through center opening on Cover.

Decorate tops of Ornaments using ribbon roses, lace, ribbon, etc., and additional pearl-head straight pins as desired *(see photo).*

COVER NO. 1 (shown at top left in photo)
Rnd 1: Ch 10, sl st in first ch to form a ring, ch 4, 29 tr in ring, join with sl st in top of ch-4 *(30 tr made)*

Rnd 2: (Ch 3, dc) in first st, dc in next 2 sts, (2 dc in next st, dc in next 2 sts) around, join with sl st in top of ch-3. *(40 dc)*

Rnd 3: (Ch 2, hdc) in first st, hdc in next st, (2 hdc in next st, hdc in next st) around, join with sl st in top of ch-2. *(60 hdc)*

Rnd 4: Ch 1 *(not worked into or counted as a st),* sc in first st, sc in each st around, join with sl st in **back lp** *(see Stitch Guide)* of first sc. *(60 sc)*

Rnd 5: Ch 7 *(counts as dc and ch 4),* skip next 2 sts, (dc in **back lp** of next st, ch 4, skip next 2 sts) around, join in third ch of ch-7. *(20 ch sps)*

Rnd 6: Ch 1, sc in first st, (sc, hdc, dc, tr, dc, hdc, sc) in next ch sp *(scallop made),* *sc in **back lp** of next dc, (sc, hdc, dc, tr, dc, hdc, sc) in next ch sp *(scallop made);* repeat from * around, join.

Rnd 7: Ch 1, sc in first st, ch 6, skip next scallop, (sc in **back lp** of next sc, ch 6, skip next scallop) around, join.

Rnd 8: *(4 sc, ch 3, 4 sc) in next ch sp, 7 sc in next ch sp; repeat from * around, join.

Rnd 9: Sl st across to first ch-3 sp, (sl st, ch 3, 2 dc, ch 3, 3 dc) in ch sp, ch 4, skip next ch sp, sc in **back lp** of center 5 sc of next 7-sc group, ch 4, *(3 dc, ch 3, 3 dc) in next ch-3 sp, ch 4, skip next ch sp, sc in **back lp** of center 5 sc of next 7-sc group, ch 4; repeat from * around, join.

Rnd 10: Sl st across to first ch sp, (sl st, ch 3, 3 dc, ch 4, 4 dc) in ch sp, ch 4, skip next ch sp, sc in **back lps** of center 3 sc in next 5-sc group, ch 4, skip next ch sp, *(4 dc, ch 4, 4 dc) in next ch sp, ch 4, skip next ch sp, sc in **back lps** of center 3 sc

in next 5-sc group, ch 4, skip next ch sp; repeat from * around, join.

Rnd 11: Sl st across to first ch sp, (sl st, ch 3, 4 dc, ch 5, 5 dc) in ch sp, ch 4, skip next ch sp, sc in **back lp** of center sc in next 3-sc group, ch 4, skip next ch sp, *(5 dc, ch 5, 5 dc) in next ch sp, ch 4, skip next ch sp, sc in **back lp** of center sc in next 3-sc group, ch 4, skip next ch sp; repeat from * around, join. Fasten off.

Finish according to General Instructions on this page.

COVER NO. 2 (shown at top right in photo)
Rnds 1–4: Work rnds 1–4 of Cover No. 1.

Rnd 5: Ch 1, sc in first st, ch 3, skip next st, (sc in **back lp** of next st, ch 3, skip next st) around, join. *(30 ch sps)*

Rnd 6: Sl st in next ch, ch 1, sc in first ch sp; ch 4, (sc in next ch sp, ch 4) around, join.

Rnd 7: Sl st in each of next 2 chs, ch 1, sc in first ch sp; ch 4, (sc in next ch sp, ch 4) around, join.

Rnd 8: (Sl st, ch 3, 2 dc, ch 3, 3 dc) in first ch sp, (ch 3, sc in next ch sp) 2 times, ch 3, *(3 dc, ch 3, 3 dc) in next ch sp, (ch 3, sc in next ch sp) 2 times, ch 3; repeat from * around, join.

Rnd 9: (Sl st, ch 3, 4 dc, ch 5, 5 dc) in first ch sp, ch 3, 3 sc in next ch sp, ch 3, *(5 dc, ch 5, 5 dc) in next ch sp, ch 3, 3 sc in next ch sp, ch 3; repeat from * around, join.

Rnd 10: (Sl st, ch 3, 6 dc, ch 6, 7 dc) in first ch sp, ch 5, sc in **back lp** of second sc of next 3-sc group, ch 5, *(7 dc, ch 6, 7 dc) in next ch sp, ch 5, sc in **back lp** of second sc of next 3-sc group, ch 5; repeat from * around, join. Fasten off.

Finish according to General Instructions on this page.

COVER NO. 3 (shown at center left in photo)
Rnds 1–4: Work rnds 1–4 of Cover No. 1.

Rnd 5: Ch 1, sc in first st, ch 3, skip next 2 sts, (sc in **back lp** of next st, ch 3, skip next 2 sts) around, join. *(20 ch sps)*

Rnd 6: Sl st in next ch, (sl st, ch 6, dc) in **back lp** of next ch, ch 3, sc in **back lp** of second ch in next ch-3 sp, ch 3, *(dc, ch 2, dc) in **back lp** of second ch in next ch-3 sp, ch 3, sc in **back lp** of second ch in next ch-3 sp, ch 3; repeat from * around, join in third ch of ch 6.

Rnd 7: (Sl st, ch 3, dc, ch 2, 2 dc) in next ch sp, ch 5, skip next 2 ch sps, *(2 dc, ch 2, 2 dc) in next ch sp, ch 5, skip next 2 ch sps; repeat from * around, join.

Rnd 8: Sl st in next st, (sl st, ch 3, 2 dc, ch 3, 3 dc) in next ch sp, ch 2, sc in center ch of next ch-5 sp, ch 2, *(3 dc, ch 3, 3 dc) in next ch sp, ch 2, sc in center ch of next ch-5 sp, ch 2; repeat from * around, join.

Rnd 9: Sl st in next 2 sts, (sl st, ch 3, 3 dc, ch 4, 4 dc) in next ch sp, ch 3, 3 sc in next ch sp, sc in **back lp** of next sc, 3 sc in next ch sp, ch 3, *(4 dc, ch 4, 4 dc) in next ch sp, ch 3, 3 sc in next ch sp, sc in **back lp** of next sc, 3 sc in next ch sp, ch 3; repeat from * around, join.

Rnd 10: Sl st across to next ch sp, (sl st, ch 3, 4 dc, ch 5, 5 dc) in next ch sp, ch 9, skip next 2 ch sps, *(5 dc, ch 5, 5 dc) in next ch sp, ch 9, skip next 2 ch sps; repeat from * around, join. Fasten off.

Finish according to General Instructions on this page.

Continued on page 60

Wedding Wonders

Wedding Ornaments

Continued from page 59

COVER NO. 4 (shown at center right in photo)
Rnds 1–4: Work rnds 1–4 of Cover No. 1.

Rnd 5: Ch 1, sc in first st, ch 3, skip next st, (sc in **back lp** of next st, ch 3, skip next st) around, join. *(30 ch sps)*

Rnd 6: Sl st in next ch, ch 1, sc in ch sp, ch 5, skip next ch sp, (sc in next ch sp, ch 5, skip next ch sp) around, join. *(15 ch sps)*

Rnd 7: Ch 1, (3 sc; for **picot, ch 3, sl st in last sc made;** 3 sc) in each ch sp around, join.

Rnd 8: Ch 12, skip next 6 sc, (sc in **back lp** of next sc, ch 12, skip next 6 sc) around, join with s l st in first ch of first ch-12.

Rnd 9: Ch 1, (5 sc, picot, 5 sc) in each ch sp around, join.

Rnd 10: Ch 16, skip next 10 sc, (sc in **back lp** of next sc, ch 16, skip next 10 sc) around, join with sl st in first ch of first ch-16.

Rnd 11: Ch 1, (7 sc, picot, 7 sc) in each ch sp around, join.

Rnd 12: Ch 20, skip next 14 sc, (sc in **back lp** of next sc, ch 20, skip next 14 sc) around, join with sl st in first ch of first ch-20. Fasten off.

Finish according to General Instructions on page 59.

COVER NO. 5 (shown at center in photo)
Rnds 1–4: Work rnds 1–4 of Cover No. 1.

Rnd 5: Ch 1, sc in first st, ch 16, skip next 9 sts, (sc in **back lp** of next st, ch 16, skip next 9 sts) around, join. *(6 ch sps)*

Rnd 6: Ch 1, (7 sc, ch 5, 7 sc) in each ch sp around, join.

Rnd 7: *Ch 7, (5 tr, ch 5, 5 tr) in next ch sp, ch 7, skip next 7 sc, sc in next space between sc groups; repeat from * around, **do not join.**

Rnd 8: *9 sc in next ch-7 sp, ch 3, (6 dc, ch 5, 6 dc) in next ch-5 sp, ch 3, 9 sc in next ch-7 sp, skip next sc; repeat from * around, join.

Rnd 9: *Ch 5, sc in next ch-3 sp, ch 5, (7 dc, ch 3, 7 dc) in next ch-5 sp, ch 5, sc in next ch-3 sp, ch 5, skip next 9 sc, sc in next space between sc groups; repeat from * around, join with sl st in first ch of first ch-5. Fasten off.

Finish according to General Instructions on page 59.

COVER NO. 6 (shown at bottom in photo)
Rnds 1–4: Work rnds 1–4 of Cover No. 1.

Rnd 5: (Ch 5, dc) in first st, skip next st, *(dc, ch 2, dc) in **back lp** of next st, skip next st; repeat from * around, join with sl st in third ch of ch-5. *(30 ch sps)*

Rnd 6: (Sl st, ch 5, dc) in first ch sp, (dc, ch 2, dc) in each ch sp around, join with sl st in third ch of ch-5.

Rnd 7: (Sl st, ch 3, 2 dc, ch 3, 3 dc) in first ch sp, 3 sc in each of next 4 ch sps, *(3 dc, ch 3, 3 dc) in next ch sp, 3 sc in each of next 4 ch sps; repeat from * around, join.

Rnd 8: Sl st across to first ch sp, (sl st, ch 3, 4 dc, ch 5, 5 dc) in ch sp, (ch 3, sc in **back lp** of second sc in next 3-sc group) 4 times, ch 3, *(5 dc, ch 5, 5 dc) in next ch sp, (ch 3, sc in **back lp** of second sc in next 3-sc group) 4 times, ch 3; repeat from * around, join.

Rnd 9: Sl st across to first ch sp, (sl st, ch 3, 6 dc, ch 7, 7 dc) in ch sp, ch 5, skip next ch sp, sc in next ch sp, (ch 3, sc in next ch sp) 2 times, ch 5, skip next ch sp, *(7 dc, ch 7, 7 dc) in next ch sp, ch 5, skip next ch sp, sc in next ch sp, (ch 3, sc in next ch sp) 2 times, ch 5, skip next ch sp; repeat from * around, join.

Rnd 10: Sl st across to first ch sp, (sl st, ch 3, 8 dc, ch 2, 9 dc) in ch sp, ch 7, skip next ch sp, sc in next ch sp, ch 3, sc in next ch sp, ch 7, skip next ch sp, *(9 dc, ch 2, 9 dc) in next ch sp, ch 7, skip next ch sp, sc in next ch sp, ch 3, sc in next ch sp, ch 7, skip next ch sp; repeat from * around, join. Fasten off.

Finish according to General Instructions on page 59. ❏❏

Nosegay Doily

Continued from page 57

times, 2 dc in next dc, sc in next ch sp; repeat from * around, ending with sl st at base of first ch-7.

Rnd 9: Sl st across to middle of next ch sp, *ch 8, sc in next ch sp, ch 4, (3-tr cluster, ch 4) 3 times in next ch sp, 3-tr cluster in same ch sp, ch 4, sc in next ch sp, ch 8, sc in next ch sp, (dc in next dc) 2 times, sc in next ch sp; repeat from * around, ending with sl st at base of first ch-8.

Rnd 10: Sl st across to middle of next ch sp, *(ch 6, sc in next ch sp) 6 times, dc in next dc, 2 dc in next dc, sc in next ch sp; repeat from * around, ending with sl st at base of first ch-6.

Rnd 11: Sl st across to middle of next ch sp, *ch 6, sc in next ch sp, (ch 7, sc in next ch sp) 3 times, ch 6, sc in next ch sp, dc in next dc, 2 dc in next dc, dc in next dc, sc in next ch sp; repeat from * around, ending with sl st at base of first ch-6.

Rnd 12: Sl st in 6 ch of next ch sp and 3 ch of next ch sp, *4 sc in remainder of ch sp, 4 sc in next ch sp, ch 5, sl st in sc at base of ch, 4 sc in remainder of ch sp, 8 sc in next ch sp, 4 sc in next ch sp, dc in next 2 dc, 2 dc in next dc, dc in next dc, 4 sc in next ch sp, 4 sc in next ch sp, **turn;** ch 6, **double treble (dtr—**see *Stitch Guide*) in second dc, ch 7, **triple treble (ttr—**see *Stitch Guide*) in next dc, ch 7, dtr in next dc, ch 6, join with sl st in middle st of 8-sc group, **turn;** ch 5; for **picot, sl st in third ch of ch-5;** ch 2, dc in first ch sp, (ch 5, picot, ch 2, dc in next ch sp, ch 5, picot, ch 2, dc in same ch sp) 2 times, ch 5, picot, ch 2, dc in next ch sp, ch 5, picot, ch 2, sl st in base of ch-7; repeat from * around, ending with sl st in first sc. Fasten off.

Weave ribbon through sts on rnd 1. ❏❏

Bed & Bath

The bedroom and
bathroom, collectively
known as the boudoir, together
function as the most intimate area of
the home. Here, dreams are nurtured,
beauty is enhanced, and a steaming,
scented bath beckons to soothe away
stresses at day's end.
Romanticism rules this retreat and little
luxuries abound, with fabulous
embellishments of handmade laces
adorning lampshade, tray, bedspread
and pillowcase. Day or night,
femininity and serenity unite
midst tender touches of
thread crochet.

Rose Filet Edging

Finished Size: Fits any pillowcase.

Materials:
- ❏ 400 yds. white size 20 crochet cotton thread
- ❏ Pillowcase
- ❏ Tracing paper
- ❏ Sewing thread and needle
- ❏ No. 12 steel hook or hook needed to obtain gauge

Gauge: 20 sc = 1"; 9 mesh rows = 1".

Basic Stitches: Ch, sl st, sc, dc, tr.

Special Stitches:
For **beginning block (beg block),** ch 3, dc in each of next 3 sts, or, ch 3, 2 dc in next ch sp, dc in next st.

For **block,** dc in each of next 3 sts, or, 2 dc in next ch sp, dc in next st.

For **beginning mesh (beg mesh),** ch 5, skip next 2 sts or chs, dc in next st.

For **mesh,** ch 2, skip next 2 chs or sts, dc in next st.

For **end mesh,** ch 2, skip next 2 chs, dc in third ch of ch-5.

For **beginning 1-mesh increase (beg 1-mesh inc),** ch 7, dc in first st.

For **beg 1-mesh or block decrease (beg 1-mesh or block dec),** sl st in each of first 2 chs, sl st in next st, or, sl st in each of first 3 sts.

For **end 1-mesh inc,** ch 2, tr in bottom strand at side of last dc made *(see illustration).*

For **beginning 2-mesh increase (beg 2-mesh inc),** ch 10, dc in eighth ch from hook, ch 2, skip next 2 chs, dc in next st.

For **end mesh or block dec,** leave last mesh or block unworked.

For **beginning 2-mesh decrease (beg 2-mesh dec),** sl st in next 6 chs or sts.

EDGING
Row 1: Ch 20, dc in eighth ch from hook, (ch 2, skip next 2 chs, dc in next ch, dc in each of next 3 chs) 2 times, turn. *(3 mesh, 2 blocks made)*

Row 2: Beg block *(see Special Stitches),* mesh, block 2 times, ch 2, skip next 2 chs, dc in next ch, turn.

Row 3: Beg 1-mesh inc, mesh 3 times, block, mesh, turn.

Row 4: Beg mesh, mesh, block 2 times, mesh, ch 2, skip next 2 chs, dc in next ch, turn.

Row 5: Beg 1-mesh inc, mesh, block, mesh 2 times, block, **end mesh,** turn.

Row 6: Beg mesh, block 2 times, mesh, block, mesh, ch 2, skip next 2 chs, dc in next ch, turn.

Row 7: Beg 1-mesh or block decrease, beg mesh, mesh, block 2 times, mesh, end mesh, turn.

Row 8: Beg block, mesh 4 times, end mesh, turn.

Row 9: Beg 1-mesh dec, beg mesh, mesh, block, mesh, block, turn.

Row 10: Beg block, mesh, block 2 times, end mesh, turn.

Rows 11–34: Repeat rows 3–10 consecutively.

Row 35: Beg 1-mesh inc, mesh 3 times, block, mesh, **end 1-mesh inc,** turn.

Rows 36–44: For rose design, work according to graph on page 67 across, turn.

Row 45: Beg 2-mesh inc, mesh, block 3 times, mesh 3 times, block 2 times, mesh, block 4 times, mesh 5 times, end 1-mesh inc, turn.

Rows 46–61: Work according to graph across, turn.

Row 62: Beg 1-mesh dec, beg mesh, mesh 4 times, block 4 times, mesh 2 times, block 2 times, mesh 2 times, block, mesh 3 times, block 3 times, mesh 2 times, block 2 times, mesh 2 times, block 3 times, mesh, block 3 times, mesh 3 times, block, mesh, end mesh, turn.

Row 63: Beg mesh, block, mesh 4 times, block 4 times, mesh, block 3 times, mesh 4 times, block 4 times, mesh 4 times, block 9 times, mesh 5 times, **end mesh or block dec,** turn.

Rows 64–70: Work according to graph across, turn.

Row 71: Beg 2-mesh dec, beg mesh, block, mesh 2 times, block, mesh 5 times, block, mesh 3 times, block 4 times, mesh 2 times, block, mesh 8 times, end block dec, turn.

Rows 72–90: Work according to graph across, turn.

Rows 91–328: Or until entire piece fits around edge of pillowcase; repeat rows 3–10 consecutively, ending with row 8. Fasten off. Sew first and last rows together.

Rnd 329: Working in mesh on bottom edge of piece, join with sc in mesh at end of row 35, (sc; for **picot,** ch 3, sl st in third ch from hook—*picot made;* 2 sc) in same mesh as joining sc, 2 sc in each mesh across to row 61 with (2 sc, picot, 2 sc) in each corner mesh, (sc, picot, sc) in next mesh, 2 sc in each mesh across to row 90 with (2 sc, picot, 2 sc) in each corner mesh, (2 sc, picot, 2 sc) in next mesh, 2 sc in next mesh, 4 sc in next mesh, picot, 4 sc in next mesh, 2 sc in next mesh, 4 sc in next mesh, (2 sc in each of next 2 mesh, 4 sc in next mesh, 2 sc in next mesh, 4 sc in next mesh, picot, 4 sc in next mesh, 2 sc in next mesh, 4 sc in next mesh) around to last 2 mesh, 2 sc in each of last 2 mesh, join with sl st in first sc. Fasten off.

FINISHING
Fold tracing paper in half crosswise, unfold. Place crease of folded paper under center of rose design. Using section of Edging with rose design as pattern, trace along top edge. Cut paper along tracing lines.

Remove hem from pillowcase and press open. Center paper pattern over one side of open end on pillowcase, cut out. Machine zigzag or hand stitch raw edge to secure.

Center and pin Edging over stitched edge on pillowcase. Sew in place. ❏❏

Rose Filet Bedroom

Designed by Vicki Owen

Finished Sizes: Bedspread is 110" wide × 131" long. Lampshade Cover is 10" high.

Materials:
- ❏ Size 10 crochet cotton thread:
  19,800 yds. cream *(for Bedspread)*
  450 yds. cream *(for Lampshade)*
- ❏ 24" cream ¼"-wide satin ribbon
- ❏ 10"-high fabric lampshade with 7"-diameter top and 12"-diameter bottom
- ❏ Tapestry needle
- ❏ No. 9 steel hook or hook needed to obtain gauge

Gauge: 7 blocks or mesh = 2"; 7 blocks or mesh rows = 2".

Basic Stitches: Ch, sl st, sc, dc.

Special Stitches:
For **beginning block (beg block),** ch 3, 2 dc in first ch sp, dc in next dc, or, dc in each of next 3 dc.
For **block,** dc in each of next 3 dc, or, 2 dc in next ch sp, dc in next dc.
For **beginning mesh (beg mesh),** ch 5 *(counts as dc and ch-2),* skip first ch sp or next 2 dc, dc in next dc.
For **mesh,** ch 2, skip next ch sp, dc in next dc, or, ch 2, skip next 2 dc, dc in next dc.

ROSE FILET BEDSPREAD

SIDE PANEL *(make 2)*
Row 1: Ch 206, dc in eighth ch from hook, (ch 2, skip next 2 chs, dc in next ch) 9 times, dc in next 6 chs; repeat between ( ) 43 times, dc in next 6 chs; repeat between ( ) 10 times, turn. *(76 dc made)*

Row 2: Beg mesh *(see Special Stitches)*, 9 **mesh,** 2 **blocks,** 43 mesh, 2 blocks, 10 mesh, turn. *(63 mesh, 4 blocks)*

Rows 3–67: Work across according to graph on page 66, turn.

Rows 68–469: Repeat rows 1–67 according to graph 6 more times. At end of last row, fasten off.

CENTER PANEL
NOTE: *When following the Bedspread Graph for the Center Panel, repeat the pattern between the arrows 3 times to complete the row.*

Row 1: Ch 608, dc in eighth ch from hook, (ch 2, skip next 2 chs, dc in next ch) 9 times, *dc in next 6 chs; repeat between ( ) 43 times, dc in next 6 chs; repeat between ( ) 20 times; repeat from *, dc in next 6 chs; repeat between ( ) 43 times, dc in next 6 chs; repeat between ( ) 10 times, turn. *(226 dc made)*

Row 2: Beg mesh, 9 mesh, (2 blocks, 43 mesh, 2 blocks, 20 mesh) 2 times, 2 blocks, 43 mesh, 2 blocks, 10 mesh, turn. *(189 mesh, 12 blocks)*

Rows 3–67: Work across according to graph on page 66, turn.

Rows 68–469: Repeat rows 1–67 according to graph 6 more times. At end of last row, fasten off.

ASSEMBLY
Matching design pattern, place long edges of one Side Panel and Center Panel together. Working through both thicknesses in ends of rows, join with sl st in end of first mesh row, ch 1, 2 sc in end of

Continued on page 66

Continued from page 65

same mesh row, work 2 sc in end of each mesh row and in end of each block row across, fasten off. *(Sc is wrong side of work.)*

Complete the other side of Center Panel in same manner with remaining Side Panel.

For **Top Edge of Bedspread,** with right side facing you, join with sl st in first st, ch 3, 2 dc in each mesh, dc in each dc and in each seam across, fasten off.

FRINGE

For each **Fringe,** cut five pieces each 5" long from thread. Hold all strands together and fold in half, insert hook in end of row or in mesh, pull fold through row or mesh, pull ends through fold, tighten.

Fringe in end of each mesh row and in each block row on each side and across bottom.

ROSE FILET LAMPSHADE COVER

COVER

Row 1: Ch 104, dc in eighth ch from hook, (ch 2, skip next 2 ch, dc in next ch) across, turn. *(34 dc made)*

Row 2: Beg mesh *(see Special Stitches),* 15 **mesh,** 1 **block,** 16 mesh, turn. *(32 mesh, 1 block—Front of row 2 is right side of work.)*

Rows 3–57: Work across according to graph on page 67, turn.

Rows 58–114: Repeat rows 1–57 according to graph. At end of last row, fasten off leaving a 20" end for sewing.

Fold in half and sew row 1 and row 114 together with 20" end.

For **Top Edging,** working in ends of rows on one side, join with sc in end of first mesh row at seam, 5 dc in end of next mesh row, (sc in end of next mesh row, 5 dc in end of next mesh row) around, join with sl st in first sc. Fasten off.

For **Bottom Edging,** working in ends of rows on opposite side, join with sc in end of first mesh row at seam, (3 dc; for **picot,** ch 3, sc in third ch from hook—*picot made;* 3 dc) in end of next mesh row, *sc in end of next mesh row, (3 dc, picot, 3 dc) in end of next mesh row; repeat from * around, join with sl st in first sc, fasten off.

Starting at center front, weave ribbon through mesh at top of Cover. Place over lampshade and tie ribbon in bow. ❑❑

BEDSPREAD GRAPH

☐ = BEG MESH or MESH   ◼ = BEG BLOCK or BLOCK

Work three times between arrows for Center Panel.

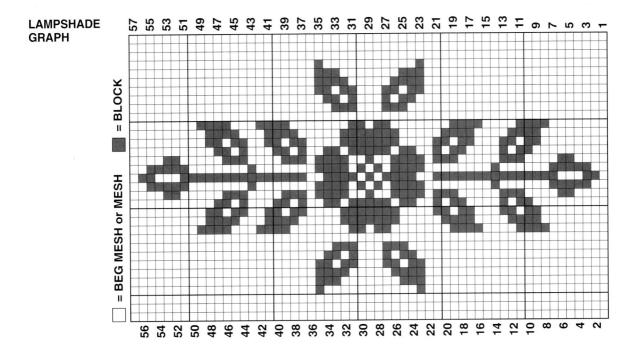

= BLOCK

= BEG MESH or MESH

Rose Filet Edging

Continued from page 63

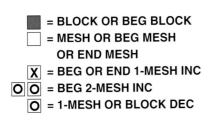

= BLOCK OR BEG BLOCK

= MESH OR BEG MESH OR END MESH

X = BEG OR END 1-MESH INC

OO / O = BEG 2-MESH INC

O = 1-MESH OR BLOCK DEC

TOP EDGE

TOP EDGE

67

Finished Size: 9¼" tall.

Materials:
- ❏ 200 yds. ecru size 10 crochet cotton thread
- ❏ 28" of ¼" picot ribbon
- ❏ 29" of 1" lace
- ❏ Silk rosebud spray
- ❏ Small amount of small dried flowers
- ❏ Fabric stiffener or heavy starch
- ❏ Craft glue or glue gun
- ❏ Sewing thread and needle
- ❏ Plastic wrap
- ❏ No. 0 steel hook

Gauge: 6 tr and 6 ch sps = 2"; 3 tr rows = 2½".

Basic Stitches: Ch, sl st, hdc, dc, tr.

BOOT

NOTE: Work all sts loosely.

Rnd 1: Starting at **Heel**, ch 4, sl st in first ch to form ring, ch 4 *(counts as first dc and ch-1)*, dc in ring, ch 1, (dc in ring, ch 1) 10 times, join with sl st in third ch of second ch-4. *(12 dc made)*

Rnd 2: Ch 5 *(counts as first tr and ch-1)*, (tr in next st, ch 1) around, join with sl st in fourth ch of ch-5; for **bottom of foot**, ch 39, tr in sixth ch from hook *(bottom of toe made)*, ch 1, skip next ch, (tr in next ch, ch 1, skip next ch) 16 times, join with sl st in second st from first joining. *(18 ch sps)*

Rnd 3: Working in ch sps only, sl st in next ch sp, ch 5, (tr in next ch sp, ch 1) 9 times, tr in next ch sp, ch 1; working in skipped chs on opposite side of ch-39, tr in first ch, ch 1, (tr in next ch, ch 1) 16 times, (tr around ch on bottom of toe, ch 1) 6 times, (tr in next ch sp, ch 1) 16 times, tr in next ch sp, ch 1, skip next ch sp on rnd 2, join with sl st in fourth ch of ch-5. *(51 ch sps)*

Rnd 4: Working in ch sps only, sl st in first ch sp, ch 5, tr in next ch sp, (ch 1, tr in next ch sp) 29 times, ch 1, skip next ch sp, tr in next ch sp, (ch 1, tr in next ch sp) 18 times, ch 1, join. *(50 ch sps)*

Rnd 5: Sl st in first ch sp, ch 5, (tr in next ch sp, ch 1) around, join.

Rnd 6: Sl st in first ch sp, ch 5, tr in next ch sp, (ch 1, tr in next ch sp) 14 times, tr in next 24 ch sps, (ch 1, tr in next ch sp) 10 times, ch 1, join. Fasten off. *(26 ch sps, 50 tr)*

Row 7: Working in rows, skip first 29 sts, join with sl st in next st, ch 5, skip next st, tr in next st, (ch 1, skip next st, tr in next st) 5 times, (ch 1, tr in next st) 10 times; working in skipped sts, (ch 1, tr in next st) 16 times, (ch 1, skip next st, tr in next st) 5 times leaving last st unworked, turn. *(38 tr)*

Rows 8–12: Ch 5, tr in next st, (ch 1, tr in next st) across, turn. At end of last row, fasten off.

TONGUE

Row 1: Starting at bottom, ch 15, tr in seventh ch from hook, (ch 1, skip next ch, tr in next ch) across, turn. *(6 tr made)*

Rows 2–4: Ch 5, tr in next st, (ch 1, tr in next st) across, turn.

Row 5: (Ch 5, tr) in first st, (ch 1, tr in next st) across to last st, (tr, ch 1, tr) in last st, turn. *(8 tr)*

Rows 6–7: Ch 5, tr in next st, (ch 1, tr in next st) across, turn.

Row 8: (Ch 5, tr) in first st, (ch 1, tr in next st) across to last st, (tr, ch 1, tr) in last st, turn. *(10 tr)*

Rows 9–10: Ch 5, tr in next st, (ch 1, tr in next st) across, turn.

Rnd 11: Working around outer edge, ch 2, hdc in each st and in each ch with 3 hdc in end of each row around, join with sl st in top of ch-2. Fasten off.

FINISHING

Stiffen crochet pieces *(see General Instructions on page 159)*. Stuff Boot with plastic wrap, shaping as it dries. Place Tongue over flat surface covered with plastic wrap, remove before completely dry. Fold in half. Let dry.

Cut 18" piece from ribbon. Glue or sew over top of rnd 6 with ends touching at center front of Boot.

Glue or tack row 1 on bottom of Tongue to inside of row 6 on on front of Boot.

Glue or sew lace over ends of rows 7-12 and over sts on row 12 on Boot with ends touching at center front.

Glue or tack center of top edge on Tongue to center of row 5 on front of Boot *(see photo)*.

Make a bow from remainder of ribbon. Trim ends to same length.

Glue dried flowers, bow and rose spray to front of Tongue. ❏❏

Victorian Boot

Designed by Wendy Johnson

Tray Place Mat

Designed by Dot Drake

Finished Size: 12½" × 19".

Materials:
- ❏ Size 10 crochet cotton thread:
    - 150 yds. aqua
    - 150 yds. pink
    - 300 yds. yellow
- ❏ No. 7 steel hook or hook needed to obtain gauge

Gauge: Large Motif rnds 1–6 = 3½" across.

Basic Stitches: Ch, sl st, sc, hdc, dc, tr.

Special Stitch:
For **picot**, ch 3, sl st in top of last st made.

LARGE MOTIF (make 6)

Rnd 1: With aqua, ch 5, sl st in first ch to form ring, 12 sc in ring, join with sl st in first sc. Fasten off. *(12 sc made)*

Rnd 2: Working this rnd in **front lps** (see Stitch Guide), join pink with sc in any sc, ch 3, skip next sc, (sc in next sc, ch 3, skip next sc) around, join. *(6 ch sps)*

Rnd 3: Ch 1, (sc, hdc, 2 dc, hdc, sc) in each ch sp around, join. Fasten off.

Rnd 4: For **petals**, working behind rnds 2 and 3 into remaining **back lps** of rnd 1, join yellow with sc in any sc, (ch 11, sc in second ch from hook, dc in each ch across, sc in next sc on rnd 1) around, ch 11, sc in second ch from hook, dc in each ch across, join. Fasten off. *(12 petals)*

Rnd 5: Join aqua with sc in tip of any petal, ch 7, (sc in tip of next petal, ch 7) around, join. *(12 ch sps)*

Rnd 6: Ch 1, 9 sc in each ch sp around, join. *(108 sc)*

Rnd 7: Ch 1, sc in first 9 sts, (*picot—*see Special Stitch, sc in next 4 sc, ch 10 for corner, **turn**, skip 4 sc past picot, sc in each of next 2 sc, **turn**, work 16 sc in corner ch sp*, sc in next 23 sts on rnd 6) 3 times; repeat between first and second *, sc in last 14 sc, join. Fasten off.

Rnd 8: With wrong side of rnd 7 facing you, join pink with sc in first sc worked into any corner ch sp *(work the following steps to complete the rnd)*:
- **A:** (Ch 4, skip next 2 sc, sc in next sc) 5 times, **turn**;
- **B:** For **scallops**, skipping each sc, (sc, hdc, 2 dc, hdc, sc) in each of next 5 ch sps, **turn**;
- **C:** Working behind scallops into skipped sc of step A, (ch 5, skip next ch sp, sc in back of next sc) 5 times;
- **D:** Sc in next sc on rnd 7, (ch 3, skip next 3 sc, sc in next sc, ch 3, sc in next sc, ch 3, skip next 3 sc, sc in next sc) 2 times;
- **E:** Sc in first sc worked into next corner ch sp;
- **F:** Repeat steps A–E 2 more times;
- **G:** Repeat steps A–D, join. Fasten off.

Rnd 9: Join aqua with sl st in first ch-5 sp behind scallops at any corner, ch 1, *(sc, hdc, 3 dc, picot, 2 dc, hdc, sc) in each ch-5 sp around corner, ch 2, skip next ch-3 sp; for **fan, (dc, picot, ch 2, tr, picot, ch 2, dc, picot, ch 2)** in next ch-3 sp; skip next 2 ch-3 sps, work fan in next ch-3 sp, skip next ch-3 sp; repeat from * around, join. Fasten off.

Rnd 10: *Work on first Large Motif only:* Join yellow with sc in center picot at any corner, (ch 7, sc in next picot) 2 times, *(ch 7, sc in center picot of next fan) 2 times, (ch 7, sc in next picot) 5 times; repeat from * 2 more times, (ch 7, sc in center picot of next fan) 2 times, (ch 7, sc in next picot) 2 times, ch 7, join. Fasten off.

Joining Rnd 10: *Work on last 5 Large Motifs as follows, forming a piece 2 Motifs wide and 3 Motifs long:* Join yellow with sc in center picot at any corner; to **join side,** *(ch 3, sc in corresponding ch sp on adjacent Motif, ch 3, sc in next picot on this Motif) 2 times, (ch 3, sc in next ch sp on adjacent Motif, ch 3, sc in center picot of next fan on this Motif) 2 times, (ch 3, sc in next ch sp on adjacent Motif, ch 3, sc in next picot on this Motif) 3 times*; *(when needed, to **join next side,** repeat between first and second *)* then complete remainder of rnd as follows: **(ch 7, sc in next picot) 2 times, (ch 7, sc in center picot of next fan) 2 times, (ch 7, sc in next picot) 3 times; repeat from ** around ending last repeat with sl st in first sc. Fasten off.

FILL-IN MOTIF (make 2)

Rnd 1: With pink, ch 6, sl st in first ch to form ring, ch 1, 16 sc in ring, join with sl st in first sc. *(16 sc made)*

Rnd 2: Ch 3, sc in any ch-3 sp on edge of opening between Large Motifs, ch 2, (sc in each of next 2 sc on this Motif, ch 2, sc in next ch-3 sp on edge of Large Motif, ch 2) 7 times, sc in last sc on this Motif, join with sl st in first ch of ch-3. Fasten off.

BORDER

Rnd 1: Working around outer edge of Motifs, join yellow with sc in any ch sp, ch 7, (sc in next ch sp, ch 7) around, join with sl st in first sc.

Rnd 2: Sl st in each of next 2 chs, (ch 3, 6 dc) in first ch sp, ch 2, (7 dc, ch 2) in each ch sp around, join with sl st in top of ch-3.

Rnd 3: Ch 6, sl st in fourth ch from hook *(first picot made)*, (ch 2, skip next dc, dc in next dc, picot) 2 times, *ch 2; skipping ch-3 sp, dc next dc and first dc of next dc group tog, picot, (ch 2, skip next dc, dc in next dc, picot) 2 times; repeat from * around ending with ch 2, dc in last dc, join with sl st in third ch of ch-6 at base of first picot. Fasten off. ❏❏

71

Hangers & Sachets

Designed by Dot Drake

HANGER & SACHET NO. 1

Finished Sizes: Fits 16" garment hanger. Sachet is 3½" across.

Materials:
- ❏ Size 10 crochet cotton thread:
  - 225 yds. white
  - 30 yds. pink
  - 50 yds. purple
- ❏ 5" square pink tulle
- ❏ Potpourri
- ❏ Nine white 4-mm. pearl beads
- ❏ One 16" padded garment hanger with bow
- ❏ Pink and white sewing thread
- ❏ Hot glue gun
- ❏ Sewing and tapestry needles
- ❏ No. 8 steel hook or hook needed to obtain gauge

Gauge: 1 shell = ½"; 3 shell rows = 1".

Basic Stitches: Ch, sl st, sc, hdc, dc, tr.

HANGER
Sleeve (make 2)
Rnd 1: With white, ch 8, sl st in first ch to form ring, (ch 3, sc in ring) 7 times, ch 3, join with sl st in first ch of first ch-3. *(8 ch sps made)*
Rnd 2: Sl st in first ch-3 sp, (ch 5, sc in next sp) around, ch 2, join with dc in first ch of first ch-5.
Rnd 3: (Ch 5, sc in next ch sp) around, ch 2, join.
Rnd 4: Ch 3, (dc, ch 3, 2 dc) in first ch sp; for **shell,** (2 dc, ch 3, 2 dc) in next ch sp *(shell made);* shell in each ch sp around, join with sl st in top of ch-3.
Rnd 5: Sl st in next st, sl st in next ch sp, (ch 3, 1 dc, ch 3, 2 dc) in same ch sp, shell in each ch-3 sp around, join.
Repeat rnd 5 until Sleeve fits one end of hanger. Fasten off.
Place Sleeves on each end of hanger and sew together at center.

SACHET
Flower
Rnd 1: With white, ch 2, 5 sc in second ch from hook, join. *(5 sc made)*
Rnd 2: For **petals,** (sc, hdc, dc, hdc, sc) in each st around, **do not join rnds.** *(5 petals).*
Rnd 3: Working behind petals, (ch 3, sl st in sp between next 2 petals) around, ch 3.
Rnd 4: For **petals,** (sc, hdc, 3 dc, hdc, sc) in each ch sp around.
Rnd 5: Working behind petals, (ch 4, sl st in sp between next 2 petals) around, ch 4.
Rnd 6: For **petals,** (sc, ch 1, dc, 5 tr, dc, ch 1, sc) in each ch sp around, join with sl st in first sc. Fasten off.
Rnd 7: Join pink with sc in sp between any 2 petals, sc in next ch sp, sc in next 4 sts; for **picot,** ch 3, sl st in top of last st made *(picot made);* sc in each of next 3 sts, sc in next ch sp, (sc in next sp between petals, sc in next ch sp, sc in next 4 sts, picot, sc in each of next 3 sts, sc in next ch sp) around, join. Fasten off.
Sew three pearl beads to center of Flower *(see photo).* Reversing colors, make two more Flowers.
Cut one 4" circle from tulle. Place potpourri in center of circle and gather edge with thread to close into small pouch.

Pillow Side (make 2)
Rnd 1: With purple, ch 10, sl st in first ch to form ring, ch 12, ***dtr** (see Stitch Guide)* in ring, ch 7; repeat from * 5 more times, join with sl st in fifth ch of ch-12. *(7 ch sps made)*
Rnd 2: 12 sc in each ch sp around, join with sl st in first sc. For **first Side,** fasten off; for **second Side,** do not fasten off. *(84 sc)*
Rnd 3: Hold Pillow Sides with wrong sides together; working through both thicknesses, in **back lps** *(see Stitch Guide)* on front piece and **both lps** on back piece, sc in each sc around, inserting tulle pouch inside before completing rnd, join.
Rnd 4: *Sc in next st, hdc in next st, dc in next st, tr in next st, 2 dtr in next st, dtr in next st, picot, 5 sc around post of last dtr made; repeat from * around, join.
For **hanging loop,** *ch 3, hdc in third ch from hook; repeat from * 9 more times, join with sl st in first ch of first ch-3. Fasten off.
Tack or glue Flowers over one side of Sachet. Sachet can be hung on hanger if desired.

HANGER & SACHET NO. 2

Finished Size: Hanger fits 16" garment hanger. Sachet is 3¾" across.

Materials:
- ❏ Size 10 crochet cotton thread:
  - 230 yds. yellow
  - 70 yds. lavender
  - 30 yds. pink
- ❏ One 16" padded garment hanger with bow
- ❏ 18 white 4-mm. pearl beads
- ❏ Two 3½" squares of desired color tulle
- ❏ White sewing thread
- ❏ Hot glue gun
- ❏ Sewing and tapestry needles
- ❏ No. 8 steel hook or hook needed to obtain gauge

Gauge: 4 dc = ½"; 7 rows = 2". Flower is 3" across.

Basic Stitches: Ch, sl st, sc, hdc, dc.

HANGER
Sleeve (make 2)
NOTE: *Back of sts is right side of work.*
Rnd 1: With yellow, ch 6, sl st in first ch to form ring, ch 4 *(counts as dc and ch-1),* (dc in ring, ch 1) 9 times, join with sl st to third ch of ch-4. *(10 dc made)*
Rnd 2: Sl st into ch-1 sp, ch 5, (dc in next ch sp, ch 2) around, join with sl st in third ch of ch-5.
Rnd 3: Ch 3, dc in next ch sp; for **picot,** ch 3, sl st in top of last st made *(picot made),* dc in same sp, dc in next dc, ch 2, *dc in next dc, (dc, picot, dc) in next ch sp, dc in next dc, ch 2; repeat from * around, join with sl st in top of ch-3.
Rnd 4: Ch 6, *[skip next 2 dc and picot, dc in next dc, (dc, picot, dc) in next ch sp], dc in

Continued on page 74

next dc, ch 2; repeat from * 3 more times; repeat between [ ], join.

Rnd 5: Ch 3, *(dc, picot, dc) in next ch sp, dc in next dc, ch 2, skip next 2 dc and picot, dc in next dc; repeat from * 3 more times, (dc, picot, dc) in next ch sp, dc in next dc, ch 2, skip next 2 dc and picot, join.

Repeat rnds 4 and 5 alternately until Sleeve fits one end of hanger. Fasten off.

Place Sleeves on each end of hanger and sew together at center.

FLOWER
Rnd 1: With pink, ch 5, sl st in first ch to form ring, ch 1, 10 sc in ring, join with sl st in first sc. *(10 sc made)*

Rnd 2: Ch 1, 2 sc in each st around, join. Fasten off. *(20 sc)*

Rnd 3: Join yellow with sc in first st, sc in each of next 3 sts, ch 10, (sc in next 4 sts, ch 10) around, join. *(5 ch sps)*

Rnd 4: *Sl st in second and third sts of 4-sc group; for **petal,** (3 sc, hdc, 13 dc, hdc, 3 sc) in next ch sp; repeat from * around.

Rnd 5: Sl st across to first sc of next petal, *sl st in first 2 sc on petal, sc in next sc, ch 3, skip next hdc, 1 dc in next dc, (ch 1, skip next dc, dc in next dc) 3 times, ch 3, dc in same st as last dc; repeat between ( ) 3 times, ch 3, skip next hdc, sc in next sc, sl st in each of next 2 sc; skipping sl st between petals, repeat from * around, join with sl st in first sl st on first petal. Fasten off.

Rnd 6: Join pink with sc in first sl st on any petal, *[sc in next sl st, sc in next sc, 3 sc in first ch-3 sp on petal, (sc in next dc, 2 sc in next ch-1 sp) 3 times, sc in next dc, (2 sc, picot, 2 sc) in next ch-3 sp, (sc in next dc, 2 sc in next ch-1 sp) 3 times, sc in next dc, 3 sc in ch-3 sp, sc in next sc, sc in each of next 2 sl sts], sc in first sl st on next petal; repeat from * 3 more times; repeat between [ ], join with sl st in first sc. Fasten off.

Tack or glue beads in a circle to center of Flower *(see photo)*.

Tack or glue back of Flower to center on one side of Hanger.

SACHET
Flower
Reversing colors, work same as Hanger Flower.

SACHET
NOTE: *Back of sts is right side of work.*
Back
Rnd 1: With lavender, ch 7, sl st in first ch to form ring, ch 3, 3 dc in ring, (ch 3, 4 dc in ring) 3 times, ch 1, join with dc in top of ch-3. *(Counts as joining ch sp—16 dc, 4 ch sps made.)*

> **Rnd 2:** (Ch 3, 3 dc) in joining ch sp, *ch 2, (4 dc, ch 3, 4 dc) in next ch sp; repeat from * 2 more times, ch 2, 4 dc in joining ch sp, ch 1, join with dc in top of ch-3.

Rnd 3: (Ch 3, 3 dc) in joining ch sp, *ch 2; for **shell, 4 dc in next ch sp, ch 2;** for **corner, (4 dc, ch 3, 4 dc) in next ch sp;** repeat from * 2 more times, ch 2, shell, 4 dc in joining ch sp, ch 1, join with dc in top of ch-3.

Rnds 4–6: (Ch 3, 3 dc) in joining ch sp, (ch 2, shell across to next corner, corner) 3 times, ch 2, shell across, 4 dc in joining ch sp, ch 1, join. At end of last rnd, fasten off.

Front
Rnd 1: Ch 40, join with sl st in first ch to form ring, ch 3, 3 dc in ring, *ch 2, 4 dc in ring, ch 2, (4 dc, ch 3, 4 dc) in ring; repeat from * 2 more times, (ch 2, 4 dc in ring) 2 times, ch 1, join with dc in top of first ch-3.

Rnd 2: Ch 3, 3 dc in joining ch sp, (ch 2, shell 2 times, corner) 3 times, ch 2, shell 2 times, 4 dc in joining ch sp, ch 1, join with dc in top of ch-3.

Rnds 3–4: Repeat rnd 4 of Back. At end of last rnd, fasten off.

Sew edges of tulle squares together, stuffing with potpourri before closing.

Trim
Hold Front and Back with wrong side of sts facing out; working through both thicknesses, join pink with sc in first ch-2 sp after any corner, sc in same ch sp, *(sc in each of next 2 dc, picot, sc in each of next 2 dc, 2 sc in next ch-2 sp) across to next corner, sc in each of next 2 dc, picot, sc in each of next 2 dc, 2 sc in corner ch sp, ch 5, sl st in second ch from hook, ch 1, dc in top of last sc made, (ch 5, sl st in second ch from hook, ch 1, dc in top of last dc made) 2 times, 2 sc in same corner ch sp; repeat from * 3 more times, sc in each of next 2 dc, picot, sc in each of next 2 dc, join with sl st in first sc. Fasten off.

Tack or glue center of Flower to tulle at center front of Sachet.

HANGER & SACHET NO. 3
Finished Size: Hanger fits 16" garment hanger. Sachet is 3¾" across.

Materials:
❑ Size 10 crochet cotton thread:
　265 yds. white
　40 yds. lt. pink
　15 yds. green
　8 yds. yellow
　30 yds. dk. pink
❑ One 16" padded garment hanger with bow
❑ Two 3½" squares desired color tulle
❑ Sewing thread
❑ Potpourri
❑ Hot glue gun
❑ Sewing and tapestry needles
❑ No. 8 steel hook or hook needed to obtain gauge

Gauge: 1 shell = ¾"; 3 shell rows = 1¼". Large Flower is 2½" across.

Basic Stitches: Ch, sl st, sc, hdc, dc, tr.

HANGER
Sleeve (make 2)
Rnd 1: With white, ch 8, sl st in first ch to form ring,

(ch 3, sc in ring) 7 times, ch 3, join with sl st in first ch of first ch-3. *(8 ch sps made)*

Rnd 2: Sl st in first ch-3 sp, (ch 5, sc in next sp) around, ch 2, join with dc in first ch of first ch-5.

Rnd 3: (Ch 5, sc in next sp) around, ch 2, join with dc in first ch of first ch 5.

Rnd 4: For **beginning shell (beg shell), ch 5, tr in first ch sp, (ch 1, tr in same ch sp) 3 times;** *ch 2, sc in next sp, ch 2; for **shell, (tr, ch 1) 4 times in third ch of next ch-5 sp, tr in same ch sp; repeat from * 2 more times;** ch 2, sc in next sp, ch 2, join with sl st in fourth ch of ch 5 (4 shells). *First ch-5 counts as tr and ch 1. Back of rnd 4 is right side of work.*

Rnd 5: Sl st to third tr of beg shell, *ch 2, shell in sc, ch 2, sc in third tr of next shell; repeat from * 2 more times, ch 2, shell in sc, ch 2, join with sl st in same sl st as first ch-2.

Rnd 6: Beg shell, *ch 2, sc in third tr of next shell, ch 2, shell in next sc; repeat from * 2 more times, ch 2, sc in third tr of next shell, ch 2, join in fourth ch of ch-5.

Repeat rnds 5 and 6 alternately until Sleeve fits one end of hanger. Fasten off.

Place Sleeves on each end of hanger and sew together at center.

Large Flower

Rnd 1: With yellow, ch 2, 6 sc in second ch from hook, join with sl st in first sc. *(6 sc made)*

Rnd 2: 2 sc in each st around, join. *(12 sc)*

Rnds 3–4: Sc in each st around, join. At end of last rnd, fasten off.

Rnd 5: With lt. pink, join with sc in any st, (ch 3, skip next st, sc in next st) around to last st, ch 3, skip last st, join, **turn.** *(6 ch-3 sps)*

Rnd 6: For **petals,** (sc, ch 1, 5 dc, ch 1, sc) in each ch sp around, **do not join.** *(6 petals)*

Rnd 7: Working behind petals, (ch 3, sc in sp between next 2 petals) around, ch 3, join with sl st in first ch of first ch-3.

Rnd 8: For **petals,** (sc, ch 1, dc, 3 tr, dc, ch 1, sc) in each ch sp around, **do not join.**

Rnd 9: Repeat rnd 7. Fasten off.

Rnd 10: For **petals,** join dk. pink with sc in any ch sp, (ch 1, dc, 3 tr, dc, ch 1, sc) in same ch sp, (sc, ch 1, dc, 3 tr, dc, ch 1, sc) in each ch sp around, **do not join.**

Rnd 11: Working behind petals, (ch 4, sl st in sp between next 2 petals) around, ch 4.

Rnd 12: For **petals,** (sc, ch 2, dc, 8 tr, dc, ch 2, sc) in each ch sp around, join with sl st in first sc. Fasten off.

Rnd 13: Join lt. pink with sc in sp between any 2 petals, sc in next ch-2 sp, sc in next 5 sts; for **picot,**

ch 3, sl st in top of last st made *(picot made),* sc in next 5 sts, sc in ch-2 sp, *sc in next sp between petals, sc in next ch-2 sp, sc in next 5 sts, picot, sc in next 5 sts, sc in next ch-2 sp; repeat from * around, join. Fasten off.

Rnd 14: Join green with sl st in center back of any petal, *ch 6, sl st in center back of next petal; repeat from * around, ch 6.

Rnd 15: (Sc, hdc, 2 dc, 4 tr, picot, 4 tr, 2 dc, hdc, sc) in each ch sp around, join. Fasten off.

Small Flower

Rnd 1: With yellow, ch 2, 5 sc in second ch from hook, join with sl st in first sc. *(5 sc made)*

Rnd 2: For **petals,** (sc, hdc, dc, hdc, sc) in each st around, **do not join.**

Rnd 3: Working behind petals, (ch 3, sl st in sp between sts of next 2 petals) around, ch 3, join with sl st in first ch of first ch-3. Fasten off.

Rnd 4: Join dk. pink with sc in any ch sp, (hdc, 5 dc, hdc, sc) in same ch sp, (sc, hdc, 5 dc, hdc, sc) in each ch sp around.

Rnd 5: Working behind petals, (ch 4, sl st in sp between sts of next 2 petals) around, ch 4, join with sl st in first ch of first ch-4. Fasten off.

Rnd 6: Join green with sc in any ch-4 sp, 3 sc in same ch-4 sp, *(sc, hdc, dc, 2 tr, 2 dtr) in next ch-4 sp, picot, 5 sc around post of last dtr, sc in same ch-4 sp*, 4 sc in next ch sp; repeat between first * 2 more times, join with sl st in first sc. Fasten off.

Tack or glue Flowers to each Sleeve on one side of Hanger.

SACHET
Side (make 2)

Rnd 1: With white, ch 7, sl st in first ch to form ring, ch 3, 3 dc in ring, (ch 3, 4 dc in ring) 3 times, ch 1, join with dc in top of ch-3. *(Counts as joining ch sp—16 dc, 4 ch sps made)*

Rnd 2: (Ch 3, 3 dc) in joining ch sp, *ch 2, (4 dc, ch 3, 4 dc) in next ch sp; repeat from * 2 more times, ch 2, 4 dc in joining ch sp, ch 1, join with dc in top of ch-3.

Rnd 3: (Ch 3, 3 dc) in joining ch sp, *ch 2; for **shell, 4 dc in next ch sp, ch 2; for corner, (4 dc, ch 3, 4 dc) in next ch sp;** repeat from * 2 more times, ch 2, shell, 4 dc in joining ch sp, ch 1, join with dc in top of ch-3.

Rnds 4–6: (Ch 3, 3 dc) in joining ch sp, (ch 2, shell across to next corner, corner) 3 times, ch 2, shell across, 4 dc in joining ch sp, ch 1, join. At end of last rnd, fasten off.

Make one Large Flower and sew to center of one side of Sachet. ❑❑

Victorian Baskets

FLUTED FLORAL
Finished Size: 11" tall including Handle.

Materials:
- ❏ 200 yds. size 10 crochet cotton thread
- ❏ Fabric stiffener *(see General Instructions)*
- ❏ No. 7 steel hook or hook needed to obtain gauge

Gauge: 8 sts = 1"; 4 dc rows = 1"; 5 tr rows = 2".

Basic Stitches: Ch, sl st, sc, dc, tr.

Note: When working in stitches, insert hook through center of stitch instead of under 2 top loops *(see illustration).*

BASE
Rnd 1: Ch 18, sl st in first ch to form ring, ch 3, 47 dc in ring, join with sl st in top of ch-3. *(48 dc made)*
Rnd 2: Ch 3, dc in each st around, join.
Rnd 3: Ch 5, (tr, ch 1) in each st around, join with sl st in fourth ch of ch-5.

Rnds 4–5: Ch 4, skip next ch-1, (dc in next st, ch 1, skip next ch-1) around, join with sl st in third ch of ch-4.

Rnd 6: Sl st in first ch sp; for **beginning shell (beg shell), (ch 4, tr, ch 2, 2 tr) in same ch sp;** *skip next 2 ch sps, ch 4; for **shell, (2 tr, ch 2, 2 tr)** in next ch sp; repeat from * around, join with sl st in top of ch-4. *(16 shells)*

Rnd 7: Sl st in next st, sl st in next ch sp, beg shell, ch 5, (shell in ch sp of next shell, ch 5) around, join.

Rnd 8: Sl st in next st, sl st in next ch sp, beg shell; *ch 4, sc around ch lps of rnds 6 and 7 *(see illustration)*, ch 4, shell in ch sp of next shell; repeat from * 14 more times, ch 4, sc around ch lps of rnds 6 and 7, ch 4, join. Fasten off.

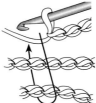

SIDE

Rnd 1: Working in unworked ch-1 sps on rnd 3 of Base, join with sl st in any ch-1 sp, ch 4, (dc, ch 1) in each ch-1 sp around, join with sl st in third ch of ch-4.

Rnds 2–10: Ch 4, (dc, ch 1) in each st around, join.

Rnd 11: Sl st in next ch sp, beg shell, (skip next ch sp, shell in next ch sp) around, join. *(24 shells)*

Rnd 12: Sl st in next st, sl st in ch sp of first shell, beg shell, (ch 1, shell) in ch sp of each shell around, ch 1, join.

Rnd 13: Sl st in next st, sl st in ch sp of first shell, beg shell, (ch 2, shell) in ch sp of each shell around, ch 2, join.

Rnd 14: Sl st in next st, sl st in ch sp of first shell, beg shell, (ch 3, shell) in ch sp of each shell around, ch 3, join.

Rnd 15: Sl st in next st, sl st in ch sp of first shell, beg shell, (ch 4, shell) in ch sp of each shell around, ch 4, join.

Rnd 16: Sl st in next st; for **beginning large shell (beg large shell), (sl st, ch 4, 2 tr, ch 2, 3 tr) in ch-2 sp of first shell;** *ch 6; for **large shell, (3 tr, ch 2, 3 tr)** in ch-2 sp of next shell; repeat from * around, join.

Rnd 17: Sl st in each of next 2 sts, beg large shell, *ch 7, large shell in ch-2 sp of next shell; repeat from * around, ch 7, join.

Rnd 18: Sl st in each of next 2 sts, beg large shell, *ch 4, sc around ch lps of last 2 rnds, ch 4, large shell in ch-2 sp of next shell; repeat from * around, ch 4, sc around ch lps of last 2 rnds, ch 4, join.

Rnd 19: Sl st in each of next 2 sts, beg large shell, (ch 7, large shell) in ch-2 sp of each shell around, ch 7, join.

Rnd 20: Sl st in each of next 2 sts, beg large shell, (ch 8, large shell) in ch-2 sp of each shell around, ch 8, join.

Rnd 21: Sl st in each of next 2 sts, beg large shell, *ch 5, sc around ch lps of last 2 rnds, ch 5, large shell in ch-2 sp of next shell; repeat from * around, ch 5, sc around ch lps of last 2 rnds, ch 5, join. **Do not fasten off.**

HANDLE

Row 1: Sl st in each of next 2 sts, beg large shell, ch 4, large shell in ch-2 sp of next shell, ch 4, turn.

Row 2: Large shell in ch-2 sp of first shell, ch 5, large shell in ch-2 sp of next shell, ch 4, turn.

Row 3: Large shell in ch-2 sp of first shell, ch 4, sc around ch lps of last 2 rows, ch 4, large shell in ch-2 sp of next shell, ch 4, turn.

Row 4: Large shell in ch-2 sp of first shell, ch 4, large shell, ch 4, turn.

Row 5: Large shell in ch-2 sp of first shell, ch 5, large shell in ch-2 sp of next shell, ch 4, turn.

Rows 6–23: Repeat rows 3–5 consecutively.

Row 24: 3 dc in ch-2 sp of first shell, skip next 10 shells on Basket Side, sc in ch-2 sp of next shell; 3 dc in ch-2 sp of first shell on row 23 of Handle, ch 4, sc around ch lps of last 2 rows, ch 4, 3 dc in ch-2 sp of next shell, sc in ch-2 sp of next shell on Basket Side, 3 dc in ch-2 sp of next shell on row 23, ch 4, sl st in ch-2 sp of same shell on Basket Side. Fasten off.

FINISHING

Apply fabric stiffener to Basket, shape and allow to dry completely.

Decorate Basket as desired.

Finished Size: 11" tall including Handle.

Materials:
- ❏ 130 yds. size 10 crochet cotton thread
- ❏ Fabric stiffener *(see General Instructions)*
- ❏ No. 7 steel hook or hook needed to obtain gauge

Gauge: 9 sts = 1"; dc = ⅜" tall; tr = ½" tall.

Basic Stitches: Ch, sl st, sc, dc, tr.

BASE

Rnd 1: Ch 8, sl st in first ch to form ring, ch 4, 29 tr in ring, join with sl st in top of ch 4. *(30 tr made)*

Rnd 2: Ch 5, (skip next st, dc in each of next 2 sts, ch 2) around to last 2 sts, skip next st, dc in last st, join with sl st in third ch of ch-5. *(10 ch sps)*

Rnd 3: (Sl st, ch 3, 2 dc) in next ch sp, (ch 3, 3 dc in next ch sp) 9 times, ch 3, join with sl st in top of ch-3.

Rnd 4: Sl st in each of next 2 sts, (sl st, ch 3, 3 dc) in next sp, (ch 4, 4 dc in next sp) 9 times, ch 4, join.

Rnd 5: Sl st in each of next 2 sts, ch 5, *(tr, **dtr**—*see Stitch Guide;* for **picot,** ch 3, sl st in third ch from hook—*picot made;* dtr, tr) in next ch sp *(shell made)*, ch 4, sc in third dc of next 4-dc group, ch 4; repeat from * around, join with sl st in first ch of first ch-5. Fasten off.

SIDE

Rnd 1: Working in ch-4 sps of rnd 4 on Base, join with sl st in first ch sp on either side of the shell already worked into that ch sp, ch 3, 2 dc in same ch sp, 3 dc in each ch sp on each side of each shell, join with sl st in top of ch-3. *(60 dc made)*

Rnd 2: (Ch 4, tr) in first st, tr in next 9 sts, (2 tr in next, tr in next 9 sts) around, join with sl st in top of ch-4. *(66 tr)*

Rnd 3: (Ch 4, tr) in first st, tr in next 6 sts, (2 tr in next st, tr in next 5 sts, 2 tr in next st, tr in next 6 sts) 4 times, 2 tr in next st, tr in next 6 sts, join. *(76 tr)*

Rnd 4: Ch 3, dc in next st, (ch 2, skip next 2 sts, dc in each of next 2 sts) 18 times, ch 2, skip last 2 sts, join. *(38 sts, 19 ch sps)*

Rnd 5: Sl st in next st, (sl st, ch 4, 2 tr) in next ch sp, (ch 2, 3 tr in next ch sp) 18 times, ch 2, join.

Rnd 6: Sl st in each of next 2 sts, (sl st, ch 3, dc) in next ch sp, (ch 3, 2 dc in next sp) 18 times, ch 3, join.

Continued on page 78

77

Bed & Bath

Rnds 7–12: Repeat rnds 5–6 three more times.

Rnd 13: Ch 4, tr in next st, 4 tr in next ch sp, (tr in each of next 2 sts, 3 tr in next ch sp) 8 times, tr in each of next 2 sts, 4 tr in next ch sp, (tr in each of next 2 sts, 3 tr in next ch sp) 9 times, join. *(97 tr)*

Rnd 14: Ch 4, (tr in next 31 sts, 2 tr in next st) around, join. *(100 sts)*

Rnd 15: (Ch 5, 2 dtr) in first st, ch 2, 3 dtr in next st; *ch 1, skip next 3 sts, 3 dtr in next st, ch 2, 3 dtr in next st; repeat from * 18 more times, ch 1, skip last 3 sts, join with sl st in top of ch-5; working into first sts of this rnd, sl st in each of next 2 sts and in next ch-2 sp *(mark this ch-2 sp for working Edging later),* **turn. Do not fasten off.**

HANDLE

Row 1: For **first half of Handle,** ch 7, (3 dc, ch 2, 3 dc) in next ch-2 sp, ch 4, dc in next ch-2 sp, turn.

Rows 2–14: Ch 7, (3 dc, ch 2, 3 dc) in ch-2 sp, ch 4, dc in third ch of ch-7, turn. At end of last row, fasten off.

Row 1: For **second half of Handle,** skip next 7 ch-2 sps on rnd 15, join with sl st in next ch-2 sp, ch 7, (3 dc, ch 2, 3 dc) in next ch-2 sp, ch 4, dc in next ch-2 sp, turn. *(Mark this ch-2 sp also.)*

Rows 2–13: Repeat rows 2–13 of first half of Handle.

Row 14: Ch 3, sl st in third ch of ch-7 on row 14 of first half of Handle, ch 4, 3 dc in ch-2 sp on row 13 of second half of Handle, sl st in ch-2 sp of row 14 of first half, 3 dc in same ch-2 sp on row 13 of second half, ch 4, sl st in top of dc on row 14 of first half, dc in third ch of ch-7 on second half. Fasten off.

EDGING

For first half of Edging, join with sc in one marked ch-2 sp on rnd 15 of Basket, *ch 3, sc in next ch-1 sp, ch 3, (2 dc, picot, 2 dc) in next ch-2 sp; repeat from * 6 more times, ch 3, sc in next ch-1 sp, ch 3; sc in ch-2 sp that row 1 of Handle was worked into, (4 sc, ch 2) in end of each row across side of assembled Handle, join with sl st in first sc. Fasten off. Joining in other marked ch-2 sp, repeat for second half of Edging.

FINISHING

Apply stiffener to Basket, shape and allow to dry completely. Decorate Basket as desired.

DELICATE DELIGHTS

Finished Size: 2" tall excluding Handle.

Materials for one Basket:
❏ 60 yds. size 10 crochet cotton thread
❏ Fabric stiffener *(see General Instructions)*
❏ No. 8 steel hook or hook needed to obtain gauge

Gauge: 9 sts = 1"; 4 dc rows = 1".

Basic Stitches: Ch, sl st, sc, dc.

BASE

Rnd 1: Ch 4, sl st in first ch to form ring, ch 4, (dc in ring, ch 1) 9 times, join with sl st in third ch of ch-4. *(10 ch sps made)*

Rnd 2: (Sl st, ch 4, dc) in first ch sp, (ch 1, dc, ch 1, dc) in each ch sp around, ch 1, join. *(20 ch sps)*

Rnd 3: Sl st in first ch sp, ch 5, (dc, ch 2) in each ch sp around, join with sl st in third ch of ch-5.

Rnd 4: (Sl st, sc) in first ch sp, *[ch 3, 2 dc in next ch sp; for **picot,** ch 3, sc in left bar at top of last dc made *(see illustration—picot made),* 2 dc in same ch sp, ch 3], sc in next ch sp; repeat from * 8 more times, repeat between [ ], join with sl st in first sc. Fasten off.

SIDE

Rnd 1: Working in ch-1 sps of rnd 2 again *(these sps have already been worked into),* join with sl st in any ch sp, ch 3, 2 dc in same ch sp, 2 dc in next 4 ch sps, (3 dc in next ch sp, 2 dc in next 4 ch sps) around, join with sl st in top of ch-3. *(44 dc made)*

Rnd 2: Ch 3, dc in next 9 sts, (ch 1, skip next st, dc in next 10 sts) 3 times, ch 1, skip next st, join. *(40 dc, 4 ch sps)*

Rnd 3: Sl st in next st, ch 3, dc in next 7 sts, (ch 1, skip next st, 3 dc in next ch sp, ch 1, skip next st, dc in next 8 sts) 3 times, ch 1, skip next st, 3 dc in next ch sp, ch 1, join.

Rnd 4: Sl st in next st, ch 3, dc in next 5 sts, *ch 1, skip next st, (3 dc in next ch sp, ch 1) 2 times, skip next st, dc in next 6 sts; repeat from * 2 more times, ch 1, skip next st, (3 dc in next ch sp, ch 1) 2 times, join.

Rnd 5: Sl st in next st, ch 3, dc in each of next 3 sts, *ch 1, skip next st, (3 dc in next ch sp, ch 1) 3 times, skip next st, dc in next 4 sts; repeat from * 2 more times, ch 1, skip next st, (3 dc in next ch sp, ch 1) 3 times, join.

Rnd 6: Sl st in next st, ch 3, dc in next st, *ch 1, skip next st, (3 dc in next ch sp, ch 1) 4 times, skip next st, dc in each of next 2 sts; repeat from * 2 more times, ch 1, skip next st, (3 dc in next ch sp, ch 1) 4 times, join.

Rnd 7: Sl st in next st and in next ch sp, ch 3, 2 dc in same sp, ch 1, (3 dc in next ch sp, ch 1) around, join.

Rnd 8: Sl st in each of next 2 sts and in next ch sp, ch 3, (2 dc, picot, 3 dc) in same sp, *ch 3, sc in next ch sp, ch 3, (3 dc, picot, 3 dc) in next ch sp *(shell made);* repeat from * 8 more times, ch 3, sc in next ch sp, ch 3, join, **turn. Do not fasten off.**

HANDLE

Row 1: Ch 3, dc in next ch sp, ch 2, 2 dc in next ch sp, turn.

Rows 2–15 or to desired length: Ch 3, dc in next st, ch 2, skip ch sp, dc in each of next 2 sts, turn.

Row 16: Ch 3, skip next 5 picots of shells on right side of Handle, sc in next ch sp between shells on rnd 8, ch 3, sl st in next st on row 15 of Handle, sl st in each of next 2 chs on row 15, sc in next ch sp on rnd 8, ch 3, sl st in next st on row 15. Fasten off.

FINISHING

Apply fabric stiffener to Basket, shape and allow to dry completely. Decorate Basket as desired. ❏❏

Gifts for Giving

Why crochet?
When asked, stitchers
often answer simply,
"To give it away."
While needlework was born of
necessity, it flourishes as a boon of
celebrations and a handy means of
cosseting loved ones with tactile talismans
of rejoicing. Sharing small niceties—a filet
pillow, a flower-strewn bookmark, a pair
of exquisite baby booties—reminds us
that our kindred lives are linked
together by providential design, the
intricate grandness of which
only time can reveal.

Mother Pillow

Designed by Elizabeth White

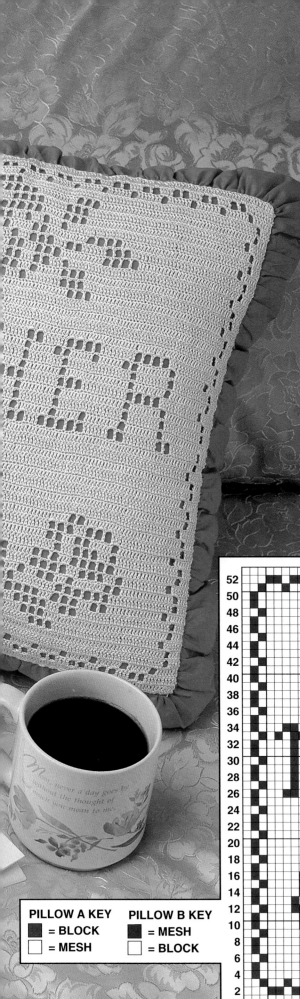

Finished Size: Pillow Front is 12½" square.

Materials:
- ❏ Size 10 crochet cotton thread:
  350 yds. *(for Pillow Front A)*
  500 yds. *(for Pillow Front B)*
  13" square pillow for each Pillow Front
- ❏ Sewing thread to match crochet cotton
- ❏ Sewing needle
- ❏ No. 10 steel hook or hook needed to obtain gauge

Gauge: 13 dc = 1", 8 dc rows = 2".

Special Stitches:
For **mesh**, ch 2, skip next 2 sts or ch, dc in next st.
For **block**, dc in each of next 3 sts or 2 dc in next ch sp, dc in next st.

PILLOW FRONT A
Row 1: Ch 164, dc in eighth ch from hook, (ch 2, skip next 2 chs, dc in next ch) across, turn. *(53 mesh made)*
Row 2: Ch 3, 3 mesh, 2 blocks, (mesh, 2 blocks) across to last 3 mesh, 3 mesh, turn.
Rows 3–53: Ch 3, work according to graph across, turn. At end of last row, fasten off.
Sew edges of Pillow Front to pillow.

PILLOW FRONT B
Row 1: Ch 162, dc *(see Special Stitches)* in fourth ch from hook, dc in each ch across, turn. *(160 dc made)*
Row 2: Ch 3, 3 blocks, 2 mesh, (block, 2 mesh) across to last 9 dc, 3 blocks, turn.
Rows 3–53: Ch 3, work according to graph across, turn. At end of last row, fasten off.
Sew edges of Pillow Front to pillow. ❏❏

PILLOW A KEY
■ = BLOCK
□ = MESH

PILLOW B KEY
■ = MESH
□ = BLOCK

Finished Size: 3" × 10½" without tassel.

Materials:
- ❑ Size 10 white crochet cotton thread:
    - 80 yds. white
    - 50 yds. lilac
    - 35 yds. green
- ❑ 3½" square cardboard
- ❑ No. 8 steel hook or hook needed to obtain gauge

Gauge: Rnds 1–2 = 2" across.

Basic Stitches: Ch, sl st, sc.

Special Stitches:

For **beginning cluster (beg cl)**, ch 4, (yo 2 times, insert hook in ring or ch sp, yo, pull lp through ring or ch sp, yo, pull through 2 lps, yo, pull through 2 lps) 3 times, yo, pull through all 4 lps on hook.

For **cluster (cl)**, (yo 2 times, insert hook in ring or ch sp, yo, pull lp through ring or ch sp, yo, pull through 2 lps, yo, pull through 2 lps) 4 times, yo, pull through all 5 lps on hook.

MOTIF (make 3)

Rnd 1: With lilac, ch 4, sl st in first ch to form ring, **beg cl** *(see Special Stitches)*, ch 8, ***cl** *(see Special Stitches)*, ch 8; repeat from * 3 more times, join with sl st in top of beg cl. Fasten off. *(5 cls made)*

Rnd 2: Join green with sl st in any ch-8 sp, (beg cl, ch 12, cl) in same ch-8 sp, (cl, ch 12, cl) in each ch-8 sp around, join. Fasten off. *(10 cls)*

Rnd 3: Join white with sl st in space between first and last cls, ch 4, *(sl st, ch 4) 2 times in next ch-12 sp, sl st in sp between next 2 cls, ch 4; repeat from * around, join with sl st in first sl st. *(15 ch sps)*

Rnd 4: (5 sc in next ch sp, sl st in next sl st) around. Fasten off. Mark beginning of rnd 4.

BORDER

Rnd 1: Beginning at top, join white with sc in center sc of first 5-sc group on any Motif, ch 5; for **corner**, *yo 2 times, insert hook in center sc of next 5-sc group, yo, pull through st, (yo, pull through 2 lps on hook) 2 times, repeat from *, yo, pull through all 3 lps on hook, ch 12, sl st in same st as ch-12 *(corner made)*, (ch 5, sc in center sc of next 5-sc group) 3 times, ch 5; *work steps A–I to finish rnd:*

    A: Yo 2 times, insert hook in center sc of next 5-sc group on this Motif, yo, pull through st, yo, pull through 2 lps on hook, yo, pull through 2 lps on hook;

    B: Yo 2 times; with right sides of both pieces facing you, insert hook in center sc of next 5-sc group on this Motif and in last sl st on next Motif at the same time, yo, pull through sts, (yo, pull through 2 lps on hook) 2 times;

    C: (Yo 2 times, insert hook in center sc of first 5-sc group on next Motif, yo, pull through st, (yo, pull through 2 lps on hook) 2 times, yo, pull through all 4 lps on hook, ch 12, sl st in same st as ch-12;

    D: Continuing across second Motif, (ch 5, sc in center sc of next 5-sc group) 5 times, ch 5, repeat steps A, B and C;

    E: Continuing around third Motif, (ch 5, sc in center sc of next 5-sc group) 3 times, ch 5, work corner, ch 5, sc in center sc of next 5-sc group, ch 5, sc in center sc of next ch-5 group, ch 12, sl st in same st as ch-12, ch 5, sc in center sc of next 5-sc group, ch 5, work corner, (ch 5, sc in center sc of next 5-sc group) 3 times, ch 5, repeat step A;

    F: Yo 2 times, insert hook in bottom of st joining two Motifs, yo, pull through st, (yo, pull through 2 lps on hook) 2 times;

    G: Yo 2 times, insert hook in center sc of next 5-sc group on next Motif, yo, pull through st, (yo, pull through 2 lps on hook) 2 times, yo, pull through all 4 lps on hook, ch 12, sl st in same st as ch-12;

    H: Continuing across opposite side of second Motif, (ch 5, sc in center sc of next 5-sc group) 5 times, ch 5, repeat step A, step F and step G;

    I: Continuing across opposite side of first Motif, (ch 5, sc in center sc of next ch-5 group) 3 times, ch 5, work corner, ch 5, sc in center sc of next 5-sc group, ch 5, join with sl st in first sc.

Rnd 2: Ch 1, work 6 sc in each ch-4 sp, 20 sc in each ch-12 sp and sl st in each sc around, join with sl st in first sc. Fasten off.

For **Tassel,** wrap lilac 50 times around 3½" cardboard. Tie separate 12" strand lilac around loops on one edge of cardboard, cut loops at other edge. Pull one end of strands through ch-12 loop at bottom of Border, pull through to fold; wrap same 12" strand several times around all strands ½" below fold, tie knot and hide ends on inside. ❑❑

Violet Bookmark

Designed by Ann Kirtley

Antique Baby Bib

Finished Size: 8½" across.

Materials:
- ❐ 170 yds. size 10 white crochet cotton thread
- ❐ 2 yds. of ¼" double-faced satin ribbon
- ❐ Sewing thread to match ribbon
- ❐ Sewing needle
- ❐ No. 12 steel hook or hook needed to obtain gauge

Gauge: 5 sc = ½"; 4 sc back lp rows = ½".

Basic Stitches: Ch, sl st, sc, dc.

Note: Work in **back lps** (*see Stitch Guide*) unless otherwise stated.

Bib

Row 1: Ch 46, sc in second ch from hook, sc in each ch across, turn. *(45 sc made)*

Rows 2–28: Ch 1, sc in first st, skip next st, sc in next 5 sts, (3 sc in next st, sc in next 6 sts, skip next 2 sts, sc in next 6 sts) 2 times, 3 sc in next st, sc in next 5 sts, skip next st, sc in last st, turn. At end of last row, fasten off. Join with sl st in end of row 28 on right-hand side, ch 14. Fasten off.

Row 29: Ch 15, sc in second ch from hook, sc in each ch across, sc in end of row 28 on left-hand side, sc in end of each row across; working in remaining lps on opposite side of starting ch on row 1, 3 sc in first ch for corner, sc in each ch across to last ch, 3 sc in last ch for corner; sc in end of each row across to ch-14 at opposite end of row 28, sc in each ch across, turn. *(133 sc)*

Row 30: Working this row in **both lps,** ch 3, dc in each st across with 3 dc in center st of each corner, turn. *(137 dc)*

Row 31: Ch 4, skip next st, *(dc in each of next 2 sts, ch 1, skip next st) across to center st of next corner, (2 dc, ch 1, 2 dc) in center st*, ch 1, skip next 2 sts; repeat between first *, ch 1, skip next st, (dc in each of next 2 sts, ch 1, skip next st) across to last st, dc in last st, turn.

Row 32: Ch 3, dc in each st and in each ch across to ch-4, dc in each of next 2 chs, turn. *(144 dc)*

Row 33: Ch 1, sc in each st across, **do not turn.** Fasten off.

EDGING

Row 1: Working in ends of rows and in sts, join with sl st in row 29 on left-hand side, ch 5, dc in next row, ch 2, (dc, ch 2) 2 times in each of next 2 rows, skip next row, (dc, ch 2, dc) in first st on row 33, ch 2, skip next st, (dc in next st, ch 2, skip next st) 22 times, (dc, ch 2, dc) in next st, ch 2, skip next st, (dc in next st, ch 2, skip next st) 24 times, (dc, ch 2, dc) in next st, ch 2, skip next st, (dc in next st, ch 2, skip next st) 21 times, dc in next st, ch 2, skip next 2 sts, (dc, ch 2, dc) in last st, ch 2, skip next row, dc in next row, ch 2, (dc, ch 2) 2 times in each of next 2 rows, dc in last row, turn. *(88 dc, 87 ch sps made)*

Row 2: Ch 5, skip first ch sp, (dc in next ch sp, ch 2) 5 times; for **scallop, (2 dc, ch 3, 2 dc) in next ch sp;** *ch 2, (dc in next ch sp, ch 2) 7 times, scallop*; repeat between first * 2 more times, ch 2, (dc in next ch sp, ch 2) 8 times, scallop; repeat between first *, ch 2, (dc in next ch sp, ch 2) 8 times, scallop; repeat between first * 3 times, (ch 2, dc in next ch sp) 5 times, ch 2, skip next 2 chs, dc in next ch, turn. *(10 scallops)*

Row 3: Ch 5, skip first ch sp, *(dc in next ch sp, ch 2) across to ch sp before next scallop, skip next ch sp, dc in each of next 2 sts, (3 dc, ch 3, 3 dc) in next ch sp, dc in each of next 2 sts, ch 2, skip next ch sp; repeat from * 9 more times, (dc in next ch sp, ch 2) across to ch-5, skip next 2 chs, dc in next ch, turn.

Row 4: Ch 5, skip first ch sp, *(dc in next ch sp, ch 2) across to ch sp before next scallop, skip next ch sp, dc in each st across scallop to ch-3 sp, (2 dc, ch 3, 2 dc) in ch-3 sp, dc in each st across scallop, ch 2, skip next ch sp; repeat from *9 more times, (dc in next ch sp, ch 2) across to ch-5, skip next 2 chs, dc in next ch, turn.

Row 5: Ch 5, skip first ch sp, *(dc in next ch sp, ch 2) across to ch sp before next scallop, skip next ch sp, dc in each st across scallop to ch-3 sp, 2 dc in ch-3 sp, dc in each st across scallop, ch 2, skip next ch sp; repeat from * 9 more times, (dc in next ch sp, ch 2) across to ch-5, skip next 2 chs, dc in next ch, turn.

Row 6: Ch 5, skip first ch sp, *(dc in next ch sp, ch 2) across to first st on scallop, skip first st on scallop, dc in next st, (ch 2, skip next st, dc in next st) 7 times, ch 2; repeat from *9 more times, (dc in next ch sp, ch 2) 2 times, skip next 2 chs, dc in next ch, **do not turn.** Fasten off.

Row 7: Join with sc in end of row 1 on Edging, (2 dc, sc) in same row as first sc, (sc, 2 dc, sc) in end of each row and in each ch sp around to opposite side of row 1. Fasten off.

Cut piece ribbon 56" long. Weave through sts of row 1 on Edging, folding at corners and leaving ends for ties. Tack in place at each end of row 1.

Cut 2 pieces ribbon each 8" long. Tie each in bow. Tack to ribbon at each bottom corner. ❐❐

Flower Caches

Designed by Patricia Hall

Finished Sizes: Fits 2-oz. pimento jar; changes for 4-oz. baby food jar are in [ ].

Materials:
- ❏ Size 10 white crochet cotton thread:
  - 120 yds. bright green
  - 90 yds. brown
  - 70 yds. white
  - 55 yds. variegated yellow
  - 50 yds. ecru
  - 35 yds. each orange, red, variegated pink and yellow
- ❏ 4 yellow and 1 orange berry beads
- ❏ ¼" ribbon:
  - 34" dk. yellow
  - 17" each lt. yellow, pink and orange

Gauge: Rnds 1–2 = 1".

Basic Stitches: Ch, sl st, sc, hdc, dc, tr.

POPPY CACHE
Cover
Rnd 1: Beginning at bottom with brown, ch 4, sl st in first ch to form ring, ch 3, 13 dc in ring, join with sl st in top of ch-3. *(14 dc made)*

Rnd 2: Ch 3, dc in same st, 2 dc in each st around, join. *(28 dc)*

Rnd 3: Ch 3, dc in same st, (2 dc in next st, dc in each of next 2 sts) around, join. *(38 dc)*

Rnd 4: Ch 3, dc in next st, (2 dc in next st, dc in next st) around, join. *(56 dc)*

*Notes: For **beginning popcorn (beg pc)**, ch 3, 3 dc in same st, drop lp from hook, insert hook in third ch of ch 3, pull dropped lp through ch.*

*For **popcorn (pc)**, 4 dc in next st, drop lp from hook, insert hook in top of first dc of group, pull dropped lp through st.*

Rnd 5: Working this rnd in **back lps** *(see Stitch Guide)*; **beg pc** *(see Notes above)*, ch 1, skip next st; ***pc** (see Notes above), ch 1, skip next st; repeat from * around, join with sl st in top of first pc. *(28 pc)*

Rnds 6–9 [6–14]: (Sl st, beg pc) in next ch-1 sp, ch 1, skip next st, (pc in next ch-1 sp, ch 1, skip next st) around, join. At end of last rnd, fasten off.

Rnd 10 [15]: Join green with sl st in any ch-1 sp, ch 7, skip next 2 pc, (tr in next ch-1 sp, ch 3, skip next 2 pc) around, join with sl st in fourth ch of ch-7, **turn**. *(14 ch sps)*

Rnd 11 [16]: Ch 1, *(sc, ch 1, dc, tr, 6 **dtr**—*see Stitch Guide*) in next ch sp, (6 dtr, tr, dc, ch 1, sc) in next ch sp; repeat from * around, join with sl st in first sc. Fasten off.

Place Cover on jar. Weave orange ribbon through rnd 10 [15], tie ends in bow.

Flower
Rnd 1: With orange, ch 12, sl st in first ch to form ring, ch 2, 23 hdc in ring, join with sl st in top of ch-2. *(24 hdc made)*

Rnd 2: Ch 9, skip next 3 sts, (sl st in next st, ch 9, skip next 3 sts) around, join with sl st in first ch of ch-9. *(6 ch sps)*

Rnd 3: For **petals,** ch 1, (sc, 2 dc, 10 tr, 2 dc, sc) in each ch sp around, join with sl st in first sc. *(6 petals)*

Rnd 4: Working in front of petals in skipped sts of rnd 1, sl st in each of next 2 hdc, ch 7, (sl st in center st of next 3 skipped sts, ch 7) around, join with sl st in first ch of first ch-7.

Rnd 5: Ch 1, (sc, 2 dc, 8 tr, 2 dc, sc) in each ch sp around, join.

Rnd 6: Working in skipped sts of rnd 1, ch 1, sl st in next st, ch 7, (skip next st, sl st in next st, ch 7) around, join.

Rnd 7: Repeat rnd 5.

Rnd 8: Working in skipped sts of rnd 1, ch 1, sl st in next st, ch 5, (sl st in next st, ch 5) around, join with sl st in first ch of ch 5.

Rnd 9: Ch 1, (sc, 2 dc, 6 tr, 2 dc, sc) in each ch sp around, join. Fasten off.

Sew 1 yellow bead to center of Flower. Glue Flower to jar lid.

WILD ROSE CACHE
Cover
Rnds 1–4: With white, work rnds 1–4 of Poppy Cache Cover.

Rnd 5: Ch 1, (sc in next 5 sts, sc next 2 sts tog) around, join with sl st in first sc. *(48 sc)*

*Notes: For **beginning shell (beg shell)**, (ch 3, dc, ch 2, 2 dc) in first st or ch sp.*

*For **shell**, (2 dc, ch 2, 2 dc) in next st or ch sp.*

Rnd 6: Working this rnd in **back lps** *(see Stitch Guide)*, **beg shell** *(see Notes above)*, skip next 3 sts, ***shell** (see Notes above) in next st, skip next 3 sts; repeat from * around, join with sl st in top of ch-3. *(12 shells)*

Rnds 7–10 [7–14]: Sl st in next st, (sl st, beg shell) in ch sp of next shell, shell in ch sp of each shell around, join. At end of last rnd, fasten off.

Rnd 11 [15]: Join green with sl st in any shell, ch 9, (tr in next shell, ch 5) around, join with sl st in fourth ch of ch-9, **turn**. *(12 ch sps)*

Rnd 12 [16]: Ch 1, *(sc, ch 1, dc, 3 tr, 4 dtr—*see Stitch Guide*) in next ch sp, ch 3, sl st in third ch from hook, (4 dtr, 3 tr, dc, ch 1, sc) in next ch sp; repeat from * around, join with sl st in first sc. Fasten off.

Place Cover on jar. Weave pink ribbon through rnd 11 [15], tie ends in bow.

Flower
Rnd 1: With variegated pink, ch 6, sl st in first ch to form ring, ch 5, (dc, ch 2) 7 times in ring, join with sl st in third ch of ch-5. *(8 dc, 8 ch sps made)*

Rnd 2: For **petals,** ch 1, (sc, ch 1, 4 dc, ch 1, sc) in each ch sp around, join with sl st in first sc. *(8 petals)*

Rnd 3: (Ch 4, sc around first sc on next petal) around, join with sl st in first ch of first ch-4.

Rnd 4: Ch 1, (sc, ch 1, 6 dc, ch 1, sc) in each ch sp around, join.

Rnd 5: Repeat rnd 3.

Rnd 6: Ch 1, (sc, ch 1, 8 dc, ch 1, sc) in each ch sp around, join. Fasten off.

Rnd 7: Working on petals of rnd 2, join variegated pink with sl st in first sc of first petal, ch 1, *sc in first st, ch 3, sc in next ch-1 sp, (ch 3, sc in next dc) across to next ch-1 sp, ch 3, sc in next ch-1 sp, ch 3, sc in last sc; repeat from * on each petal around, join. Fasten off.

Rnd 8: Working on petals of rnd 4, join variegated pink with sl st in first sc of first petal, ch 1, *sc in first st, ch 4, sc in next ch-1 sp, (ch 4, sc in next dc) across to next ch-1 sp, ch 4, sc in next ch-1 sp, ch 4, sc in last sc; repeat from * on each petal around, join. Fasten off.

Rnd 9: Working on petals of rnd 6, join variegated pink with sl st in first sc of first petal, ch 1, *sc in first st, ch 5, sc in next ch-1 sp, (ch 5, sc in next dc) across to next ch-1 sp, ch 5, sc in next ch-1 sp, ch 5, sc in last sc; repeat from * on each petal around, join. Fasten off.

Sew 1 yellow bead to center of Flower. Glue Flower to jar lid.

Continued on page 91

Finished Size: Each pair of Booties fits up to 4"-long foot.

Materials For One Pair:
- ❏ 300 yds. size 10 crochet cotton thread
- ❏ 30" of desired color ¼" ribbon
- ❏ Tapestry needle
- ❏ No. 8 steel hook or hook needed to obtain gauge

Gauge: 9 sts = 1"; 9 sc rows = 1".

Basic Stitches: Ch, sl st, sc, hdc, dc, tr.

BASIC SOLE

Rnd 1: Ch 21 loosely, 3 sc in second ch from hook, sc in next 18 chs, 3 sc in last ch; working in remaining lps on opposite side of ch, sc in next 18 chs, join with sl st in first sc. *(42 sc made)*

Rnd 2: Ch 1, sc in first sc, 3 sc in next sc, sc in next 20 sc, 3 sc in next sc, sc in last 19 sc, join. *(46)*

Rnd 3: Ch 1, sc in first sc; for **toe end of Sole,** 2 sc in next sc, 3 sc in next sc, 2 sc in next sc; sc in next 21 sc, 3 sc in next sc, sc in last 20 sc, join. *(52)*

Rnd 4: Ch 1, sc in each of first 3 sc, 2 sc in next sc, sc in each of next 3 sc, 2 sc in next sc, sc in next 23 sc, 3 sc in next sc, sc in last 20 sc, join. *(56)*

Rnd 5: Ch 1, sc in each of first 3 sc, 2 sc in each of next 2 sc, sc in next sc, 2 sc in each of next 2 sc, sc in next 26 sc, 3 sc in next sc, sc in last 21 sc, join. *(62)*

Rnd 6: Ch 1, sc in first sc, (2 sc in next sc, sc in next sc, 2 sc in next sc) 2 times, sc in next sc, (2 sc in next sc, sc in next sc, 2 sc in next sc) 2 times, sc in next 25 sc, 3 sc in next sc, sc in last 22 sc, join. *(72)*

Rnd 7: Ch 1, sc in first 4 sc, (2 sc in next sc, sc in each of next 2 sc, 2 sc in next sc), sc in next 7 sc; repeat between ( ), sc in next 28 sc, 3 sc in next sc, sc in last 24 sc, join. *(78)*

Rnd 8: Ch 1, sc in first 8 sc, (2 sc in next sc, sc in each of next 3 sc, 2 sc in next sc), sc in next sc; repeat between ( ), sc in next 33 sc, 3 sc in next sc, sc in last 25 sc, join. *(84)*

Rnd 9: Ch 1, sc in first 9 sc, 2 sc in next sc, (sc in each of next 3 sc, 2 sc in next sc) 3 times, sc in next 35 sc, 3 sc in next sc, sc in last 26 sc, join. *(90)*

Rnd 10: Ch 1, sc in each st around, join. Fasten off.

YELLOW RIBBON BOOTIES

SOLE

Make 2 Basic Soles; at end of last rnd, **do not fasten off.**

SIDES (work on each Sole)

Rnd 1: Working in **back lps** *(see Stitch Guide)* of rnd 10 on Sole, ch 3, dc in each dc around, join with sl st in top of ch-3. *(90 dc made)*

Rnd 2: Working in **both lps,** ch 3, dc in each dc around, join, **turn.**

Rnd 3: Working in **back lps,** ch 1, sc in first st, skip next 2 dc, 7 dc in next dc *(scallop made)*, skip next 2 dc, (sc in next dc, skip next 2 dc, 7 dc in next dc, skip next 2 dc) around, join with sl st in first sc, **turn.** *(15 scallops)*

Rnd 4: Working in remaining **front lps** of rnd 2, sl st in first st, ch 3, dc in each dc around, join, **turn.** *(90 dc)*

Rnd 5: Repeat rnd 3.

Rnd 6: Working in remaining **front lps** of rnd 4, sl st in first st, ch 3, dc in each dc around, join, **do not turn.**

Rnd 7: (Ch 3, skip next dc, sl st in **front lp** of next dc) around, join with sl st in joining sl st of last rnd. Fasten off. *(45 ch-3 sps)*

TOP (make 2)

Rnd 1: Ch 48 loosely; being careful not to twist ch, sl st in first ch to form ring, ch 3, dc in each ch around, join with sl st in top of ch-3. *(48 dc made)*

Rnd 2: Working in **front lps,** ch 1, sc in first st, skip next 2 dc, 7 dc in next dc, skip next 2 dc, (sc in next dc, skip next 2 dc, 7 dc in next dc, skip next 2 dc) around, join. *(8 scallops)*

Rnd 3: Working behind last rnd into remaining **back lps** of rnd before last, ch 3, dc in each dc around, join. *(48 dc)*

Rnds 4–9: Repeat rnds 2 and 3 alternately.

Rnd 10: Working in **both lps,** ch 3, dc in each dc around, join. **Do not turn or fasten off.**

Instep

Row 1: Working in **front lps** of rnd 10 on Top, (ch 3, dc) in first st, dc in next 18 dc, 2 dc in next dc leaving remaining dc unworked, turn. *(22 dc made)*

Row 2: Working in **both lps,** (ch 3, dc) in first st, dc in next 10 dc, 2 dc in next dc, dc in next 9 dc, 2 dc in last dc, turn. *(25)*

Row 3: Working in **front lps,** ch 1, sc in first st, (skip next 2 dc, 7 dc in next dc, skip next 2 dc, sc in next dc) across, turn. *(4 scallops)*

Row 4: Working in remaining **back lps** of row 2, ch 2, dc in next dc, (dc in each of next 3 dc, dc next 2 dc tog) 2 times, dc in next dc, dc next 2 sts tog, (dc in each of next 3 dc, dc next 2 dc tog) 2 times, turn. *(19 dc)*

Row 5: Working in **front lps,** ch 1, sc in first st, (skip next 2 dc, 7 dc in next dc, skip next 2 dc, sc in next dc) across, turn. *(3 scallops)*

Row 6: Working in remaining **back lps** of row 4, ch 3, dc in each dc across, turn. *(19 dc)*

Row 7: Working in **front lps,** ch 1, sc in first st, (skip next 2 dc, 7 dc in next dc, skip next 2 dc, sc in next dc) across, turn. *(3 scallops)*

Rows 8–9: Repeat rows 6 and 7.

Row 10: Working behind last row into remaining **back lps** of row before last, ch 2, dc in next st, dc in next dc, dc next 2 sts tog 2 times, dc in next 5 dc, dc next 2 sts tog 2 times, dc in next dc, dc next 2 sts tog. *(13 dc)*

Row 11: Working in **front lps,** ch 1, sc in first st, (skip next 2 dc, 7 dc in next dc, skip next 2 dc, sc in next dc) across, turn. *(2 scallops)*

Rows 12–14: Working in **both lps,** ch 3, dc in each st across, turn. *(13 dc)*

Row 15: Ch 3, (dc next 2 sts tog) 6 times. Fasten off.

Row 16: Join with sl st in remaining **back lp** of first st

Continued on page 90

Gifts for Giving

Heirloom Booties

Designed by Ann Kirtley

on rnd 10 of Top, work 62 sc evenly spaced around edge of Instep, ending with sl st in **back lp** of same st as last st of Instep. Fasten off.

Top Edging
Working in remaining lps on opposite side of starting ch on Top, join with sl st in any ch, ch 3, skip next ch, (sl st in next ch, ch 3, skip next ch) around, join with sl st in first sl st. Fasten off.

ASSEMBLY & FINISHING
1: With wrong sides together and working through **inside lps,** matching row 15 on Instep to center of toe on Sole, sew edge of Instep and Top to last rnd of Side.

2: Cut ribbon in half. On each Bootie, weave one piece through rnd 10 on Top, tie in bow at center front.

3: If desired, using photograph as a guide, sew pearl beads, pearl trim and flowers to Booties.

LIGHT PINK BOOTIES
SOLE
Make 2 Basic Soles on page 88.

TOP, SIDES & INSTEP (make 2)
Top
Row 1: Ch 21 loosely, dc in fourth ch from hook and in last 17 chs, turn. *(9 dc made)*

Row 2: For **ruffles,** working in **front lps** *(see Stitch Guide),* ch 1, sc in first dc, (skip next 2 dc, 7 dc in next dc, skip next 2 dc, sc in next dc) 3 times, turn.

Row 3: Working in **back lps** of row before last, ch 3, dc in each dc across, turn. *(19 dc)*

Rows 4–38: Repeat rows 2 and 3 alternately, ending with row 2. Mark last dc on row 19 for center.

Row 39: With wrong sides together, match remaining lps of starting ch and **back lps** of row 38; working through both thicknesses, sl st in each st across, **do not fasten off.**

Sides
Rnd 1: Ch 1, 2 sc in end of next dc row, (skip next ruffle row, 2 sc in end of next dc row) 6 times, sc in sc at end of next ruffle row, ch 60 loosely, skip next 9 rows; being careful not to twist ch, sc in sc at end of next ruffle row, (2 sc in end of next dc row, skip next ruffle row) 7 times, join with sl st in first sc. *(90 sts and chs)*

Rnd 2: Working in **front lps,** ch 1, sc in first sc, skip next 2 sc, (7 dc in next sc, skip next 2 sc, sc in next sc, skip next 2 sc) 2 times, (7 dc in next ch, skip next 2 chs, sc in next ch, skip next 2 chs) 10 times, 7 dc in next sc, skip next 2 sc, (sc in next sc, skip next 2 sc, 7 dc in next sc, skip next 2 sc) 2 times, join.

Rnd 3: Working behind rnd 2 into **back lps** of rnd 1, ch 5, dtr in each st and in each ch around, join with sl st in top of ch-5. *(90 dtr)*

> **NOTE:** For **cross st,** skip next st, dc in next st; working in front of last dc made, dc back into skipped st.

Rnd 4: Working in **back lps,** ch 3, dc back into last st on last rnd *(first cross st made),* work cross st around *(see Note above),* join with sl st in top of ch-3. *(45 cross sts)*

Rnd 5: For **ruffle,** working in **front lps,** ch 1, sc in first dc, skip next 2 dc, 7 dc in next dc, skip next 2 dc, (sc in next dc, skip next 2 dc, 7 dc in next dc, skip next 2 dc) around, join with sl st in first sc. Fasten off.

Instep
Row 1: Ch 12 loosely; with wrong side of Top facing you, sl st in end of marked center dc row, sl st in sc at end of next ruffle row on Top, **turn;** sc in next 11 chs, 2 sc in end ch; working on opposite side of ch, sc in last 11 chs, sl st in sc at end of next ruffle row on Top, ch 3, sl st in sc at end of next ruffle row, turn.

NOTES: *For **inc cross st,** dc in next st; working in front of last dc made, dc back into same st as last st of last cross st.*

Cross st or inc cross st counts as 2 dc.

Row 2: Work 6 cross sts, work (inc cross st) 2 times *(see Note above),* work 5 cross sts, skip next dc row on Top, sl st in sc at end of next ruffle row, ch 3, sl st in end of next dc row, turn. *(27 dc)*

Row 3: Dc in top of skipped dc row on Top, work cross sts across row 2, sl st in end of next dc row on Top, ch 3, sl st in end of next ruffle row at base of ch-60, turn. *(28 dc)*

Row 4: Dc in next dc on row 3, (dc in next sp between dc, dc in each of next 2 dc) 4 times, (3 dc in next sp between dc, dc in each of next 2 dc) 5 times, (dc in next sp between dc, dc in each of next 2 dc) 4 times, dc in top of ch 3, sl st in end of ruffle row at base of ch-60, turn. *(52 dc)*

Row 5: Ch 1, sc in first 2 dc; working in **back lps,** work 24 cross sts; sc in **both lps** of next dc, sc in top of ch-3, sl st in next sl st. Fasten off.

ASSEMBLY & FINISHING
1: Easing to fit, sew last rnd of Instep to remaining lps on opposite side of ch-60.

2: With wrong sides together and ruffles on outside, matching center front of Sides to center of toe on Sole, sew inside lps of last rnd on Sole and rnd 4 on Sides together.

3: Cut ribbon in half. On each Bootie, weave one piece of ribbon through ends of rows at base of Top, tie in bow at center front.

4: If desired, on each Bootie, sew 3 buttons to ch-12 at center of Instep. Using photograph as a guide, sew pearl beads and pearl trim to Booties.

PEACH RIBBON BOOTIES
SOLE
Make 2 Basic Soles on page 88.

INSTEP & SIDES (make 2)
Rnd 1: For **Heart Instep,** ch 3, 17 hdc in third ch from hook, join with sl st in top of ch-3. *(18 hdc made) Front of rnd 1 is right side of work.*

Rnd 2: Hdc in next hdc, 2 dc in next hdc, 2 tr in each of next 3 hdc, 2 dc in next hdc, dc in next hdc, hdc in next hdc, ch 1, dc in next hdc *(point made),* ch 1, hdc in next hdc, dc in next hdc, 2 dc in next hdc, 2 tr in each of next 3 hdc, 2 dc in next hdc, hdc in next hdc, sl st in joining sl st on rnd 1. *(29 sts and chs)*

Rnd 3: Working in **back lps,** sl st in each of first 2 sts on rnd 2, dc in next st, 2 dc in each of next 3 sts, dc in next st, hdc in next st, sc in each of next 3 sts, sl st in each of next 2 sts, skip ch-1, 3 sc in point st, skip ch-1, sl st in each of next 2 sts, sc in each of next 3 sts, hdc in next st, dc in next st, 2 dc in each of next 3 sts, dc in next st, sl st in each of next 2 sts. *(35 sts)*

Rnd 4: Sl st in **both lps** of each st around, join with sl st in first sl st at **center** of Heart.

Rnd 5: Working in **back lps** of rnd 3, ch 3; sl st in next st, (ch 3, skip next st, sl st in next st) 16 times, ch 1, dc in same st as first ch-3. *(Dc and ch-1 count as joining ch sp—18 ch sps made.)*

Rnd 6: For **Side,** sl st in joining ch sp, ch 39 loosely; being careful not to twist ch, sl st in first ch-3 sp to **left** of center of Heart, (ch 3, sl st in next ch sp) 16 times.

Rnd 7: Ch 3, dc in next 39 chs, sl st in next ch-3 sp, (ch 3, sl st in next ch-3 sp) 15 times, join with sl st in top of first ch-3. *(40 dc, 15 ch sps)*

Rnd 8: Ch 3, dc in next 39 dc; for **Instep,** 3 dc in each of next 15 ch-3 sps, join. *(85)*

Rnds 9–10: Ch 3, dc in each dc around, join.

Rnd 11: For **scallops,** *(sc, dc) in **front lp** of next dc, ch 1, skip next dc, sl st in **front lp** of next dc;

repeat from * around leaving joining sl st unworked. Fasten off.

TOP
Rnd 1: With right side of work facing you, working into ch-3 sps of rnd 7 on Instep and Sides beside and between sts already worked, join with sl st in first ch-3 sp, ch 3, 6 dc in same ch sp, 7 dc in each ch-3 sp across to ch-39; working on opposite side of ch, 3 tr in each of next 6 chs, 3 **dtr** *(see Stitch Guide)* in each of next 6 chs, 3 **ttr** *(see Stitch Guide)* in each of next 15 chs, 3 dtr in each of next 6 chs, 3 tr in each of next 6 chs, join with sl st in top of first ch-3. *(229 sts)*

Rnd 2: For **scallops,** *(sc, dc) in **back lp** of next dc, ch 1, skip next dc, sl st in **back lp** of next dc; repeat from * around. Fasten off.

ASSEMBLY & FINISHING
1: With wrong sides together and scallops on outside, working through **back lps,** matching center front of Instep to center of toe on Sole, sew rnd 9 of Instep and Sides to last rnd of Sole.

2: Cut ribbon in half; on each Bootie, weave one piece through dc on rnd 7 of Sides, tie in bow at center front.

3: If desired, using photograph as a guide, sew pearl beads, pearl trim and flowers to Booties. ❒❒

Flower Caches

Continued from page 87

RED ROSE CACHE
Cover
Rnds 1–4: With ecru, work rnds 1–4 of Poppy Cache Cover on page 87.

Rnd 5: Ch 1, (sc in next 13 sts, 2 sc in next st) around, join with sl st in first sc. *(60 sc)*

Notes: *For **dc cluster (dc cl),** yo, insert hook in next st, yo, pull through st, yo, pull through 2 lps on hook, (yo, insert hook in same st, yo, pull through st, yo, pull through 2 lps on hook) 3 times, yo, pull through all 5 lps on hook, ch 1.*

*For **V st,** (dc, ch 2, dc) in next st.*

Rnd 6: Working this rnd in **back lps** *(see Stitch Guide),* ch 5, dc in same st, skip next 2 sts, **dc cl** *(see Notes above),* skip next 2 sts, ***V st** (see Notes above)* in next st, skip next 2 sts, dc cl in next st, skip next 2 sts; repeat from * around, join with sl st in third ch of ch-5. *(10 cl, 10 V sts)*

Rnd 7: Sl st in next ch sp, ch 3, (yo, insert hook in same sp, yo, pull through sp, yo, pull through 2 lps on hook) 3 times, yo, pull through all 4 lps on hook, ch 1, V st in top of next cl, (dc cl in ch sp of next V st, V st in top of next cl) around, join with sl st in top of first cl.

Rnd 8: (Ch 5, dc) in first cl, dc cl in next V st, (V st in top of next cl, dc cl in next V st) around, join with sl st in third ch of ch-5.

Rnds 9–10 [9–14]: Repeat rnds 7 and 8 alternately. At end of last rnd, fasten off.

Rnd 11 [15]: Join green with sl st in ch sp of any V st, ch 9, (tr in next V st, ch 5) around, join with sl st in fourth ch of ch-9, **turn.** *(10 ch sps)*

Rnd 12 [16]: Ch 1, *(sc, hdc, dc, tr, 5 **dtr**—see Stitch Guide) in next ch sp, (5 dtr, tr, dc, hdc, sc) in next ch sp; repeat from * around, join with sl st in first sc.

Rnd 13 [17]: Ch 1, *sc in next st, (sc, ch 3, sc) in each of next 16 sts, sc in next st; repeat from * around, join. Fasten off.

Place Cover on jar. Weave 17" dk. yellow ribbon through rnd 11 [15], tie ends in bow.

Flower
Rnd 1: With red, ch 6, sl st in first ch to form ring, ch 3, 11 dc in ring, join with sl st in top of ch-3. *(12 dc made)*

Rnd 2: (Ch 2, hdc) in first st, 2 hdc in each st around, join with sl st in top of ch-2. *(24 hdc)*

Rnd 3: Ch 1, (sc in next st, ch 7, skip next 3 sts) around, join with sl st in first sc. *(6 ch sps)*

Rnd 4: For **petals,** ch 1, (sc, hdc, dc, 10 tr, dc, hdc, sc) in each ch sp around, join. *(6 petals)*

Rnd 5: Ch 1, *sc in next st, (sc, ch 2, sc) in each of next 14 sts, sc in next st; repeat from * around, join. Fasten off.

Rnd 6: Working in front of petals in skipped sts of rnd 2, join with sc in center st of any 3 skipped sts, ch 5, (sc in center st of next 3 sts, ch 5) around, join with sl st in first sc. *(6 ch sps)*

Rnd 7: Ch 1, (sc, hdc, dc, 7 tr, dc, hdc, sc) in each ch sp around, join.

Rnd 8: Ch 1, *sc in next st, (sc, ch 2, sc) in each of next 11 sts, sc in next st; repeat from * around, join. Fasten off.

Continued on page 92

Continued from page 91

Rnd 9: Working in front of petals in skipped sts of rnd 2, join yellow with sc in any st, (ch 6, sc in same st) 3 times, *sc in next st, (ch 6, sc in same st) 3 times; repeat from * around, join. Fasten off.

Sew 1 yellow bead to center of Flower. Glue Flower to lid of jar.

DAISY CACHE
Cover
Rnds 1–4: With variegated yellow, repeat rnds 1–4 of Poppy Cache Cover on page 87.

Rnd 5: Ch 1, (sc in next 13 sts, 2 sc in next st) around, join with sl st in first sc. *(60 sc)*

Rnd 6: Working this rnd in **back lps** *(see Stitch Guide)*, ch 3, dc in each of next 3 sts, ch 3, (dc in next 5 sts, ch 3) around to last st, dc in last st, join with sl st in top of ch-3.

Note: For **slanted shell**, *(4 dc, ch 3, sc) in next ch sp.*

Rnd 7: Sl st in next st ch 2, **slanted shell** *(see Note above)* in next ch sp; (skip next 2 sts, sl st in next st, ch 2, slanted shell in next ch sp) around, join with sl st in first ch-2 sp. *(12 shells)*

Rnds 8–10 [8–14]: (Ch 2, slanted shell in ch-3 sp of next slanted shell, sc in next ch-2 sp) around.

Rnd 11 [15]: Ch 8, (tr in next ch-2 sp, ch 4) around, join with sl st in fourth ch of ch-8, **turn.** Fasten off. *(12 ch sps)*

Note: For **dtr cluster (dtr cl)**, *yo 3 times, insert hook in ch sp, yo, pull through sp, (yo, pull through 2 lps on hook) 3 times, *yo 3 times, insert hook in same ch sp, yo, pull through sp, (yo, pull through 2 lps on hook) 3 times; repeat from * number of times needed for dtr in cl, yo, pull through all lps on hook, ch 1.*

Rnd 12 [16]: Join green with sc in any ch sp, ch 4, **7-dtr cl** *(see Note above)* in same ch as last sc, ch 4, sc in same ch sp, (sc, ch 4, 7-dtr cl, ch 4, sc) in each ch sp around, join with sl st in first sc. Fasten off.

Place Cover on jar. Weave lt. yellow ribbon through rnd 11 [15], tie in bow.

First Flower
Rnd 1: With white, ch 12, sl st in first ch to form ring, ch 4, (dc, ch 1) in each ch around, join with sl st in third ch of ch-4. *(12 dc, 12 ch sps made)*

Rnd 2: Ch 1, skip first st, sc in next ch sp, (ch 4, **4-dtr cl**, ch 4, sc) in same ch sp, (sc, ch 4, 4-dtr cl, ch 4, sc) in each ch sp around, join with sl st in first sc. Fasten off.

Second Flower
Rnd 1: With white, ch 9, sl st in first ch to form ring, ch 4, (dc, ch 1) in each ch around, join with sl st in third ch of ch-4. *(9 sc, 9 ch sps made)*

Rnd 2: Ch 1, skip first st, sc in next ch sp, (ch 4, **4-dtr cl**, ch 4, sc) in same ch sp, (sc, ch 4, 4-dtr cl, ch 4, sc) in each ch sp around, join with sl st in first sc. Fasten off.

Place Second Flower on top of First, sew 1 yellow bead to center to secure. Glue to jar lid.

ZINNIA CACHE
Cover
Rnds 1–4: With green, work rnds 1–4 of Poppy Cache Cover on page 87.

Rnd 5: Ch 1, sc in first 5 sts, (2 sc in next st, sc in next 4 sts) 10 times, sc in last st, join with sl st in first sc. *(66 sc)*

Rnd 6: Ch 3, dc in same st, ch 2, skip next 2 sts, (2 dc in next st, ch 2, skip next 2 sts) around, join with sl st in top of ch-3. *(44 dc, 22 ch sps)*

Rnds 7–10 [7–14]: Sl st in next st, (sl st, ch 3, dc, ch 1) in next ch sp, (2 dc, ch 1) in each ch sp around, join.

Rnd 11 [15]: Sl st in next st, (sl st, ch 5) in next ch sp, (tr, ch 1) in each ch sp around, join with sl st in fourth ch of ch-5, **turn.** Fasten off.

Rnd 12 [16]: Join yellow with sc in any tr, (hdc, dc, tr, **dtr**—see Stitch Guide, tr, dc, hdc) in next ch sp, *sc in next tr, (hdc, dc, tr, dtr, tr, dc, hdc) in next ch sp; repeat from * around, join with sl st in first sc. Fasten off.

Place Cover on jar. Weave 17" dk. yellow ribbon through rnd 11 [15], tie ends in bow.

Flower
NOTE: *Do not join rnds unless otherwise stated. Mark first st of each rnd.*

Rnd 1: With yellow, ch 2, 5 sc in second ch from hook. *(5 sc made)*

Rnd 2: 2 sc in each st around. *(10 sc)*

Rnd 3: Working this rnd in **back lps** *(see Stitch Guide)*, 2 sc in each st around. *(20 sc)*

Rnd 4: Sc in each of first 2 sts, (2 sc in next st, sc in each of next 2 sts) around. *(26 sc)*

Rnd 5: Working this rnd in **back lps,** sc in each st around.

Rnd 6: (2 sc in next st, sc in next st) around to last st, 2 sc in last st. *(40 sc)*

Rnd 7: Repeat rnd 5.

Rnd 8: (2 sc in next st, sc in each of next 3 sts) around. *(50 sc)*

Rnd 9: Repeat rnd 5, join with sl st in first sc. Fasten off.

Rnd 10: For **petals,** working in **front lps** of rnd 2, join with sc in any st, (hdc, dc, tr) in same st, (tr, dc, hdc, sc) in next st, *(sc, hdc, dc, tr) in next st, (tr, dc, hdc, sc) in next st; repeat from * around, join. Fasten off.

Rnds 11–13: Working in **front lps** of rnds 4, 6 and 8, repeat rnd 10. Fasten off.

Sew orange bead to center of Flower. Glue Flower to jar lid. ❐❐

Kitchen Creations

The kitchen shines
as the radiant epicenter
of the household, the hot spot
where the cook, children, chatty
guests and the cat all amiably collide.
If home is where the hearth is,
equipping it with crochet makes it even
more inviting. Flowery motifs lend
elegance to the tabletop, while playful
doilies spice up decor and mother and
daughter aprons make family
congeniality complete. Whatever
the project, cozying up with
crochet is a recipe for
contentment.

Tabletop Elegance

Finishes Sizes: Place Mat is 14" × 17½". Tablecloth is 59½" × 87½".

Materials:
- ❒ Size 30 crochet cotton:
    - 575 yds. ecru for place mat
    - 25 ecru 500-yd. balls for tablecloth
- ❒ No. 13 steel hook or hook needed to obtain gauge

Gauge: Large Motif is 3½" across.

Basic Stitches: Ch, sl st, sc, hdc, dc.

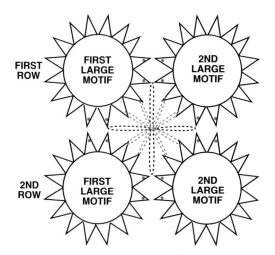

FIRST ROW
First Large Motif
Rnd 1: Ch 6, sl st in first ch to form ring, ch 4, (hdc in ring, ch 2) 7 times, join with sl st in 2nd ch of ch-4. *(8 hdc, 8 ch sps)*

Rnd 2: (Sl st, ch 3, 2 dc) in first ch sp, ch 2, (3 dc, ch 2) in each ch sp around, join with sl st in top of ch-3. *(24 dc)*

Rnd 3: Ch 3, dc in same st, (*dc in next st, 2 dc in next st, ch 2, skip next ch sp*, 2 dc in next st) 7 times; repeat between first *, join.

Rnd 4: Ch 3, dc in same st, (*dc in each of next 3 sts, 2 dc in next st, ch 2, skip next ch sp*, 2 dc in next st) 7 times; repeat between first *, join.

Rnd 5: Ch 3, (*dc in each of next 2 sts, 2 dc in next st, dc in each of next 3 sts, ch 5, skip next ch sp*, dc in next st) 7 times; repeat between first *, join.

Rnd 6: Sl st in next st, ch 3, (*dc in next 6 sts, ch 3, sc in next ch sp, ch 3*, skip next st, dc in next st) 7 times; repeat between first *, join.

Rnd 7: Sl st in next st, ch 3, (*dc in next 4 sts, ch 3, skip next dc, sc in next ch sp, sc in next st, sc in next ch sp, ch 3, skip next dc*, dc in next st) 7 times; repeat between first *, join.

Rnd 8: Sl st in next st, ch 3, (*dc in each of next 2 sts, ch 4, skip next dc, sc in next ch sp, sc in each of next 3 sts, sc in next ch sp, ch 4, skip next st*, dc in next st) 7 times; repeat between first *, join.

Rnd 9: Ch 1, *(sc, ch 2, sc) in next st, ch 6; for **shell, (2 dc, ch 3, 2 dc)** in center st of next 5-sc group; ch 6, skip next dc; repeat from * around, join with sl st in first sc.

Rnd 10: (Sl st, ch 5, dc) in next ch sp, *[ch 3, sc in next ch sp, ch 3, shell in ch sp of next shell, ch 3, sc in next ch sp, ch 3], (dc, ch 2, dc) in next ch-2 sp; repeat from * 6 more times; repeat between [ ], join with sl st in third ch of ch-5.

Rnd 11: Sl st in next ch sp, ch 7, sl st in third ch from hook, ch 2, dc in same ch sp, *[ch 3, sc in next ch sp, ch 3, sc in next sc, ch 3, sc in next ch sp, ch 3], (dc; for **picot,** ch 4, sl st in third ch from hook— *picot made;* ch 1, dc) in next ch sp; repeat from * 14 more times; repeat between [ ], join with sl st in third ch of ch-7. Fasten off.

Second Large Motif
Rnds 1–10: Repeat rnds 1–10 of First Large Motif.

Rnd 11: Sl st in next ch sp, ch 3; (working on side of last Motif according to Joining Illustration, sl st in marked picot, ch 1, dc in same ch sp, *[ch 3, sc in next ch sp, ch 3, sc in next sc, ch 3, sc in next ch sp, ch 3], dc in next ch sp) 2 times, (picot, ch 1, dc) in same ch sp; repeat from * 13 more times; repeat between [ ], join with sl st in top of ch-3. Fasten off.

Repeat Second Large Motif 3 more times for Place Mat, 15 more times for Tablecloth or to desired width.

SECOND ROW
First Large Motif
Working on bottom of First Large Motif on last row *(see Joining Illustration)*, repeat Second Large Motif of First Row.

Second Large Motif
Rnds 1–10: Repeat rnds 1–10 of First Large Motif on First Row.

Rnd 11: Sl st in next ch sp, ch 3; (working on bottom of next Motif on last row, sl st in marked picot, ch 1, dc in same ch sp, ch 3, sc in next ch sp, ch 3, sc in next sc, ch 3, sc in next ch sp, ch 3, dc in next ch sp) 2 times, (picot, ch 1, dc) in same ch sp, *[ch 3, sc in next ch sp, ch 3, sc in next sc, ch 3, sc in next ch sp, ch 3], (dc, picot, ch 1, dc) in next ch sp*, (ch 3, sc in next ch sp, ch 3, sc in next sc, ch 3, sc in next ch sp, ch 3, dc in next ch sp, ch 3; working on side of last Motif on this row, sl st in marked picot, ch 1, dc in same ch sp) 2 times; repeat between first * 10 times; repeat between [ ] , join with sl st in top of ch-3. Fasten off.

Repeat Second Large Motif three more times for Place Mat, 15 more times for Tablecloth or to desired width.

NEXT ROWS
Work same as Second Row two more times for Place Mat, 23 more times for Tablecloth or to desired length.

SMALL MOTIF
Rnd 1: Repeat rnd 1 of First Large Motif on First Row.

Rnd 2: Ch 1, sc in first ch sp; working in sp between Large Motifs, *[ch 16, sl st in joining of Large Motifs *(see dot on Joining Illustration)*, ch 16, sc in same ch sp on this Motif], (ch 8, sl st in next picot on Large Motif, ch 8, sc in next ch sp on this Motif) 2 times; repeat from * 2 more times; repeat between [ ], ch 8, sl st in next picot on Large Motif, ch 8, sc in next ch sp on this Motif, ch 8, sl st in next picot on Large Motif, ch 8, join with sl st in first sc. Fasten off.

Repeat in each sp between Large Motifs on inside of Place Mat or Tablecloth. ❒❒

Rose Kitchen Set

Designed by Elizabeth White

Finished Sizes: Jar Lid Cover fits small mouth jar. Potholder is 7" across.

Materials:
- ❏ Size 10 crochet cotton:
  - 200 yds. dk. red
  - 200 yds. white
  - 50 yds. green
- ❏ 26" red ¼" ribbon
- ❏ Tapestry needle
- ❏ No. 5 steel hook or hook needed to obtain gauge

Gauge: Rose is 2" across; 4 dc= ½", 2 dc rows = ½".

Basic Stitches: Ch, sl st, sc, hdc, dc, tr.

Special Stitches:
For **beginning dtr cl,** ch 5, *yo 3 times, insert hook in

same sp as last sl st, yo, pull through sp, (yo, pull lp through 2 lps on hook) 4 times; repeat from * 3 more times, yo, pull through all 6 lps on hook.

For **dtr cluster (dtr cl),** yo 3 times, insert hook in next st or sp, yo, pull through sp, (yo, pull through 2 lps on hook) 3 times, *yo 3 times, insert hook in same sp, yo, pull through sp, (yo, pull through 2 lps on hook) 3 times; repeat from * 3 more times, yo, pull through all 6 lps on hook.

For **shell,** (2 dc, ch 2, 2 dc) in next st or sp.

POTHOLDER
Front
Rnd 1: Starting at **rose,** with dk. red, ch 6, sl st in first ch to form ring, ch 1, sc in ring, ch 3, (sc in ring, ch 3) 5 times, join with sl st in first sc. *(6 ch sps)*

Rnd 2: Ch 1; for **petals,** (sc, hdc, 3 dc, hdc, sc) in each ch sp around, join.

Rnd 3: Ch 5, (sc in sp between next 2 petals, ch 5) around, join with sl st in first ch of first ch-5.

Rnd 4: Ch 1; for **petals,** (sc, hdc, 5 dc, hdc, sc) in each ch sp around, join.

Rnd 5: Ch 7, (sc in sp between next 2 petals, ch 7) around, join with sl st in first ch of first ch-7.

Rnd 6: Ch 1; for **petals,** (sc, hdc, 7 dc, hdc, sc) in each ch sp around, join. Fasten off.

Rnd 7: Join green with sl st in sp between any 2 petals; **beginning dtr cl** *(see Special Stitches),* ch 12, (**dtr cl** in sp between next 2 petals, ch 12) around, join with sl st in top of first leaf. Fasten off. *(6 ch sps)*

Rnd 8: Join white with sl st in any ch sp, (ch 3, 18 dc) in same sp, 19 dc in each ch sp around, join with sl st in top of ch-3. *(114 dc)*

Rnd 9: Sl st in next 8 sts, (ch 3, dc, ch 2, 2 dc) in next st, ch 4, skip next 8 sts; **shell** *(see Special Stitches)* in sp between next 2 sts; ch 4, *skip next 9 sts, shell in next st, ch 4, skip next 8 sts, shell in sp between next 2 sts, ch 4; repeat from * around, join. *(12 shells)*

Rnd 10: Sl st in next st, (sl st, ch 3, dc, ch 2, 2 dc) in next ch sp, ch 5, skip next ch sp, *(shell in ch sp of next shell, ch 5) around, join.

Rnd 11: Sl st in next st, (sl st, ch 3, 2 dc, ch 2, 3 dc) in next ch sp, ch 5, skip next ch sp, *(3 dc, ch 2, 3 dc) in next shell, ch 5; repeat from * around, join.

Rnd 12: Sl st in each of next 2 sts, (sl st, ch 3, 2 dc, ch 2, 3 dc) in next ch sp, ch 6, skip next ch sp, *(3 dc, ch 2, 3 dc) in next ch-2 sp, ch 6, skip next ch sp; repeat from * around, join.

Rnd 13: Ch 5, skip next 2 sts, (*dc in next ch-2 sp, ch 2, skip next 2 sts, dc in next st, ch 2, dc in next ch-6 sp, ch 2, dc in same ch sp, ch 2*, dc in next st, ch 2) 11 times; repeat between first * join with sl st in third ch of ch-5. Fasten off. *(60 ch sps)*

Back
Rnd 1: With white, ch 6, sl st in first ch to form ring, ch 3, 11 dc in ring, join with sl st in top of ch-3. *(12 dc)*

Rnd 2: Ch 3, dc in same st, 2 dc in each st around, join. *(24)*

Rnds 3–5: Ch 3, dc in same st, dc in next st, (2 dc in next st, dc in next st) around, join. At end of last rnd *(81)*.

Rnd 6: Ch 3, dc in same st, dc in next st, (2 dc in next st, dc in next st) around to last st, dc in last st, join. Fasten off. *(121)*

Rnd 7: Join dk. red with sl st in any st, ch 3, dc in each st around, join.

Rnds 8–9: Ch 3, dc in each st around, join.

Rnd 10: Ch 3, dc in each of next 2 sts, (2 dc in next st, dc in next st) around. Fasten off. *(180)*

Rnd 11: Join white with sl st in any st, ch 5, skip next 2 sts, (dc in next st, ch 2, skip next 2 sts) around, join. Fasten off. *(60 ch sps)*

Assembly
Rnd 1: Hold Front and Back wrong sides together, matching sts; working through both thicknesses, join white with sc in any ch sp, 7 dc in next ch sp, (sc in next ch sp, 7 dc in next ch sp) around, join with sl st in first sc.

Rnd 2: For **hanging loop,** sl st in back of next st, ch 19, skip next 5 sts, sl st in back of next st, **turn;** 21 sc in ch-19 sp, join with sl st in first sl st. Fasten off.

Rnd 3: Join dk. red with sc in first st of **hanging loop,** (ch 2, skip next st, sc in next st) around loop, (sc in next st on Front, ch 2, skip next st) around, join with sl st in first sc on Front. Fasten off.

JAR LID COVER
Rnd 1: With white, ch 4, 11 dc in fourth ch from hook, join with sl st in top of ch-3. *(12 dc)*

Rnds 2–3: Ch 3, dc in same st, 2 dc in each st around, join. *(24, 48)*

Rnd 4: Ch 3, dc in each st around, join.

Rnd 5: Ch 3, dc in same st, dc in next st, (2 dc in next st, dc in next st) around, join. *(72)*

Rnd 6: Ch 3, dc in each st around, join.

Rnd 7: Ch 5, skip next 2 sts, (dc in next st, ch 2, skip next st) around, join with sl st in third ch of ch-5. *(24 ch sps)*

Rnd 8: Ch 1, (sc, hdc, dc, 3 tr, dc, hdc, sc) in each sp around, join with sl st in first sc. Fasten off.

Rnd 9: Join dk. red with sc in any st, sc in each st around, join. Fasten off.

Rose
Rnd 1: With dk. red, ch 5, sl st in first ch to form ring, ch 5, (dc in ring, ch 2) 5 times, join with sl st in third ch of ch-5. *(6 ch sps)*

Rnd 2: Ch 1; for **petals,** (sc, 3 dc, sc) in each ch sp around, join with sl st in first sc.

Rnd 3: Ch 4, (sc in sp between next 2 petals, ch 4) around, join with sl st in first ch of first ch-4.

Rnd 4: Ch 1; for **petals,** (sc, 5 dc, sc) in each ch sp around, join.

Rnd 5: Ch 5, (sc in sp between next 2 petals, ch 5) around, join with sl st in first ch of first ch-5.

Rnd 6: Ch 1; for **petals,** (sc, 3 dc, tr, 3 dc, sc) in each ch sp around, join. Fasten off.

Sew Rose to center of Jar Lid Cover.

Leaf (make 2)
With green, ch 10, sc in second ch from hook, (hdc in next ch, dc in next ch, tr in each of next 3 chs, dc in next ch, hdc in next ch), 3 sc in last ch; working on opposite side of ch, repeat between ( ), 2 sc in last ch, join with sl st in first sc. Fasten off.

Sew one Leaf to each side of Rose on Jar Lid Cover.

Weave ribbon through sts of rnd 7 on Jar Lid Cover; tie ends in bow. ❑❑

Finished Size: 19" × 45½"

Materials:
- ❏ Size 10 crochet cotton:
  - 600 yds. green
  - 600 yds. black
  - 150 yds. each of lt. peach, dk. peach, lt. pink, dk. pink, yellow, purple and rose (for Flower colors)
- ❏ No. 8 steel hook or hook needed to obtain gauge

Gauge: Flower is 2" across.

Basic Stitches: Ch, sl st, sc, hdc, dc, tr.

FIRST ROW
First Large Motif
Rnd 1: For **Flower,** with any Flower color, ch 7, dc in seventh ch from hook, ch 3, (dc in same ch, ch 3) 4 times, join with sl st in third ch of ch-7. (6 ch sps made)

Row 2: Ch 1; for **Petals,** (sc, hdc, 2 dc, hdc, sc) in each ch sp around, join with sl st in first sc. (6 Petals)

Rnd 3: Ch 3, (sl st in sp between next 2 Petals, ch 3) around.

Rnd 4: Ch 1; for **Petals,** (sc, hdc, 3 dc, hdc, sc) in each ch sp around, join.

Rnd 5: Ch 4, (sl st in sp between next 2 Petals, ch 4) around.

Rnd 6: Ch 1; for **Petals,** (sc, ch 2, dc, 3 tr, ch 3, sl st in top of last st made, 3 tr, dc, ch 2, sc) in each ch sp around, join with sl st in first sc. Fasten off.

Rnd 7: Join black with sc in sp between any 2 Petals on last rnd, ch 5, (sc between next 2 Petals, ch 5) around, join.

Rnd 8: (Sl st, ch 3, 4 dc, ch 3, 5 dc) in first ch sp, *ch 3, (5 dc, ch 3, 5 dc) in next ch sp; repeat from * around, join with dc in top of ch-3 (dc counts as joining ch sp).

Rnd 9: (Ch 3, 4 dc) in joining ch sp, (ch 3, 5 dc in next ch sp) around, join.

Rnd 10: (Ch 3, 2 dc, ch 3, 3 dc) around post of joining dc, ch 3; *for **shell, (3 dc, ch 3, dc)** in next ch sp; ch 3; repeat from * around, join with sl st in top of ch-3.

Rnd 11: Sl st in next 2 sts, (sl st, ch 3, 2 dc, ch 3, 3 dc) in next ch sp, ch 4 (shell in ch sp of next shell, ch 4) around, join. Fasten off.

Rnd 12: Join green with sc in ch sp of any shell, ch 2; working over next ch sp on rnd 11, 5 dc in next ch sp on rnd 10, ch 2, (sc in ch sp of next shell on rnd 11; working over next ch sp on rnd 11, 5 dc in next ch sp on rnd 10, ch 2) around, join with sl st in first sc.

Rnd 13: Ch 1, *(sc, ch 3, sc) in next ch sp, ch 3; repeat from * around, join. Fasten off.

Second Large Motif
Rnds 1–12: Repeat rnds 1–12 of First Large Motif.

Rnd 13: Ch 1, (sc, ch 3, sc) in next ch sp, *ch 3; working on side of last Motif according to arrows marked on Joining Illustration, sc in marked ch-7 sp, ch 3, (sc, ch 3, sc) in next ch sp on this Motif, ch 1, sc in marked ch sp on other Motif, ch 1, (sc, ch 3, sc) in next ch sp on this Motif; repeat from *, ch 3, sc in next marked ch-7 sp on other Motif, ch 3, (sc, ch 3, sc) in next ch sp on this Motif, ch 3, [sc in next ch sp, (ch 3, sc) in same ch sp as last sc, ch 7, (sc, ch 3, sc) in next ch sp ch 3]; repeat between [ ] around, join with sl st in first sc. Fasten off.

Repeat Second Large Motif two more times or to desired width.

SECOND ROW
First Large Motif
Working on bottom of First Large Motif on last row (see illustration), repeat Second Large Motif of First Row.

Second Large Motif
Rnds 1–12: Repeat rnds 1–12 of First Large Motif.

Rnd 13: Ch 1, (sc, ch 3, sc) in next ch sp, *[ch 3; working on bottom of next Motif on last row, sc in marked ch-7 sp, ch 3, (sc , ch 3, sc) in next ch sp on this Motif, ch 1, sc in marked ch sp on other Motif, ch 1, (sc, ch 3, sc) in next ch sp on this Motif; repeat from *, ch 3, sc in next marked ch-7 sp on other Motif, ch 3], (sc, ch 3, sc) in next ch sp on this Motif, ch 3, (sc, ch 3, sc) in next ch sp; working on side of last Motif on this row, repeat between [ ], (sc, ch3, sc in next ch sp, ch 3, (sc in next ch sp, ch 3, sc in same ch sp as last sc, ch 7, sc in next ch sp, ch 3, sc in same ch sp as last sc, ch 3) around, join with sl st in first sc. Fasten off.

Repeat Second Large Motif two more times or to desired width.

NEXT ROWS
Work Second Row eight more times or to desired length.

SMALL MOTIF
Rnd 1: With green, ch 9, sl st in first ch to form ring, ch 1, 24 sc in ring, join with sl st in first sc. (24 sc made)

Rnd 2: *[Working in sp between Large Motifs, ch 2, sc in ch-3 sp on Large Motif (see dot on Joining Illustration), ch 2, sc in next 2 sts on this Motif; repeat from * 2 more times]; working on remaining Large Motifs, repeat between [ ] 3 times, join with sl st in first ch of first ch-2. Fasten off.

Repeat in each space between Large Motifs on inside of Tablecloth.

EDGING
Join green with sc in first unjoined ch-7 sp past any joining, (ch 3, sc in same sp) 3 times, ch 5, skip next ch-3 sp, sc in next ch-3 sp, [*ch 5, sc in next ch-7 sp, (ch 3, sc in same ch sp) 3 times, ch 5, skip next ch-3 sp, sc in next ch-3 sp; repeat from * across to last ch-3 sp before next joined ch-7 sps, ch 5, skip next ch-3 sp, tr next 2 joined ch-7 sps tog, ch 5, skip next ch-3 sp, sc in next ch-3 sp]; repeat between [ ] around, ch 5, join with sl st in first sc. Fasten off. ❏❏

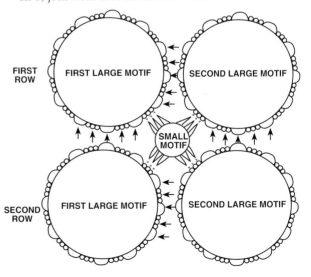

Floral Runner

Designed by Dot Drake

Finished Size: Each Doily is 11½" across.

Materials:
- ❑ Size 30 crochet cotton:
  - 500 yds. cream
  - 500 yds. ecru
- ❑ No. 12 steel hook or hook needed to obtain gauge

Gauge: 13 mesh = 2"; 7 mesh rows = 1".

Basic Stitches: Ch, sl st, sc, dc, tr.

Special Stitches: For **beginning mesh (beg mesh)**, ch 5, skip next 2 chs, dc in next st.

For **mesh**, ch 2, skip next 2 chs or sts, dc in next st or ch.

For **end mesh**, ch 2, skip next 2 chs, dc in third ch of ch-5.

For **block**, 2 dc in next ch sp, dc in next st, **or** dc in each of next 3 sts, **or** 3 dc in next bar.

For **bar**, ch 5, skip next lacet, dc in next st.

For **lacet**, ch 3, skip next 2 chs or sts, sc in next st, ch 3, skip next 2 chs or sts, dc in next st, **or** ch 3, sc in ch sp of next bar, ch 3, dc in next st.

For **beg 1-mesh inc**, ch 7, dc in first dc.

For **end 1-mesh inc**, ch 2, tr in bottom strand at side of last dc made.

For **beginning 1-mesh decrease (beg 1-mesh dec)**, sl st in first st, in each of next 2 chs and in next st.

For **end 1-mesh dec**, leave last mesh unworked.

For **beginning 2-mesh increase (beg 2-mesh inc)**, ch 10, dc in eighth ch from hook, ch 2, skip next 2 chs, dc in next st.

For **end 2-mesh inc**, ch 2, tr in bottom strand at side of last dc made, ch 2, tr in bottom strand at side of last tr made.

For **beg 2-mesh dec**, sl st in first 7 sts and ch.

For **end 2-mesh dec**, leave last 2 mesh unworked.

For **tr decrease (tr dec)**, *yo 2 times, insert hook in next st, yo, pull through st, (yo, pull through 2 lps on hook) 2 times; repeat from * number of times needed for decrease, yo, pull through all lps on hook.

DOILY

Row 1: Ch 44, dc in eighth ch from hook, **mesh** *(see Special Stitches)* across, turn. *(13 mesh made— beginning 7 chs counts as first mesh)*

Row 2: Ch 13, dc in eighth ch from hook, ch 2, skip next 2 chs, dc in next ch, ch 2, skip next 2 chs, dc in next st, mesh 12 times, ch 2, skip next 2 chs, dc in next ch, ch 2, tr in **bottom strand** at side of last dc made *(see illustration 1)*, *ch 2, tr in **bottom strand** at side of last tr made *(see illustration 2)*; repeat from *, turn. *(19 mesh)*

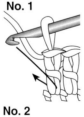

No. 1

No. 2

Row 3: Beginning 2-mesh inc *(see Special Stitches)*, mesh 18 times, ch 2, skip next 2 chs, dc in next ch, **end 2-mesh inc** *(see Special Stitches)*, turn. *(23 mesh)*

Rows 4–5: Work across according to graph of your choice on page 105, turn.

Row 6: Beginning 1-mesh inc *(see Special Stitches)*, work according to graph across to ch-7, ch 2, skip next 2 chs, dc in next ch **end 1-mesh inc,** turn. *(33 mesh)*

Rows 7–31: Work according to graph across, turn.

Row 32: Beginning 1-mesh dec, work according to graph across to last mesh, **end 1-mesh dec,** turn.

Rows 33–45: Work according to graph across, turn.

Row 46: Beg 2-mesh dec, work according to graph across to last 2 mesh, **end 2-mesh dec,** turn.

Rows 47–48: Work according to graph across, turn.

Row 49: Sl st in first 10 sts and chs; beg mesh, mesh 12 times. **Do not fasten off.**

Edging

Rnd 1: Working around outer edge, ch 3, 2 dc in first mesh, 3 dc in each mesh and in end of each row around, join with sl st in top of ch-3. *(420 dc)*

Rnd 2: Ch 3, dc in each of next 2 sts, ch 5, skip next 3 sts, (dc in each of next 3 sts, ch 5, skip next 3 sts) around, join.

Rnd 3: Sl st in each of next 2 sts (sl st, ch 4, 3 tr, ch 3, tr, ch 3, 4 tr) in first ch sp, ch 3, skip next 6 sts and ch sp, *(4 tr, ch 3, tr, ch 3, 4 tr) in next ch sp, ch 3, skip next 6 sts and ch sp; repeat from * around, join with sl st in top of ch-4.

Rnd 4: Ch 4, **3-tr dec** *(see Special Stitches)*, (*ch 3, 4 tr in next ch sp, ch 3, tr in next st, ch 3, 4 tr in next ch sp, ch 3, 4-tr dec, skip next ch sp*, cl) 34 times; repeat between first *, join with sl st in top of first dec.

Rnds 5–6: Sl st in each of first 3 chs, sl st in next st, ch 4, 3-tr dec, (*ch 3, 4 tr in next ch sp, ch 3, tr in next st, ch 3, 4 tr in next ch sp, ch 3, 4-tr dec, skip next ch sp*, cl) 34 times; repeat between first *, join with sl st in top of first dec.

Continued on page 105

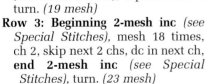

100

Kitchen Doilies

Designed by Nancy Hearne

Mother & Daughter Aprons

Designed by Karen Nordhausen

Finished Sizes: For **lady's,** Bib is 8½" × 10"; Pockets are 6" × 7½"; Straps are 2" × 12". For **child's,** Bib is 5" × 6"; Pockets are 3" × 3½".

Materials:
- ❏ Size 20 crochet cotton:
  - 555 yds. taupe
  - 350 yds. white
- ❏ Broadcloth:
  - 1½ yds. khaki
  - ½ yd. white
- ❏ ½" Velcro fastener
- ❏ White and khaki sewing thread
- ❏ Sewing needle
- ❏ No. 10 steel hook or hook needed to obtain gauge

Gauge: 13 dc = 1"; 11 mesh rows = 2".

Basic Stitches: Ch, sl st, sc, dc, tr.

Special Stitches:
For **beginning mesh (beg mesh),** ch 5, skip next 2 sts or ch, dc in next st.
For **mesh,** ch 2, skip next 2 sts or chs, dc in next st.
For **block,** dc in each of next 3 sts, or 2 dc in next ch sp, dc in next st.
For **end mesh,** ch 2, skip next 2 sts or chs, dc in third ch of ch-5.

LADY'S APRON
Skirt
1: From khaki, cut 22" × 36" piece for Skirt, 5" × 21" piece for Waistband and two 5" × 38" pieces for Sashes.

2: Press under ½" on each short edge of Skirt piece, press under again ½"; topstitch over each fold. Repeat on one long edge. Run gathering thread across ¼" from raw edge of Skirt. Gather to 20".

3: With right sides together, allowing ½" for seams, sew one short edge of each Sash piece to each short edge of Waistband. Press seams open.

4: Press under ½" on each short edge of Sash. Press under ½" on one long edge. Hold wrong side of gathered edge on Skirt and right side of raw edge on Waistband together; allowing ½" for seam, sew together. Press seam toward Waistband and press ½" under on long raw edge of each Sash.

5: Fold Waistband and Sashes in half lengthwise wrong sides together. Topstitch around open edges of Waistband and Sashes to close edges.

Bib
Row 1: Beginning at bottom with taupe, ch 126, dc in fourth ch from hook, dc in each ch across, turn. *(124 dc)*

Row 2: Beg mesh *(see Special stitches),* mesh across, turn. *(41 mesh)*

Row 3: Beg mesh, mesh 2 times, (block 3 times, mesh 7 times) 2 times, block 5 times, mesh 7 times, block 3 times, mesh 2 times, end mesh, turn.

Rows 4-44: Work according to Bib Graph on page 104, turn.

Rnd 45: Working around outer edge, ch 1, 3 sc in each mesh across, 2 sc in end of each row across; working in remaining lps on opposite side of starting ch, sc in each ch across, 2 sc in end of each row across, join with sl st in first sc. Fasten off. *(423 sc)*

Bib Edging
Row 1: With wrong side facing you, join taupe with sc in first st in end of first row on bottom right-hand corner, sc in next st, (ch 5, skip next 2 sts, sc in each of next 3 sts) 17 times, ch 5, skip next 3 sts, sc in each of next 3 sts, ch 5, skip next 4 sts, sc in each of next 3 sts, *ch 5, skip next 3 sts, sc in each of next 3 sts; repeat from * 16 more times, ch 5, skip next 4 sts, sc in each of next 3 sts, ch 5, skip next 3 sts, sc in each of next 3 sts; repeat between ( ) 16 times, ch 5, skip next 2 sts, sc in each of next 2 sts leaving last 124 sts unworked, turn.

Row 2: Ch 1, sc in each of first 2 sts, 3 sc in next ch sp, *skip next 3 sts; for **shell, (5 dc, ch 5, 5 dc)** in next ch sp; skip next 3 sts, 3 sc in next ch sp; repeat from * around to last 2 sts, sc in each of last 2 sts. Fasten off.

Pocket (make 2)
Row 1: With taupe, ch 92, dc in eighth ch from hook, (ch 2, skip next 2 ch, dc in next ch) across, turn. *(29 mesh)*

Rows 2–29: Work according to Pocket Graph on page 104, turn. At end of last row, **do not turn.**

Rnd 30: Working around outer edge, ch 1, (3 sc in end of next row, 2 sc in end of next 27 rows, 3 sc in end of next row, 2 sc in each of next 2 mesh, 3 sc in next 25 mesh, 2 sc in each of next 2 mesh) 2 times, join with sl st in first sc. Fasten off. *(286 sc)*

Pocket Edging
Row 1: With wrong side facing you, join taupe with sl st in top left-hand corner, (ch 5, skip next 3 sts, sc in each of next 3 sts) 10 times, *ch 5, skip next st, sc in each of next 3 sts*; repeat between ( ) 13 times; repeat between first *; repeat between ( ) 9 times, ch 5, skip next 2 sts, sl st in next st leaving last 82 sts unworked, turn.

Row 2: Sl st in first ch sp, (ch 3, 4 dc, ch 5, 5 dc) in same ch sp, (skip next 3 sts, 3 sc in next ch sp, skip next 3 sts, shell in next ch sp) across, sl st in last sl st. Fasten off.

Neck Strap (make 2)
Row 1: With taupe, ch 32, dc in eighth ch from hook, (ch 2, skip next 2 chs, dc in next ch) across, turn. *(9 mesh)*

Rows 2–45: Work according to Strap Graph on page 104, turn.

Rows 46–67: Or to desired length; repeat rows 2–23 of graph. At end of last row, **do not turn.**

Rnd 68: Working around outer edge, ch 1, 3 sc in each mesh and 2 sc in end of each row around, join with sl st in first sc. Fasten off.

Finishing
Center Waistband of Apron over row 1 of Bib. Sew in place.

With right side of Bib and Straps facing you, sew row 1 of one Strap to top of Bib at each corner, behind edging. Sew Velcro to opposite end of each Strap.

With unworked edge as top, sew Pockets to front of Apron 4¾" from bottom of Waistband centered 14½" apart.

CHILD'S APRON
Skirt
1: From white fabric, cut 12" × 23" piece for Skirt,

Continued on page 104

103

Kitchen Creations

Mother & Daughter Aprons

Continued from page 103

3¾" × 9½" piece for Waistband, two 3¾" × 17" pieces for Sashes and two 2" × 15" pieces for Straps.

2: Press under ¼" on each short edge of Skirt piece, press under again ¼"; topstitch over each fold. Repeat on one long edge. Run gathering thread across raw edge of Skirt ¼" from edge. Gather to 9".

3: Allowing ¼" for seams, repeat step 3 of Lady's Apron Skirt.

4: Pressing under ¼", repeat step 4 of Lady's Apron Skirt.

5: Allowing ¼" for all seams, repeat step 5 of Lady's Apron Skirt.

6: Fold each Strap piece in half lengthwise with wrong sides together. Allowing ¼" for seam, sew together across long edge and one end. Clip corners. Turn. Fold ¼" on raw edge to inside; press.

Bib
Row 1: With white, ch 87, dc in fourth ch from hook, dc in each ch across, turn. *(85 dc)*

Row 2: Beg mesh *(see Special Stitches)*, mesh across, turn. *(28 mesh)*

Row 3: Beg mesh, mesh 8 times, block 3 times, mesh 4 times, block 3 times, mesh 8 times, end mesh, turn.

Rows 4–29: Work according to Child's Bib Graph, turn. At end of last row, fasten off.

Bib Edging
With right side facing you, working in mesh at ends of rows and across top of Bib, join white with sc in mesh at end of row 2, (dc, tr) in same mesh, 3 tr in

Continued on page 108

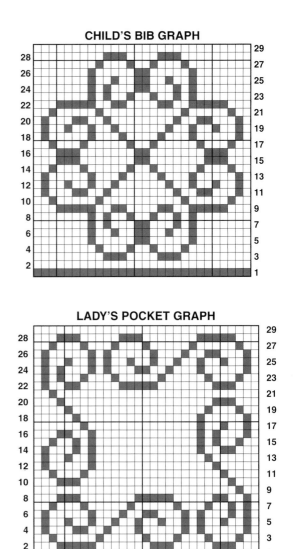

□ = MESH
■ = BLOCK

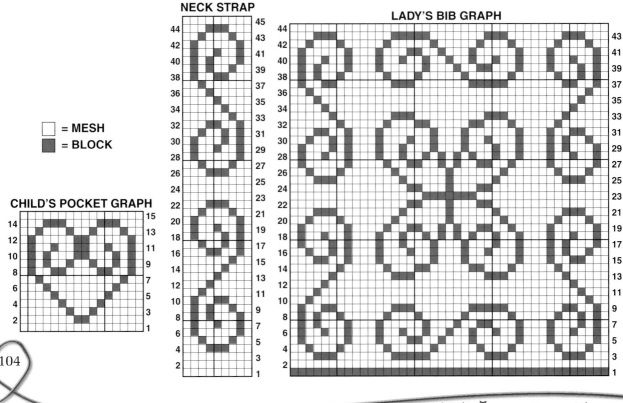

Kitchen Doilies

Continued from page 100

Rnd 7: Sl st in each of first 3 chs, sl st in next st, ch 4, 3-tr dec, (*ch 4, skip next ch sp, 4 tr in next st, ch 4, skip next ch sp, 4-tr dec, ch 3, skip next ch sp, next 2 dec and next ch sp*, 4-tr dec) 34 times; repeat between first *, join.

Rnd 8: Sl st in each of first 3 ch, sl st in next st, ch 4, 3-tr dec, (*ch 9, skip next ch sp and next dec, sc in next ch sp, ch 9, skip next dec and next ch sp*, 4-tr dec) 34 times; repeat between first *, join.

Rnd 9: Ch 4, sc in top of first dec, (*7 sc in next ch sp, skip next st, 7 sc in next ch sp*, ch 4, sc in top of next dec) 34 times; repeat between first *, join with sl st in first ch of first ch-4. Fasten off. ❏❏

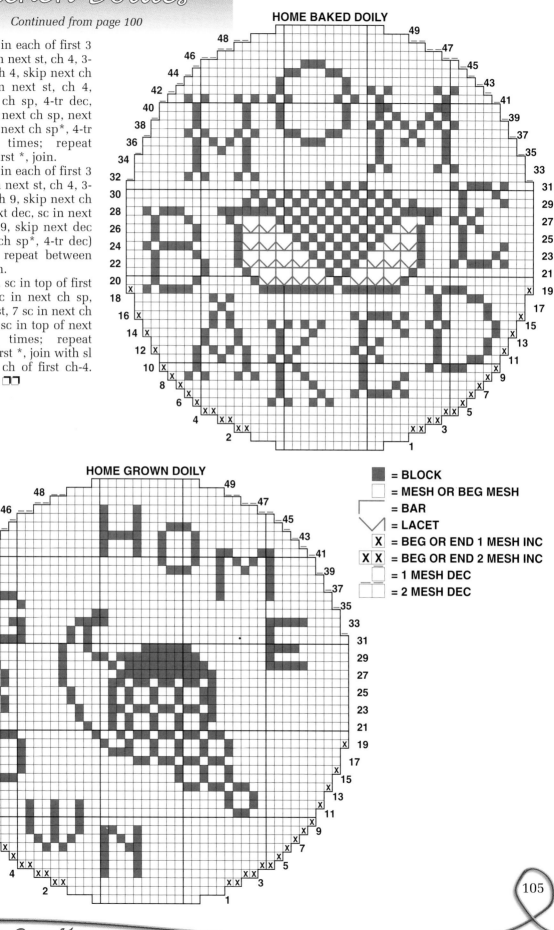

HOME BAKED DOILY

HOME GROWN DOILY

■ = BLOCK
□ = MESH OR BEG MESH
⌐ = BAR
⋁ = LACET
[X] = BEG OR END 1 MESH INC
[X][X] = BEG OR END 2 MESH INC
☐ = 1 MESH DEC
☐☐ = 2 MESH DEC

105

Kitchen Creations

Finished Sizes: Coaster is 4½" across. Place Mat is 12" × 17".

Materials:
- ❏ 400 yds. size 10 crochet cotton
- ❏ No. 7 steel hook or hook needed to obtain gauge

Gauge: 10 dc = 1"; 4 dc rows = 1".

Basic Stitches: Ch, sl st, sc, dc.

COASTER

MOTIF
Rnd 1: Ch 5, sl st in first ch to form ring, ch 4, (dc in ring, ch 1) 7 times, join with sl st in third ch of ch 4. *(8 dc, 8 ch sps made)*

Rnd 2: (Sl st, ch 3, 2 dc) in first ch sp, ch 2, dc in next ch sp, ch 2; (for **Heart,** 3 dc in next ch sp; ch 2, dc in next ch sp, ch 2) around, join with sl st in top of ch-3.

Rnd 3: (Ch 3, dc) in first st, *3 dc in next st, 2 dc in next st, ch 2, dc in next st, ch 2*, 2 dc in next st) 3 times; repeat between first *, join.

Rnd 4: (Ch 3, dc) in first st, *(dc in each of next 2 sts, 3 dc in next st, dc in each of next 2 sts, 2 dc in next st, ch 2, dc in next st, ch 2*, 2 dc in next st) 3 times; repeat between first *, join.

Rnd 5: (Ch 3, dc) in first st, *(dc in next 4 sts, 3 dc in next st, dc in next 4 sts, 2 dc in next st, ch 2, dc in next st, ch 2*, 2 dc in next st) 3 times; repeat between first *, join.

Rnd 6: (Ch 3, dc) in first st, *(dc in next 6 sts, 3 dc in next st, dc in next 6 sts, 2 dc in next st, ch 2, dc in next st, ch 2*, 2 dc in next st) 3 times; repeat between first *, join.

Row 7: For **First Heart Side,** ch 3, dc next 2 sts tog, dc in next 4 sts, dc next 3 sts tog leaving last 9 sts unworked, turn. *(7dc)*

Row 8: Ch 3, (dc next 3 sts tog) 2 times, turn. Fasten off.

Row 7: For **Second Heart Side,** join with sl st in center st of 3-dc group on rnd 6 of same Heart, ch 3, dc next 2 sts tog, dc in next 4 sts, dc next 3 sts tog, turn. *(7dc)*

Row 8: Ch 3, (dc next 3 sts tog) 2 times, turn. Fasten off.

For **remaining three Hearts,** join with sl st in first st of next Heart and repeat First and Second Heart Sides.

Rnd 9: Join with sc in first st of last row on First Heart Side, (*ch 6, skip next st, sc in next st, ch 6, sc in top of row 7, ch 6, sc in top of row 7 on next Heart Side, ch 6, sc in first st on row 8, ch 6, skip next st, sc in next st, ch 6, sc in top of row 7, ch 6, sc in next dc on row 6, ch 6, sc in top of row 7 on next Heart Side, ch 6*, sc in first st of row 8) 3 times; repeat between first and second *, join with sl st in first sc.

Rnd 10: Ch 1, 3 sc in first ch sp; for **picot,** ch 3, sl st in third ch from hook *(picot made);* 3 sc in same ch sp, (3 sc, picot, 3 sc) in next ch sp, *[5 sc in next ch sp, (3 sc, picot, 3 sc) in each of next 3 ch sps, 3 sc in each of next 2 ch sps], (3 sc, picot, 3 sc) in each of next 3 ch sps; repeat from * 2 more times; repeat between [ ], (3 sc, picot, 3 sc) in last ch sp, join. Fasten off.

PLACE MAT

FIRST ROW
First Large Motif
Rows 1–8: Work rows 1–8 of Coaster Motif.
Rnd 9: Join with sc in center st of last row on First Heart Side, (*ch 6, sc in top of row 7, ch 6, sc in top of row 7 on next Heart Side, ch 6, sc in center st of row 8, ch 6, sc in top of row 7, ch 6, sc in next dc on row 6, ch 6, sc in top of row 7 on next Heart Side, ch 6*, sc in center st of row 8) 3 times; repeat between first and second *, join with sl st in first sc. Fasten off.

Second Large Motif
Rows 1–8: Work rows 1–8 of Coaster Motif.
Rnd 9: Join with sc in center st of last row on first Heart Side, ch 3; working on side of last Motif according to X's on Joining Illustration on page 108, sl st in marked ch sp, ch 3, sc in top of row 7 on this Motif, ch 3, sl st in next ch sp of last Motif, ch 3, sc in top of ch-7 on next Heart Side of this Motif, ch 3, sc in next ch sp on last Motif, ch 3, sc in center st of row 8 on this Motif, *[ch 6, sc in top of row 7, ch 6, sc in next dc on row 6, ch 6, sc in top of row 7 on next Heart Side, ch 6], sc in center st of row 8, ch 6, sc in top of row 7, ch 6, sc in top of row 7 on next Heart Side, ch 6, sc in center st of row 8; repeat from * 2 more times; repeat between [ ], join with sl st in first sc. Fasten off.

Repeat Second Large Motif two more times or to desired width.

SECOND ROW
First Large Motif
Working on bottom of First Motif on last row *(see Joining Illustration on page 108),* work same as Second Large Motif of First Row.

Second Large Motif
Rows 1–8: Work rows 1–8 of Coaster Motif.
Rnd 9: Join with sc in center st of last row on First Heart Side, ch 3; working on side of Motif above, (sl st in marked ch sp, ch 3, sl st in top of row 7 on this Motif, ch 3, sl st in next ch sp on other Motif, ch 3, sl st in top of row 7 on next Heart Side of this Motif, ch 3, sl st in next ch sp on other Motif, ch 3, sc in center st of row 8 on this Motif, ch 6, sc in end of row 7, ch 6, sc in next dc on row 6, ch 6, sc in top of row 7 on next Heart Side, ch 6, sc in center st of row 8); ch 3; working in last Motif on this row, repeat between ( ), *ch 6, sc in top of row 7, ch 6, sc in top of row 7 on next Heart Side, ch 6, sc in center st of row 8, ch 6, sc in top of row 7, ch 6, sc in next dc on row 6, ch 6, sc in top of row 7 on next Heart Side, ch 6*, sc in center of row 8; repeat between first and second *, join with sl st in first sc. Fasten off.

Repeat Second Large Motif two more times or to desired width.

THIRD ROW
Work Second Row one more time.

SMALL MOTIF
Rnd 1: Ch 5, sl st in first ch to form ring, ch 3, 15 dc in ring, join with sl st in top of ch-3. *(16 dc)*
Rnd 2: Ch 4, 3 dc in next st, ch 1, (dc in next st, ch

Continued on page 108

Heart Place Mat Set

Designed by Sharon Compton

Heart Place Mat Set

Continued from page 106

1, 3 dc in next st, ch 1) 7 times, join with sl st in third ch of ch-4.

Rnd 3: Ch 6, dc next 3 sts tog, ch 3, (dc in next st, ch 3, dc next 3 sts tog, ch 3) around, join with sl st in third ch of ch-6.

Rnd 4: Ch 1, sc in first st; working in sp between Large Motifs *(see dots on Joining Illustration)*, (ch 3, sc in marked ch sp on Large Motif, ch 3, sc in next st on this Motif) 15 times, ch 3, sc in last ch sp on Large Motif, ch 3, join with sl st in first sc on this Motif. Fasten off.

Repeat in each space between Large Motifs on inside of Place Mat.

EDGING

Join with sc in center ch-6 sp on top right-hand Heart, (2 sc, picot, 3 sc) in same sp, *(3 sc, picot, 3 sc) in each of next 2 ch sps, 4 sc in next ch sp, picot, 4 sc in next ch sp, (3 sc, picot, 3 sc) in next ch sp, 3 sc in each of next 2 ch sps, (3 sc, picot, 3 sc) in next ch sp, 4 sc in next ch sp, picot, 4 sc in next ch sp, (3 sc, picot, 3 sc) in each of next 3 ch sps*; [repeat between first and second * 2 more times, (3 sc, picot, 3 sc) in each of next 2 ch sps, 4 sc in next ch sp, picot, 4 sc in next ch sp, (3 sc, picot, 3 sc) in each of next 3 ch sps]; repeat between [ ]; repeat between first and second * 3 times, (3 sc, picot, 3

sc) in each of next 2 ch sps; 4 sc in next ch sp, picot 4 sc in next ch sp, (3 sc, picot, 3 sc) in each of next 3 ch sps; repeat between first and second * 2 times, (3 sc, picot, 3 sc) in each of next 2 ch sps, 4 sc in next ch sp, picot, 4 sc in next ch sp, (3 sc, picot, 3 sc) in each of last 2 ch sps, join with sl st in first sc. Fasten off. ☐☐

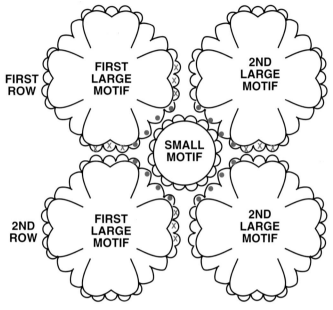

Mother & Daughter Aprons

Continued from page 104

next mesh, (tr, dc, sc) in next mesh, *(sc, dc, tr) in next mesh, 3 tr in next mesh, (tr, dc, sc) in next mesh* ; repeat between first * 7 more times, (sc, dc, 5 tr, dc, sc) in next corner mesh; repeat between first * 8 times, (sc, dc, tr) in next mesh, 3 tr in next mesh, (tr, dc, sc, sc, dc, 5 tr, dc sc) in next corner mesh; repeat between first * 9 times. Fasten off.

Pocket (make 2)

Row 1: With white, ch 53, dc in eighth ch from hook, (ch 2, skip next 2 chs, dc in next ch) across, turn. *(16 mesh)*

Rows 2–15: Work according to Pocket graph on page 104, turn. At end of last row, **do not turn.**

Pocket Edging

Working in mesh at end of rows and across bottom of Pocket, *(sc, dc, tr) in next mesh at end of first

row, 3 tr in next mesh, (tr, dc, sc) in next mesh*; repeat between first * 3 more times, [sc in next mesh, (dc, tr) in same mesh, 3 tr in next mesh, (tr, dc, sc, sc, dc, 4 tr, dc, sc) in corner mesh]; repeat between first * 4 more times, repeat between [ ]; repeat between first * 4 more times, (sc, dc, tr) in next mesh, (3 tr, dc, sc) in last mesh. Fasten off.

Finishing

Center Waistband of Apron over row 1 of Bib. Sew in place.

With right side of Bib facing you, sew open end of each Strap to top of Bib at each corner, behind edging.

With unworked edge as top, sew Pockets to front of Apron 3½" from bottom of Waistband centered 12" apart. ☐☐

Doily Delights

When thoughts turn to crochet, a word that springs naturally to mind is "doily." Now a common citizen in the creative world of needlecrafters, the doily was once its first ambassador, embarking on its claim to fame in 1711 in the shape of napkins sold by a London cloth and dry goods merchant named Doyley. Beloved by stitchers around the globe, the humble doily—by turns useful, frivolous, ornate, simplistic— decorates the very heart of thread crochet artistry.

Quilt Block Doily

Designed by Linda Mershon

Finished Size: 11" square.

Materials:
- ❒ Size 10 crochet cotton thread:
    - 350 yds. pink
    - 175 yds. burgundy
- ❒ Size 22 tapestry needle
- ❒ No. 5 steel hook or hook needed to obtain gauge

Gauge: Block is 2" square.

Basic Stitches: Ch, sl st, sc, dc, tr.

Special Stitches:
For **dc cluster (dc cl)**, yo, insert hook in st or ch sp, yo, pull through st, yo, pull through 2 lps on hook, leaving last lp of st on hook, *yo, insert hook in same st or ch sp, yo, pull through st, yo, pull through 2 lps on hook, leaving last lp of st on hook; repeat from * number of times needed for number of dc in cl, yo, pull through all lps on hook.
For **V st**, (dc, ch 2, dc) in st or ch sp.

BLOCK NO. 1 *(make 8)*
Row 1: With pink, ch 4, dc in fourth ch from hook, ch 2, 2 dc in same ch, turn. *(4 dc made)*

Row 2: Ch 3 *(counts as dc)*, dc in next dc, ch 2, (dc, ch 2, dc) in next ch-2 sp, ch 2, dc in each of last 2 dc, turn.

Row 3: Ch 3, dc in next dc, ch 2, (dc, ch 2, dc) in each of next 2 dc, ch 2, dc in each of last 2 dc, turn.

Row 4: Ch 3, dc in next dc, ch 2 (dc, ch 2, dc) in next dc, tr in next dc, ch 2, tr in next dc, (dc, ch 2, dc) in next dc, ch 2, dc in each of last 2 dc changing to burgundy *(see Stitch Guide)* in last st made, turn. Fasten off pink.

Row 5: Ch 3, dc in next dc, (dc, ch 2, tr) in next dc, tr in next dc, skip next tr, (tr, ch 3, tr) in next ch-2 sp, skip next tr, tr in next dc, (tr, ch 2, dc) in next dc, dc in each of last 2 dc, turn.

Row 6: Ch 3, dc in next dc, (dc, ch 2, dc) in next ch-2 sp, ch 1, skip next tr, dc in next tr, ch 2, tr in next tr, (tr, ch 3, tr) in second ch of next ch-3 sp, tr in next tr, ch 2, dc in next tr, ch 1, (dc, ch 2, dc) in next ch-2 sp, skip next dc, dc in each of last 2 dc, **do not turn.**

Rnd 7: Working around outer edge, ch 1, 2 sc in end of first 2 rows changing to pink in last st made, 2 sc in end of next 4 rows, 3 sc in remaining lp of starting ch at bottom of row 1 *(corner made)*, 2 sc in end of next 4 rows changing to burgundy in last st made, 2 sc in end of next 2 rows; working across row 6, 3 sc in top of ch-3 *(corner made)*, sc in each of next 2 dc, 2 sc in next ch-2 sp, sc in next dc, sc in next ch-1 sp, sc in next dc, 2 sc in next ch-2 sp, sc in each of next 2 tr, sc in next ch, 3 sc in next ch *(corner made)*, sc in next ch, sc in each of next 2 tr, 2 sc in next ch-2 sp, sc in next dc, sc in next ch-1 sp, sc in next dc, 2 sc in next ch-2 sp, sc in each of next 2 dc, 3 sc in last dc *(corner made)*, join with sl st in first sc. Fasten off both colors.

BLOCK NO. 2 *(make 8)*
Rows 1–4: With burgundy, repeat rows 1–4 of Block No.1, changing to pink at end of last row.

Row 5–Rnd 7: Repeat row 5 through rnd 7 of Block No.1, changing to burgundy at beginning of rnd 7 and pink at middle of rnd 7.

BLOCK ASSEMBLY
Working in **back lps** *(See Stitch Guide)*, sew Blocks together using matching thread, according to illustration below.

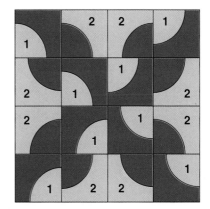

BORDER
Rnd 1: Join pink with sc in center sc of 3-sc group at any corner, 2 sc in same sc *(corner made)*; *[sc in next 13 sc, 2 sc in next sc on this Block, (sc in third sc of next 3-sc group on next Block, sc in next 13 sc) 3 times], 3 sc in next sc *(corner made)*; repeat from * 2 more times; repeat between [ ] once, join with sl st in first sc.

Rnd 2: (Sl st, ch 5, dc) in next sc, (ch 2, dc in same sc) 2 times, *(skip next 2 sc, V st in next sc—see *Special Stitches*) 19 times, skip next 2 sc, V st in next sc, ch 2, V st in same sc; repeat from * 2 more times, (skip next 2 sc, V st in next sc) 19 times, join with sl st in third ch of ch-5.

Rnd 3: Sl st in first ch-2 sp, ch 4, *[dc in next ch-2 sp, (ch 1, dc) 3 times in same ch-2 sp, ch 1, dc in next ch-2 sp, (V st in next ch-2 sp) 19 times], dc in next ch-2 sp, ch 1; repeat from * 2 more times; repeat between [ ] once, join with sl st in third ch of ch-4.

Rnd 4: Ch 2, **2-dc cl** *(see Special Stitches)* in same ch as ch-2, (ch 2, 3-dc cl in next dc) 5 times, *V st in next 19 ch-2 sps, skip next dc, 3-dc cl in next dc, (ch 2, 3-dc cl in next dc) 5 times; repeat from * 2 more times, V st in last 19 ch-2 sps, join sl st in top of first dc cl.

Rnd 5: Ch 2, 2-dc cl in first dc cl, (ch 3, 3-dc cl in next dc cl) 5 times, *V st in next 19 ch-2 sps, 3-dc cl in next dc cl, (ch 3, 3-dc cl in next dc cl) 5 times; repeat from * 2 more times, V st in last 19 ch-2 sps, join.

Rnd 6: Ch 2, 2-dc cl in first dc cl, (ch 4, 3-dc cl in next dc cl) 5 times, *V st in next 19 ch-2 sps, 3-dc cl in next dc cl (ch 4, 3-dc cl in next dc cl) 5 times; repeat from * 2 more times, V st in last 19 ch-2 sps, join.

Rnd 7: Ch 2, 2-dc cl in first dc cl, (ch-5, 3-dc cl in next dc cl) 5 times, *V st in next 19 ch-2 sps, 3-dc cl in next dc cl, (ch 5, 3-dc cl in next dc cl) 5 times; repeat from * 2 more times, V st in last 19 ch-2 sps changing to burgundy in last st made, join.

Rnd 8: Ch 1, sc in first dc cl, (4 sc in next ch-5 sp; for **picot**, ch 3, sl st in top of last sc made—*picot made*, 3 sc in same ch-5 sp, sc in next dc cl) 5 times, *[sc in next dc, (2 sc in next ch-2 sp, sc in each of next 2 dc, 2 sc in next ch-2 sp, picot, sc in same ch sp, sc in each of next 2 dc) 9 times, 2 sc in next ch-2 sp, sc in next dc], sc in next dc cl, (4 sc in next ch-5 sp, picot, 3 sc in same ch-5 sp, sc in next dc cl) 5 times; repeat from * 2 more times; repeat between [ ] once, join with sl st in first sc. Fasten off. ❒❒

Daisy Doily

Designed by Dorothy Hamilton

Finished Size: 23" across.

Materials:
- ❏ Size 10 crochet cotton thread:
    - 400 yds. main color *(MC)*
    - 30 yds. contrasting color *(CC)*
- ❏ No. 5 steel hook or size needed to obtain gauge

Gauge: Rnd 1 is ⅞" in diameter; flower is 3¼" in diameter.

Basic Stitches: Ch, sl st, sc, dc.

Special Stitches:
For **3-picot group**, ch 4, sl st in fourth ch from hook, (ch 4, sl st in same ch as first sl st) 2 times.
For **joining picot group**, ch 4, sl st in fourth ch from

hook, ch 2, sl st in center picot of any picot group on last Flower, ch 2, sl st in same ch as first sl st, ch 4, sl st in same ch as first sl st.

FLOWER (make 19)
Rnd 1: With CC, ch 6, sl st in first ch to form ring, ch 3, 17 dc in ring, join with sl st in top of ch-3. Fasten off. *(18)*

Rnd 2: Working this rnd in **back lps** *(see Stitch Guide)*, join MC with sl st in first st, (ch 10, dc in fourth ch from hook, dc in each ch across, sl st in next st on rnd 1) around with last sl st in same st as joining sl st. Fasten off. *(18 petals)*

ASSEMBLY
Center Row of Flowers
For first Flower of Row, join MC with sc in end of

any petal on one Flower, ch 3, **3-picot group** *(see Special Stitches)*, ch 3, (sc in end of next petal, ch 3, 3-picot group, ch 3) around, join with sl st in first sc. Fasten off.

For second Flower of Row, join MC with sc in end of any petal on next Flower, ch 3, work **joining picot group** *(see Special Stitches)*, ch 3, (sc in next petal on this Flower, ch 3, work joining picot group, ch 3) 2 times, (sc in end of next petal on this Flower, ch 3, 3-picot group, ch 3) around, join. Fasten off.

For third through fifth Flowers of Row, working on opposite side of last joined Flower, repeat second Flower joining.

Second Row of Flowers
For first Flower, join MC with sc in end of any petal of

Continued on page 119

Irish Garden Doily

Designed by Dot Drake

Finished Size: 19" diameter.

Materials:
- ❑ 600 yds. white size 20 crochet cotton thread
- ❑ No. 10 steel hook or hook needed to obtain gauge

Gauge: Rnds 1-12 = 4¼" across; 4 picot rnds = 1".

Basic Stitches: Ch, sl st, sc, hdc, dc, tr.

CENTER MOTIF

Rnd 1: Ch 6, sl st in first ch to form ring, ch 6, (dc in ring, ch 3) 5 times, join with sl st in third ch of ch-6. *(6 dc, 6 ch sps made)*

Rnd 2: For **petals**, ch 1, (sc, hdc, 3 dc, hdc, sc) in each ch sp around, **do not join.** *(6 petals)*

Rnd 3: Working behind petals, ch 3, (sc in dc of rnd 1 between next 2 petals, ch 3) 5 times, **do not join.**

Rnd 4: For **petals**, (sc, hdc, 5 dc, hdc, sc) in each ch sp around, **do not join.**

Rnd 5: Working behind petals, ch 4, (sc in sc of rnd 3 between next 2 petals, ch 4) 5 times, **do not join.**

Rnd 6: For **petals**, (sc, hdc, dc, 5 tr, dc, hdc, sc) in each ch sp around, **do not join.**

Rnd 7: Working behind petals, ch 5, (sc in sc of rnd 5 between next 2 petals, ch 5) 5 times, join with sl st in first ch of first ch-5. *(6 ch sps)*

Rnd 8: Ch 4, 9 tr in next ch sp, (tr in next sc, 9 tr in next ch sp) around, join with sl st in top of ch-4. *(60 tr)*

Rnd 9: Ch 4, (dc in next st, ch 1) around, join with sl st in third ch of ch-4. *(60 dc, 60 chs)*

Rnd 10: Ch 1, sc in first st, sc in next 4 sts or chs; for **picot**, ch 3, sc in third ch from hook *(picot made)*, (sc in next 10 sts or chs, picot) 11 times, sc in last 5 sts, join with sl st in first sc. *(120 sc, 12 picots)*

Rnd 11: Ch 1, sc in first st, ch 12, (sc in fifth sc after next picot, sc in next st, ch 12) 11 times, skip first 4 sts after last picot, sc in last st, join.

Rnd 12: For **petals**, ch 1, (sc, 2 hdc, 2 dc, 10 tr, 2 dc, 2 hdc, sc) in each ch sp around, join. *(12 petals)*

Rnd 13: Sl st in next 6 sts, (ch 7, picot, skip next 3 sts, sc in next st) 2 times, ch 7, picot, *skip next 11 sts, sc in next st, (ch 7, picot, skip next 3 sts, sc in next st) 2 times, ch 7, picot; repeat from * 10 times, skip last 5 sts, join with sl st in first ch of ch-7. *(36 ch sps)*

Rnds 14–18: Sl st in each of next 4 chs, ch 7, picot, (sc in next ch sp, ch 7, picot) around, join with sl st in first ch of first ch-7.

Rnds 19–22: Sl st in each of next 4 chs, ch 8, picot, (sc in next ch sp, ch 8, picot) around, join with sl st in first ch of first ch-8.

Rnd 23: Sl st in each of next 3 ch, ch 7, tr in same ch sp, ch 3, (tr, ch 3, tr, ch 3) in each ch sp around, join with sl st in fourth ch of ch-7. *(72 tr, 72 ch sps)*

Rnd 24: Ch 3, 5 dc in first ch sp, (dc in next tr, 5 dc in next ch sp) around, join with sl st in top of ch-3. *(432 dc)*

Rnd 25: Ch 8, picot, skip next 5 sts, (sc in next st, ch 8, picot, skip next 5 sts) around, join with sl st in first ch of first ch-8. Fasten off. *(72 ch sps)*

ROSE MOTIF

Rnds 1–7: Repeat rnds 1–7 of Center Motif.

Rnd 8: For **petals**, ch 1, (sc, dc, tr, 6 **dtr**—see Stitch

Guide, tr, dc, sc) in each ch sp around, join with sl st in first sc. *(72 sts)*

Rnd 9: Sl st in each of next 3 sts, ch 9, (*skip next 4 sts, dc in next st, ch 6, skip next 6 sts*, dc in next st, ch 6) 5 times; repeat between first and second *, join with sl st in third ch of ch-9.

Rnd 10: Sl st in each of next 2 chs, ch 8, picot, (sc in next ch sp, ch 8, picot) around, join with sl st in first ch of first ch-8.

Rnd 11: For **joining rnd**, *ch 8, picot, sc in next ch sp*, (ch 3, sc in any ch sp on rnd 25 of Center Motif, ch 5, sc in next ch sp on Rose Motif) 3 times; repeat between first and second * 7 times, ch 8, picot, join with sl st in first ch of first ch-8. Fasten off.

Skipping 5 ch sps on rnd 25 of Center Motif between joined ch sps *(see diagram on page 119)*, repeat Rose Motif 8 more times.

FLOWER MOTIF

Rnd 1: Ch 8, sl st in first ch to form ring, ch 4, (dc, ch 1) 11 times in ring, join with sl st in third ch of ch-4. *(12 dc, 12 ch sps made)*

Rnd 2: Sl st in first ch sp, ch 1, 3 sc in same ch sp, sc in next ch sp, ch 3, picot, 2 sc in same ch sp, *3 sc in next ch sp, (sc, ch 3, picot, 2 sc) in next ch sp; repeat from * around, join with sl st in first sc. *(36 sc, 6 picots)*

Rnd 3: Ch 8, (sc in third sc after next picot, ch 8) around, join with sl st in first ch of first ch-8. *(6 ch sps)*

Rnd 4: Ch 1, (sc, hdc, 8 dc, hdc, sc) in each ch sp around, join. *(72 sts)*

Rnd 5: Sl st in each of first 3 sts, (*ch 8, picot, skip next 4 sts, sc in next st, ch 8, picot, skip next 6 sts*, sc in next st) 5 times; repeat between first and second *, join with sl st in first ch of first ch-8.

Rnd 6: Sl st in each of next 3 sts, ch 3; holding Flower Motif between two Rose Motifs, sc in ch sp on side of Rose Motif *(see diagram on page 119)*, ch 6, picot, sc in next ch sp on Flower Motif, ch 3, sc in next ch sp on Rose Motif, ch 6, sc in first unworked ch sp on center motif, ch 6, sc in next ch sp on Flower Motif, (ch 3, sc in next ch sp on center motif, ch 6, picot, sc in next ch sp on Flower Motif) 3 times, ch 6, sc in next ch sp on center motif, ch 6, sc in first unworked ch sp on next Rose Motif, ch 6, picot, sc in next ch sp on Flower Motif, ch 3, sc in next ch sp on Rose Motif, ch 6, picot, sc in next ch sp on Flower Motif leaving last 4 ch sps unworked. Fasten off.

EDGING

Rnd 1: Working around outer edge, join with sc in first unworked ch sp of any Flower Motif, ch 8, * [sc in next ch sp, (ch 8, sc in next ch sp) 2 times, ch 10, sc in first unworked ch sp on next Rose Motif, (ch 8, sc in next ch sp) 4 times, ch 10], sc in first ch sp on next Flower Motif, ch 8; repeat from * 7 more times; repeat between [ ], join with sl st in first sc.

Rnd 2: Sl st in each of next 3 chs, (ch 10, sc in next ch sp) 2 times *[ch 5; for petal, (sc, hdc, 9 dc, hdc, sc) in next ch-10 sp *(petal made)*, ch 5, (sc in next ch sp, ch 10) 3 times, sc in next ch sp, ch 5, petal, ch 5] (sc in next ch sp, ch 10) 2 times, sc in next ch sp; repeat from * 7 more times; repeat

Continued on page 119

Doily Delights

Vase of Roses

Designed by Valmay Flint

Finished Sizes: Small Doily is 6¾" × 8¾". Large Doily is 9½" × 10¾".

Materials:
- ❏ Size 20 crochet cotton thread:
  - 140 yds. white
  - 95 yds. flower color
  - 15 yds. shaded green
- ❏ Tapestry needle
- ❏ No. 1 steel hook or size needed to obtain gauge

Gauge: 12 sts = 1"; 4 dc rows and 3 sc rows = 1".

Basic Stitches: Ch, sl st, sc, dc

SMALL DOILY
Row 1: With white, ch 27, dc in ninth ch from hook, (ch 2, skip each of next 2 chs, dc in next ch) 6 times, **do not turn.** *(7 ch-2 sps made)*

Row 2: 3 sc in end of row 1; working in remaining lps on opposite side of starting ch, sc in next ch, (2 sc in next ch-2 sp, sc in next ch) across, 3 sc in end of row 1, **do not turn.**

Row 3: Working across row 1, sl st in first st, ch 3, dc in next ch sp, dc in next st, (2 dc in next ch sp, dc in next st) across to last ch sp, dc in last sp, dc in last st, turn. *(20)*

Row 4: Ch 3, dc in next st, (ch 1, skip next st, dc in each of next 2 sts) across, turn. *(14 dc)*

Row 5: Ch 1, sc in each of first 2 sts, (ch 1, skip next ch, sc in each of next 2 sts) across, turn.

Row 6: Ch 3, dc in next st, (ch 2, skip next ch, dc in each of next 2 sts) across, turn.

NOTE: *Skip all ch sps unless otherwise stated.*

Row 19: Ch 1, sc in each of first 2 sts, (ch 6, sc in each of next 2 sts) across, turn.

Rows 20–21: Repeat rows 18 and 19.

Row 22: For **first side,** ch 3, dc in next st, (ch 7, dc in each of next 2 sts) 2 times leaving last 8 sts unworked, turn. *(6 dc)*

Row 23: Ch 1, sc in each of first 2 sts, (ch 7, sc in each of next 2 sts) 2 times, turn.

Row 24: Ch 3, dc in next st, (ch 7, dc in each of next 2 sts) 2 times, turn.

Row 25: Repeat row 23.

Row 26: Ch 3, dc in next st, (ch 8, dc in each of next 2 sts) 2 times, turn.

Row 27: Ch 1, sc in each of next 2 sts, (ch 8, sc in each of next 2 sts) 2 times, turn.

Row 28: Ch 3, dc in next st, (ch 9, dc in each of next 2 sts) 2 times, turn.

Row 29: Ch 3, dc in next st, (9 dc in next ch sp, dc in each of next 2 sts) 2 times. Fasten off.

Row 22: For **second side,** skip each of next 2 unworked sts on row 21, join white with sl st in next st, ch 3, dc in next st, (ch 7, dc in each of next 2 sts) 2 times, turn. *(6 dc)*

Rows 23–29: Repeat rows 23–29 of first side.

Flower Motif (make 6)

Rnd 1: With flower color, ch 8, sl st in first ch to form ring, ch 5, dc in ring, ch 2, (dc, ch 2) 4 times in ring, join with sl st in third ch of ch-5. *(6 ch-2 sps made)*

Rnd 2: Sl st in first ch-2 sp, ch 1; for **petals,** (sc, 4 dc, sc) in each ch sp around, join with sl st in first sc. *(24 dc, 12 sc)*

Rnd 3: Ch 1, **sc back post (sc bp—***see Stitch Guide)* around first st on rnd 1, ch 5, (sc bp around next dc on rnd 1, ch 5) around, join.

Rnd 4: Sl st in first ch-5 sp, (sc, 3 dc, ch 2, 3 dc, sc) in each ch sp around, join. Fasten off.

Rnd 5: Join white with sl st in any ch-2 sp on rnd 4, ch 3, (dc, ch 2, 2 dc) in same sp, ch 1; for **picot,** ch 4, sl st in fourth ch from hook *(picot made),* ch 1, picot, ch 1, picot, ch 1; *for **shell,** (2 dc, ch 2, 2 dc) in next ch-2 sp *(shell made),* ch 1, (picot, ch 1) 2 times; repeat from * around, join with sl st in top of ch-3. Fasten off.

Assembly

With white, sew Flower Motifs and Doily together according to Placement Diagram #1 on page 118.

Trim

Working in ch sps across outer edge of Flower Motifs, join white with sl st in end of row 27 on right edge of Doily, ch 1, (picot, ch 1) 2 times; *working in first ch sp between picots, for **cluster (cl),** (yo, insert hook in ch sp, yo, pull lp through sp, yo, pull through 2 lps on hook) 3 times in same ch sp, yo, pull through all 4 lps on hook *(cluster made),* [ch 1, (picot, ch 1) 2 times, (cl, ch 1, picot, ch 1, cl) in ch-2 sp of next shell, ch 1, (picot, ch 1) 2 times, cl in next ch sp between picots]; repeat between [ ] across to last ch sp between picots on this Motif; repeat from * across to last ch sp between picots on last Motif, ch 1, (picot, ch 1) 2 times, sl st in end of row 27. Fasten off.

Row 7: Ch 1, sc in each of first 2 sts, (ch 2, sc in each of next 2 sts) across, turn.

Row 8: Ch 3, dc in next st, (ch 3, dc in each of next 2 sts) across, turn.

Row 9: Ch 1, sc in each of first 2 sts, (ch 3, sc in each of next 2 sts) across, turn.

Row 10: Ch 3, dc in next st, (ch 4, dc in each of next 2 sts) across, turn.

Row 11: Ch 1, sc in each of first 2 sts, (ch 4, sc in each of next 2 sts) across, turn.

Rows 12–13: Repeat rows 10 and 11.

Row 14: Ch 3, dc in next st, (ch 5, dc in each of next 2 sts) across, turn.

Row 15: Ch 1, sc in each of first 2 sts, (ch 5, sc in each of next 2 sts) across, turn.

Rows 16–17: Repeat rows 14 and 15.

Row 18: Ch 3, dc in next st, (ch 6, dc in each of next 2 sts) across, turn.

Continued on page 118

Doily Delights

Leaves

Working in ch sps between picots on three joined
Motifs (*see Placement Diagram #1*), join green with
sl st in any ch sp, ch 3, (yo, insert hook in same ch
sp, yo, pull lp through ch sp, yo, pull through 2 lps
on hook) 2 times, yo, pull through all 3 lps on hook,
(cl in next ch sp of next Motif) 2 times, join with sl
st in top of ch-3. Fasten off.

Repeat for second group of Leaves, placing them
according to Placement Diagram #1.

LARGE DOILY

Row 1: With white, ch 36, dc in ninth ch from hook,
(ch 2, skip each of next 2 chs, dc in next ch) across,
turn. *(10 ch-2 sps made)*

Rows 2–21: Repeat rows 2–21 of Small Doily on pages
116–117, ending with 20 dc in last row.

Row 22: Ch 3, dc in next st, (ch 7, dc in each of next
2 sts) across, turn.

Row 23: Ch 1, sc in each of first 2 sts, (ch 7, sc in each
of next 2 sts) across, turn.

Rows 24–27: Repeat rows 22 and 23
alternately.

Row 28: For **First Side**, ch 3, dc in
next st, (ch 8, dc in each of next 2
sts) 3 times leaving last 12 sts
unworked, turn. *(8 dc)*

Row 29: Ch 1, sc in each of first 2 sts,
(ch 8, sc in each of next 2 sts)
across, turn.

Rows 30–31: Repeat rows 28 and 29.

Row 32: Ch 3, dc in next st, (ch 9, dc
in each of next 2 sts) across, turn.

Row 33: Ch 1, sc in each of first 2 sts,
(ch 9, sc in each of next 2 sts)
across, turn.

Row 34: Repeat row 32.

Row 35: Ch 3, dc in next st, (9 dc in next ch sp, dc in
each of next 2 sts) across. Fasten off.

Row 28: For **Second Side**, skip first 4 unworked sts
on row 27, join white with sl st in next st, ch 3, dc
in next st, (ch 8, dc in each of next 2 sts) across,
turn. (8 dc)

Rows 29–35: Repeat rows 29–35 of First Side.

Flower Motif (make 13)

Work same as Small Doily Flower Motif.

Assembly

With white, sew Flower Motifs and Doily together
according to Placement Diagram #2.

Trim

Joining white in end of row 28 on right side of Doily,
work same as Small Doily Trim, ending with sl st in
opposite end of row 28. Fasten off.

Leaves

Work same as Small Doily Leaves, placing them
according to Placement Diagram #2. ❏❏

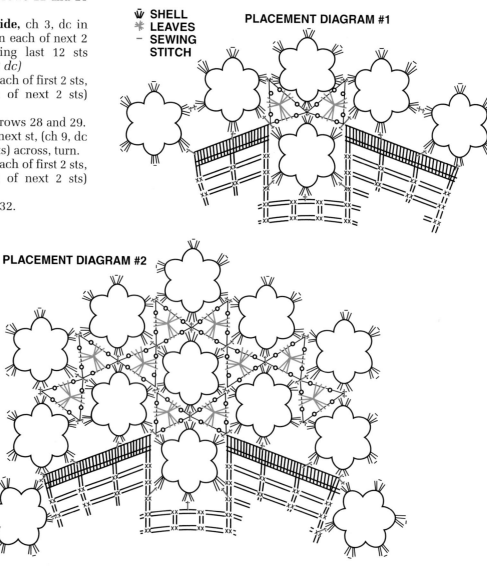

SHELL
LEAVES
SEWING STITCH

PLACEMENT DIAGRAM #1

PLACEMENT DIAGRAM #2

Irish Garden Doily

Continued from page 115

between [ ], join with sl st in first ch of first ch-10.

Rnd 3: Sl st in each of first 3 ch, ch 7, *[dc in same ch sp, ch 4, (dc, ch 4, dc) in next ch sp, ch 4, tr in next ch-5 sp, ch 4, tr in center dc of next petal, ch 4, tr in next ch-5 sp, ch 4, (dc in next ch sp, ch 4, dc in same ch sp, ch 4) 3 times, tr in next ch-5 sp, ch 4, tr in center dc of next petal, ch 4, tr in next ch-5 sp, ch 4], dc in next ch sp, ch 4; repeat from * 7 more times; repeat between [ ], join with sl st in third ch of ch-7. *(144 sts, 144 ch sps)*

Rnd 4: Ch 1, sc in each st and 5 sc in each ch sp around, join with sl st in first sc. *(864 sc)*

Rnd 5: Ch 1, sc in first 8 sts; for **first loop of first scallop**, ch 6, **turn**, sc in first sc, **turn**, *(4 sc, picot, 6 sc) in first loop, sc in next 8 sts on rnd 4; for **second loop**, ch 6, **turn**, skip next 7 sc, sc in next sc, **turn**, 4 sc in second loop; for **top loop**, ch 7, **turn**, sc in fourth sc of first loop, **turn**, (4 sc, picot, 4 sc, picot, 4 sc) in top loop, (2 sc, picot, 4 sc) in last half of second loop, sc in next 10 sts on rnd 4; for **first loop of next scallop**, ch 6, **turn**, skip next 7 sc, sc in next sc, **turn**; repeat from * around to last 2 sts, sc in each of last 2 sts, join with sl st in first sc. Fasten off. ❐❐

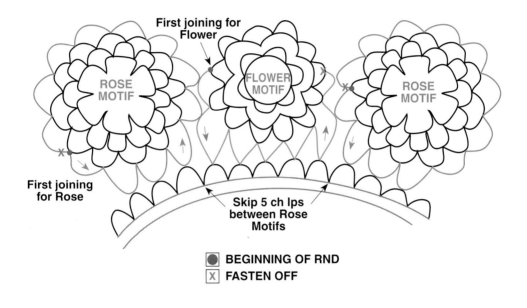

First joining for Flower

ROSE MOTIF

FLOWER MOTIF

ROSE MOTIF

First joining for Rose

Skip 5 ch lps between Rose Motifs

⬤ BEGINNING OF RND

X FASTEN OFF

Daisy Doily

Continued from page 113

one Flower, ch 3; working in picot groups of first Flower on last Row, work joining picot group in third group from last joining, ch 3, sc in end of next petal on this Flower, (ch 3, work joining picot group, ch 3, sc in end of next petal on this Flower) 2 times, ch 3; working in picot groups of next Flower on last Row, work joining picot group in first unworked group, ch 3, (sc in end of next petal on this Flower, ch 3, work joining picot group, ch 3) 2 times, (sc in end of next petal on this Flower, ch 3, 3-picot group, ch 3) around, join with sl st in first sc. Fasten off.

For second through fourth flowers of Row, join MC with sc in end of any petal on one Flower, ch 3; working in first 3-picot groups after joining on last Flower of this Row, work joining picot in third

group from joining, ch 3, (sc in end of next petal on this Flower, ch 3, work joining picot group, ch 3) 2 times; *working in next unworked groups on next Flower of last Row, (sc in end of next petal on this Flower, ch 3, joining picot group, ch 3) 3 times; repeat from *, (sc in end of next petal on this Flower, ch 3, 3-picot group, ch 3) around, join. Fasten off.

Third Row of Flowers

For first through third Flowers of Row, repeat first three Flowers of Second Row.

Fourth & Fifth Rows of Flowers

Working on opposite edge of Center Row of Flowers, repeat Second and Third Rows of Flowers. ❐❐

Roses & Leaves Doily

Finished Size: 13¾" across.

Materials:
- ❑ Size 20 crochet cotton thread:
    - 120 yds. ecru
    - 90 yds. tan
    - 90 yds. peach
- ❑ No. 10 steel hook and hook needed to obtain gauge

Gauge: Rnds 1-3 of Doily is 1¼" across. Rose is 1¼" across. Leaf is 1½" long.

Basic Stitches: Ch, sl st, sc, hdc, dc, tr.

Special Stitches:
For **V st,** (tr, ch 3, tr) in st or ch sp.
For **beginning tr cluster (beg tr cl),** ch 4, *yo 2 times, insert hook in st or ch sp, yo, pull through ch sp, (yo, pull through 2 lps on hook) 2 times; repeat from *, yo, pull through all 3 lps on hook.
For **treble crochet cluster (tr cl),** yo 2 times, insert hook in st or ch sp, yo, pull through, (yo, pull through 2 lps on hook) 2 times, leaving last lp of st on hook; *yo 2 times, insert hook in same st or ch sp, yo, pull through, (yo, pull through 2 lps on hook) 2 times, leaving last lp of st on hook; repeat from * number of times needed for number of tr in cluster; yo, pull through all lps on hook.

ROSE (make 15)
Rnd 1: With peach, ch 5, sl st in first ch to form ring, ch 4 *(counts as dc and ch sp),* (dc in ring, ch 1) 5 times, join with sl st in third ch of ch-4. *(6 dc, 6 ch sps made)*
Rnd 2: Ch 1; for **petals,** (sc, hdc, dc, hdc, sc) in each ch sp around, join with sl st in first sc. *(6 petals)*
Rnd 3: Working behind petals, ch 1, **sc back post (sc bp—**see Stitch Guide**)** around ch 3 at beginning of rnd 1, ch 3, * sc bp around next st on rnd 1, ch 3; repeat from * around, join. *(6 ch sps)*
Rnd 4: Ch 1; for **petals,** (sc, hdc, 3dc, hdc, sc) in each ch sp around, join.
Rnd 5: Working behind petals, ch 1, sc bp around first sc on rnd 3, ch 4, (sc bp around next sc on rnd 3, ch 4) around, join.
Rnd 6: Ch 1; for **petals,** (sc, hdc, 5 dc, hdc, sc) in each ch around, join. Fasten off.

LEAF (make 15)
Row 1: With tan, ch 11, sc in second ch from hook, sc in next 8 chs, 3 sc in last ch; working in remaining lp on opposite side of starting ch, sc in next 7 chs leaving last 2 chs unworked, turn. *(19 sc made)*
Rows 2–8: Working these rows in **back lps** *(see Stitch Guide),* ch 1, sc in each st across to center st of 3-sc group, 3 sc in center st, sc in each st across leaving last 2 sts unworked, turn.
Row 9: Ch 1, sc in each st across to center st of 3-sc group, sc in center st leaving remaining sts unworked. Fasten off.

DOILY
Rnd 1: With ecru, ch 6, sl st in first ch to form

121

Continued on page 122

ring, ch 3, 14 dc in ring, join with sl st in top of ch-3. *(15 dc made)*

Rnd 2: Ch 5, (dc in next st, ch 2) around, join with sl st in third ch of ch-5. *(15 dc, 15 ch sps)*

Rnd 3: Ch 6, skip next ch sp, (dc in next st, ch 3, skip next ch sp) around, join with sl st in third ch of ch-6.

Rnd 4: Sl st in first ch sp, **beg tr cl** *(see Special Stitches)*, ch 4, skip next st, ***3-tr cl** *(see Special Stitches)*, ch 4, skip next st; repeat from * around, join with sl st in first cl. *(15 cl)*

Rnd 5: Ch 1, sc in first ch sp, (ch 8, sc in next ch sp) 14 times, ch 4, join with tr in first sc *(ch-4 and tr count as last ch-8 sp)*.

Rnd 6: Ch 1, sc in last ch sp made, ch 8, (sc in next ch sp, ch 8) around, join with sl st in first sc.

Rnd 7: (Sl st, ch 4, 2 tr, ch 3, 3 tr) in first ch sp *(ch-4 counts as first tr)*, (3 tr, ch 3, 3 tr) in each ch sp around, join with sl st in top of ch-4. *(90 tr)*

Rnd 8: Ch 7, sc in next ch sp, (ch 7, sc in sp between next two 3-tr groups, ch 7, sc in next ch sp) around, ch 3, skip last 3 sts, join with tr in first ch of first ch-7.

Rnd 9: (Ch 7, sc in next ch sp) around, ch 3, join.

Rnd 10: (Ch 7, tr) in same ch sp, ch 5, sc in next ch sp, ch 5, ***V st** *(see Special Stitches)* in next ch sp, ch 5, sc in next ch sp, ch 5; repeat from * around, join with sl st in fourth ch of ch-7.

Rnd 11: (Sl st, ch 4, 2 tr) in first ch sp, (*ch 7, skip next ch sp, sc in next sc, ch 7, skip next ch sp*, 3 tr in next V st) 14 times; repeat between first and second *, join with sl st in top of ch-4.

Rnd 12: (Ch 4, tr) in first st, tr in next st, 2 tr in next st, (*ch 7, skip next ch sp, sc in next st, ch 7, skip next ch sp*, 2 tr in next st, tr in next st, 2 tr in next st) 14 times; repeat between first and second *, join.

Rnd 13: Ch 4, tr in next st, V st in next st, tr in each of next 2 sts, (*ch 4, sc in next ch sp, ch 5, sc in next ch sp, ch 4*, tr in each of next 2 sts, V st in next st, tr in each of next 2 sts) 14 times; repeat between first and second *, join.

Rnd 14: Sl st in each of next 2 sts, ch 1, sc in next ch sp, (*ch 7, skip next ch sp, V st in next ch-5 sp, ch 7, skip next ch sp*, sc in next ch sp) 14 times; repeat between first and second *, join with sl st in first sc.

Rnd 15: Ch 1, sc in first st, (*ch 8, skip next ch sp, 3 tr in next V st, ch 8, skip next ch sp*, sc in next st) 14 times; repeat between first and second *, join.

Rnd 16: Ch 1, sc in first st, (*ch 8, skip next ch sp, 2 tr in next st, tr in next st, 2 tr in next st*, ch 8, skip next ch sp, sc in next st) 14 times; repeat between first and second *, ch 4, join with tr in first sc.

Rnd 17: Ch 1, sc in last ch sp, (*ch 5, sc in next ch sp, ch 4, tr in each of next 2 sts, V st in next st, tr in each of next 2 sts, ch 4*, sc in next ch sp) 14 times; repeat between first and second *, join with sl st in first sc.

Rnd 18: (Sl st, ch 7, tr) in first ch sp, *[ch 4, sc in next ch sp, ch 4, skip next 3 sts, (2-tr cl, ch 4, 2-tr cl) in next ch sp, ch 4, skip next 3 sts, sc in next ch sp, ch 4], V st in next ch sp; repeat from * 13 more times; repeat between [ ], join with sl st in fourth ch of ch-7.

Rnd 19: (Sl st, ch 4, 2 tr) in first ch sp, *[ch 5, skip next ch sp, tr in next st, ch 5, skip next ch sp, (sc ch 3, sc) in ch sp of next shell, ch 5, skip next ch sp, tr in next st, ch 5, skip next ch sp], 3 tr in next V st; repeat from * 13 more times; repeat between [ ], join with sl st in top of ch-4.

Rnd 20: (Ch 4, tr) in first st, (*tr in next st, 2 tr in next st, ch 5, skip next ch sp, sc in next st, ch 5, skip next ch sp, shell in next ch sp, ch 5, skip next ch sp, sc in next st, ch 5, skip next ch sp*, 2 tr in next st) 14 times; repeat between first and second *, join.

Rnd 21: Ch 4, (*tr in next st, V st in next st, tr in each of next 2 sts, ch 5, skip next ch sp, sc in next st, ch 5, skip next ch sp, shell in next shell, ch 5, skip next ch sp, sc in next st, ch 5, skip next ch sp*, tr in next st) 14 times; repeat between first and second *, join. Fasten off.

Rnd 22: Join tan with sc in first st, sc in each of next 2 sts, 3 sc in next ch sp, sl st in any center dc of any Rose petal, *[3 sc in same ch sp, sc in each of next 3 sts, ch 5, skip next ch sp, dtr in next st, ch 1, sl st in center dc of next petal on same Rose, ch 1, (sc, ch 3, sc) in same dtr, ch 1, sl st in third st of row 9 on one Leaf, ch 1, sc in same dtr, ch 5, sc in next st, 3 sc in next ch sp, sl st in center st of 3-sc group on same Leaf, 3 sc in same ch sp, sc in next st, ch 5, skip next ch sp, dtr in next st, ch 1, sl st in third st of row 8 on same Leaf, ch 1, (sc, ch 3, sc) in same dtr, ch 1], sl st in center dc of any petal on next Rose, ch 1, sc in same dtr, ch 5, sc in each of next 3 sts, 3 sc in next ch sp, sl st in center dc of next petal on same Rose; repeat from * 13 more times; repeat between [ ], sl st in center st of next petal on first worked Rose, ch 1, sc in same dtr, ch 5, join with sl st in first sc. Fasten off. ❏❏

Country Home

*Though the exact
origin of crochet remains a
mystery, historians speculate it
evolved from the fabrication of nets
and snares by primitive fishermen and
shepherds, growing, by hook or by crook,
into a cottage industry and beyond.
Transcending its countrified roots, crochet
today transfigures crafter's lofts and
penthouse suites alike with comfort.
Homey accents of baskets, curtains,
dolls and coasters prove that
beautiful and sensible interior
design is within reach with
a hook and thread.*

Rose Basket & Wreath

Designed by Eunice Svinicki

Finished Sizes: Basket is 8" across × 3½" deep. Wreath is 8" across.

Materials:
- ❏ Size 10 crochet cotton thread:
  - 550 yds. ecru
  - 270 yds. pink
  - 175 yds. green
- ❏ 175 yds. ecru size 20 crochet cotton thread
- ❏ Dried baby's breath flowers
- ❏ 4 yds. of ⅛" ribbon
- ❏ 8" across × 3½" deep basket
- ❏ 8" Spanish moss wreath
- ❏ Craft glue
- ❏ Tapestry needle
- ❏ No. 7 steel hook or hook needed to obtain gauges

Gauge: **Size 10 thread,** 7 dc = 1"; 7 dc rows = 2". **Size 20 thread,** 4 rows = 1".

Basic Stitches: Ch, sl st, sc, dc, hdc, tr.

Special Stitch: For **increase (inc)**, 2 dc in next st.

ROSE BASKET
Doily
Rnd 1: With size 10 ecru, ch 6, sl st in first ch to form ring, ch 5, (dc in ring, ch 2) 5 times, join with sl st in third ch of ch-5. *(6 dc, 6 ch sps made)*

Rnd 2: (Sl st, ch 3, 4 dc) in first ch sp, 5 dc in each ch sp around, join with sl st in top of ch-3. *(30 dc)*

Rnd 3: Ch 3, dc in same st as ch-3, dc in each of next 3 sts, 2 dc in next st, ch 1; *inc (see Special Stitch), dc in each of next 3 sts, inc, ch 1; repeat from * around, join. *(42)*

Rnds 4–7: Ch 3, dc in same st, dc in each st across to next inc, dc in next st, inc, ch 1, skip next ch sp, (inc, dc in each st across to next inc, dc in next st, inc, ch 1, skip next ch sp) around, join. At end of last rnd *(90)*.

Rnds 8–10: Ch 3, dc in same st, dc in each st across to next inc, dc in next st, inc, ch 3, skip next ch sp, (inc, dc in each st across to next inc, dc in next st, inc, ch 3, skip next ch sp) around, join. At end of last rnd *(126)*.

Rnds 11–12: Sl st in next st, ch 3, dc in next 19 sts, dc in next ch sp, ch 4, (skip next st, dc in next 20 sts, dc in next ch sp, ch 4) around, join.

Rnd 13: Sl st in each of next 2 sts, ch 3, *dc in each st across to next ch sp, (dc, ch 3, sc, ch 3) in next ch sp, skip next 2 sts; repeat from * around, join. *(120 dc, 6 sc)*

Rnd 14: Sl st in each of next 2 sts, ch 3, *dc in each st across to next ch sp, (dc, ch 3, sc, ch 3) in next ch sp, sc in next ch sp, ch 3, skip next 2 sts; repeat from * around, join *(114 dc, 12 sc)*.

Rnds 15–19: Sl st in each of next 2 sts, ch 3, *dc in each st across to next ch sp, (dc, ch 3, sc, ch 3) in next ch sp, (sc in next ch sp, ch 3) across to next dc, skip next 2 sts; repeat from * around, join. At end of last rnd *(84 dc, 42 sc)*.

Rnds 20–26: Sl st in each of next 2 sts, ch 3, *dc in each st across to next ch sp, (dc, ch 4, sc, ch 4) in next ch sp, (sc in next ch sp, ch 4) across to next dc, skip next 2 sts; repeat from * around, join. At end of last rnd *(42 dc, 84 sc)*.

Rnd 27: Sl st in each of next 2 sts, ch 1, *sc in next st, ch 5, skip next 3 sts, (sc in next ch sp, ch 5) across to next dc, skip next 3 sts; repeat from * around, join with sl st in first sc. *(96 ch sps)*

Rnds 28–30: Sl st in each of next 2 chs, ch 1, sc in same ch sp, ch 5, (sc in next ch sp, ch 5) around, join.

Rnd 31: Sl st in first ch sp, ch 4, (dc, ch 1) 6 times in same ch sp, sc in next ch sp, ch 1, *(dc, ch 1) 7 times in next ch sp, sc in next ch sp, ch 1; repeat from * around, join with sl st in third ch of ch-4.

Rnd 32: Ch 1, (sc in next ch sp, ch 3) around, join. Fasten off.

Cut 1 yd. ribbon, weave through rnd 19.

Place basket centered on wrong side of Doily. Fold Doily around Basket edge, pull ribbon to fit, tie in bow. Glue Doily to Basket evenly spaced around top.

Rose (make 11)
Rnd 1: With pink, ch 5, sl st in first ch to form ring, ch 3, dc in ring, ch 4, (2 dc in ring, ch 4) 4 times, join with sl st in top of ch-3. *(10 dc, 5 ch sps made)*

Rnd 2: Sl st in next st, ch 1; for **petals,** (2 sc, 7 dc, 2 sc) in each ch sp around, join with sl st in first sc.

Rnd 3: Ch 5, (sc in space between next 2 petals, ch 5) around, join with sl st in first ch of first ch-5.

Rnd 4: Ch 1; for **petals,** (2 sc, hdc, 7 dc, hdc, 2 sc) in each ch sp around, join with sl st in first sc. Fasten off.

Bud (make 12)
With pink, ch 13, 4 dc in fourth ch from hook, 5 dc in each of next 2 chs, 5 tr in each of next 3 chs, dc in each of next 2 chs, sc in each of last 2 chs. Fasten off.

Roll piece to form Bud.

Sew one Bud to center of each Rose.

Leaf (make 11)
Row 1: With green, ch 5, 3 tr in fifth ch from hook, turn *(4 tr)*.

Rows 2–3: Ch 3, dc in same st, dc in each st across to last st, 2 dc in last st, turn. At end of last row *(8 dc)*.

Row 4: Ch 3, dc in each st across, turn.

Rows 5–7: Skip first st, sl st in next st, ch 3, dc in each st across leaving last st unworked, turn. At end of last row *(2)*, fasten off.

Tack one Leaf to back of six Roses.

Sew six Roses with Leaves evenly spaced around edge of Basket.

WREATH
Lace
Row 1: With size 20 ecru thread, ch 4, (dc, ch 1, 2 dc) in fourth ch from hook, turn. *(4 dc)*

Row 2: Sl st in each of first 2 sts, (sl st, ch 3, dc, ch 1, 2 dc) in next ch sp, turn.

Next Rows: Repeat row 2 until piece measures 48" or to desired length. At end of last row, fasten off.

Glue dried flowers around one side of Spanish moss wreath. Wrap Lace around wreath, tie in bow.

Sew one Leaf to back of two Roses, two Leaves to back of one Rose and one Leaf to back of remaining Bud.

Glue Roses and Bud as desired to top of Wreath.

Tie remaining ribbon in bow, glue to center of Lace bow. ❏❏

125

Country Home

Finished Sizes: Armrest is 5¼" × 16¾". Headrest is
16¾" × 21".

Materials:
- ❑ 1,300 yds. size 30 crochet cotton thread
- ❑ No. 9 steel hook or hook needed to obtain gauge

Gauge: 9 mesh = 2"; 5 mesh rows = 1".

Basic Stitches: Ch, sl st, sc, dc.

Special Stitches:
For **beg block**, ch 3, 2 dc in next ch sp, dc in next st,
  or ch 3, dc in each of next 3 sts.
For **block**, 2 dc in next ch-2 sp, dc in next st, **or** dc
  in each of next 3 sts.
For **mesh**, ch 2, skip next 2 chs or sts, dc in next st.

ARMREST (make 2)

Row 1: Ch 18, dc in fourth ch from hook, dc in each
ch across, turn. *(16 dc made)*

Row 2: Ch 11, dc in fourth ch from hook, dc in next
7 chs, dc in next st, mesh 4 times, block, turn.

Row 3: Ch 11, dc in fourth ch from hook, dc in next
7 chs, dc in next st, mesh 7 times, block, turn.

Row 4: Ch 8, dc in fourth ch from hook, dc in next 4
chs, dc in next st, mesh 10 times, block, turn.

Row 5: Ch 8, dc in fourth ch from hook, dc in next 4
chs, dc in next st, mesh 12 times, block, turn.

Row 6: Ch 14, dc in fourth ch from hook, dc in next
10 chs, dc in next st, mesh 14 times, block, turn.

Row 7: Ch 14, dc in fourth ch from hook, dc in next
10 chs, dc in next st, mesh 16 times, block, mesh
2 times, turn.

Row 8: Beg block, ch 2, sc in next ch sp, ch 2, dc in
next st, block, mesh 8 times, block, mesh 8 times,
block, mesh 2 times, turn.

Rows 9–84: Work according to graph across, turn.

Rnd 85: Working around outer edge, ch 1, sc in each
st and 2 sc in end of each row around with 3 sc in
each corner, join with sl st in first sc. Fasten off.

HEADREST
Panel (make 4)

Work same as Armrest.

Hold right sides of Panels together, matching sts at
ends of rows; working through both thicknesses, sl
st Panels together. ❑❑

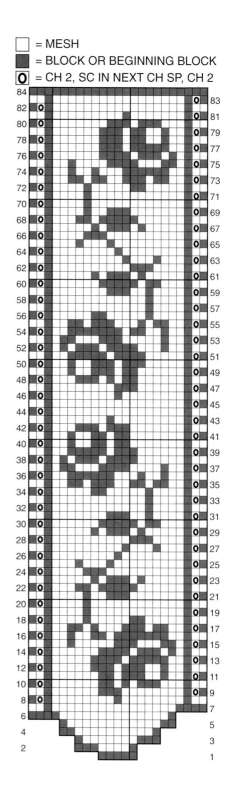

☐ = MESH
⬛ = BLOCK OR BEGINNING BLOCK
Ⓞ = CH 2, SC IN NEXT CH SP, CH 2

Rose Filet Chair Set

Designed by Dot Drake

Filet Cafe Curtains

Designed by Angelina Varona

Finished Sizes: Valance is 9¾" × 58½". Curtain is 20½" × 58½". Both fit ⅜"-diameter cafe rod.

Materials:
- ❏ Size 10 crochet cotton thread:
  - 2,400 yds. white *(for one Curtain and Valance)*
  - 200 yds. yellow or red
  - 150 yds. green
  - 150 yds. dk. brown *(for Pear Curtain)*
- ❏ No. 10 steel hook or hook needed to obtain gauge

Gauge: 9 dc = 1"; 7 dc rows = 2".

Basic Stitches: Ch, sl st, sc, dc, tr.

Special Stitches:
For **mesh**, ch 2, skip next 2 chs or sts, dc in next st.
For **block**, 2 dc in next ch sp, dc in next st, **or** dc in each of next 3 sts.

Note: When changing colors *(see Stitch Guide),* drop first color to wrong side of work, pick up when needed. Do not carry dropped color along back of work, use separate ball of thread for each section of color and fasten off each color when no longer needed.

PEAR VALANCE
NOTE: Wind 27 balls white and 7 balls each yellow, green and brown.

Row 1: With white, ch 531, dc in fourth ch from hook, dc in each ch across, turn. *(529 dc made)*

Rows 2–7: Ch 3, block, (mesh 24 times, block) 7 times, turn. *(Front of row 2 is right side of work.)*

Row 8: Ch 3, block, *mesh 9 times changing to yellow *(see Notes)* in last st made; with yellow, block, 2 dc in next ch sp changing to brown in last st made; with brown, dc in next st, 2 dc in next ch sp changing to yellow in last st made; with yellow, dc in next st, block, 2 dc in next ch sp changing to white in last st made; with white, dc in next st, mesh 10 times, block; repeat from * across, turn.

NOTE: Always change to next color in last st of last color used.

Row 9: Ch 3, block, (mesh 9 times; with yellow, block 6 times, 2 dc in next ch sp; with white, dc in next st, mesh 8 times, block) across, turn.

Row 10: Ch 3, block, (mesh 8 times; with yellow, block 6 times, dc in each of next 2 sts; with white, dc in next st, mesh 9 times, block) across, turn.

Row 11: Ch 3, block, (mesh 9 times; with yellow, block 6 times, dc in each of next 2 sts; with white, dc in next st, mesh 8 times, block) across, turn.

Row 12: Repeat row 10.

Row 13: Ch 3, block, (mesh 10 times; with yellow, block 4 times, dc in each of next 2 sts; with white, dc in next st, mesh 9 times, block) across, turn.

Row 14: Ch 3, block, (mesh 9 times; with yellow, block 4 times, dc in each of next 2 sts; with white, dc in next st, mesh 10 times, block) across, turn.

Rows 15–16: Repeat rows 13–14.

Row 17: Ch 3, block, (mesh 11 times; with yellow, block 2 times, dc in each of next 2 sts; with white, dc in next st, mesh 10 times, block) across, turn.

Row 18: Ch 3, block, (mesh 11 times; with brown, block; with green, block 2 times, 2 dc in next ch sp; with white, dc in next st, mesh 9 times, block) across, turn.

Row 19: Ch 3, block, (mesh 8 times; with green, block 2 times, dc in each of next 2 sts; with white, dc in each of next 3 sts; with brown, dc in each of next 3 sts; with white, dc in next st, mesh 11 times, block) across, turn.

Row 20: Ch 3, block, (mesh 11 times; with brown, block; with white, mesh 2 times, with green, block 2 times, 2 dc in next ch sp; with white, dc in next st, mesh 7 times, block) across, turn.

Rows 21–26: Repeat row 2.

Row 27: Ch 3, block across, turn. *(529 dc)*

Row 28: Ch 5, dtr *(see Stitch Guide)* in each of next 3 sts, (ch 3, skip next 4 sts, dtr in each of next 3 sts) 2 times, (ch 3, skip next 3 sts, dtr in each of next 3 sts) across to last 7 sts, ch 3, skip next 3 sts, dc in last 4 sts, turn.

Row 29: Ch 3, dc in each st and 3 dc in each ch sp across, turn. *(527)*

Row 30: Ch 3, skip next 3 sts, 3 dc in next st; for **picot,** ch 4, sc in fourth ch from hook *(picot made),* 3 dc in next st, (ch 3, skip next 4 sts, sc in next st, ch 4, skip next 4 sts, 3 dc in next st, picot, 3 dc in next st) across to last 4 sts, ch 3, skip next 3 sts, sl st in last st. Fasten off.

Row 31: Working in remaining lps on opposite side of starting ch, join with sl st in first ch, ch 3, skip next 4 chs, 3 dc in next ch, picot, 3 dc in next ch, (ch 3, skip next 4 chs, sc in next ch, ch 3, skip next 4 chs, 3 dc in next ch, picot, 3 dc in next ch) across to last 5 chs, ch 3, skip next 4 chs, sl st in last ch. Fasten off.

CHERRY VALANCE
NOTE: Wind 21 balls white and 14 balls each green and red.

Rows 1–7: Repeat rows 1–7 of Pear Valance.

Row 8: Ch 3, block, (mesh 6 times changing to red in last st made; with red, block 2 times, 2 dc in next ch sp changing to white in last st made; with white, dc in next st, mesh 15 times, block) across, turn.

NOTE: Always change to next color in last st of last color used.

Row 9: Ch 3, block, (mesh 14 times; with red, block 4 times, 2 dc in next ch sp; with white, dc in next st, mesh 5 times, block) across, turn.

Row 10: Ch 3, block, (mesh 5 times; with red, block 4 times, dc in each of next 2 sts; with white, dc in next st, mesh 14 times, block) across, turn.

Row 11: Ch 3, block, (mesh 14 times; with red, block 4 times, dc in each of next 2 sts; with white, dc in next st, mesh 5 times, block) across, turn.

Row 12: Ch 3, block, (mesh 6 times; with red, block 2 times, dc in each of next 2 sts; with white, dc in next st, mesh 5 times; with red, block 2 times, 2 dc in next ch sp; with white, dc in next st, mesh 7 times, block) across, turn.

Row 13: Ch 3, block, (mesh 6 times; with red, block 4 times, 2 dc in next ch sp; with white, dc in next st, mesh 5 times; with green, dc in each of next 2 sts; with white, dc in next st, mesh 7 times, block) across, turn.

Row 14: Ch 3, block, (mesh 7 times; with green, dc in each of next 2 sts; with white, dc in next st, mesh 5 times; with red, block 4 times, dc in each of next 2 sts; with white, dc in next st, mesh 6 times, block) across, turn.

Row 15: Ch 3, block, (mesh 6 times; with red, block 4 times, dc in each of next 2 sts; with white, dc in next st, mesh 4 times; with green, block; with white, mesh 8 times, block) across, turn.

Continued on page 133

LT. GREEN DOLL

Finished Size: 12" tall.

Materials:
- ❒ Size 10 crochet cotton thread:
  - 300 yds. lt. green
  - 150 yds. white
  - 25 yds. pink
- ❒ 18" piece of ¼" and 1 yd. of ⅛" white ribbon
- ❒ 12" flat dried pine broom with 3½" handle
- ❒ Small amount curly doll hair
- ❒ White sewing thread
- ❒ Sewing and tapestry needles
- ❒ Craft glue
- ❒ Polyester fiberfill
- ❒ No. 7 steel hook or hook needed to obtain gauge

Gauge: 7 dc = 1"; 5 dc rnds = 1½".

Basic Stitches: Ch, sl st, sc, dc, tr.

DRESS

Rnd 1: Leaving 9" end for gathering, starting at top, with lt. green, ch 36, sl st in first ch to form ring, ch 3, dc in each ch around, join with sl st in top of ch-3. *(First 3 chs count as first dc—36 dc made.)*

Rnds 2–4: Ch 3, dc in each st around, join.

Rnd 5: (Ch 3, dc) in first st, dc in next 5 sts, (2 dc in next st, dc in next 5 sts) around, join. *(42)*

Rnd 6: (Ch 3, dc) in first st, dc in next 6 sts, (2 dc in next st, dc in next 6 sts) around, join. *(48)*

Rnd 7: (Ch 3, dc) in first st, dc in next 7 sts, (2 dc in next st, dc in next 7 sts) around, join. *(54)*

Rnd 8: (Ch 3, dc) in first st, dc in next 8 sts, (2 dc in next st, dc in next 8 sts) around, join. *(60)*

Rnd 9: (Ch 3, dc) in first st, dc in next 9 sts, (2 dc in next st, dc in next 9 sts) around, join. *(66)*

Rnd 10: (Ch 3, dc) in first st, dc in next 10 sts, (2 dc in next st, dc in next 10 sts) around, join. *(72)*

Rnd 11: (Ch 3, dc) in first st, dc in next 11 sts, (2 dc in next st, dc in next 11 sts) around, join. *(78)*

Rnd 12: (Ch 3, dc) in first st, dc in next 12 sts, (2 dc in next st, dc in next 12 sts) around, join. *(84)*

Rnd 13: (Ch 3, dc) in first st, dc in next 13 sts, (2 dc in next st, dc in next 13 sts) around, join. *(90)*

Rnd 14: (Ch 3, dc) in first st, dc in next 14 sts, (2 dc in next st, dc in next 14 sts) around, join. *(96)*

Rnd 15: (Ch 3, dc) in first st, dc in next 15 sts, (2 dc in next st, dc in next 15 sts) around, join. *(102)*

Rnd 16: (Ch 3, dc) in first st, dc in next 16 sts, (2 dc in next st, dc in next 16 sts) around, join. *(108)*

Rnd 17: (Ch 3, dc) in first st, dc in next 17 sts, (2 dc in next st, dc in next 17 sts) around, join. *(114)*

Rnd 18: (Ch 3, dc) in first st, dc in next 18 sts, (2 dc in next st, dc in next 18 sts) around, join. *(120)*

Rnd 19: (Ch 3, dc) in first st, dc in next 19 sts, (2 dc in next st, dc in next 19 sts) around, join. *(126)*

Rnd 20: (Ch 3, dc) in first st, dc in next 20 sts, (2 dc in next st, dc in next 20 sts) around, join. *(132)*

Rnd 21: (Ch 3, dc) in first st, dc in next 21 sts, (2 dc in next st, dc in next 21 sts) around, join. *(138)*

Rnd 22: (Ch 3, dc) in first st, dc in next 22 sts, (2 dc in next st, dc in next 22 sts) around, join. *(144)*

Rnd 23: (Ch 3, dc) in first st, dc in next 23 sts, (2 dc in next st, dc in next 23 sts) around, join. *(150)*

Rnd 24: (Ch 3, dc) in first st, dc in next 24 sts, (2 dc in next st, dc in next 24 sts) around, join. Fasten off. *(156)*

Ruffle

Row 1: With white, ch 100, sc in second ch from hook, (ch 4, skip next ch, sc in next ch) across, turn. *(49 ch sps made)*

Rows 2–3: Ch 4, sc in first ch sp, (ch 4, sc in next ch sp) across, turn.

Row 4: Ch 5 *(counts as first tr and ch-1)*, (tr, ch 1, tr) in first st, ch 1, *sc in next ch sp, ch 1, (tr, ch 1) 5 times in next ch sp; repeat from * across to last st, sc in last st, turn. *(147 ch sps)*

Row 5: Ch 1, skip first st, skip next ch sp, (3 sc in each of next 4 ch sps, skip next 2 ch sps) 24 times, 3 sc in each of last 2 ch sps. Fasten off.

Sleeve

Rnd 1: With lt. green, ch 4, 11 dc in fourth ch from hook, join with sl st in top of ch-4. *(12 dc made)*

Rnd 2: (Ch 3, dc) in first st, 2 dc in each st around, join. *(24)*

Rnds 3–4: Ch 3, dc in each st around, join.

Rnd 5: Ch 3, dc next 2 sts tog, (dc in next st, dc next 2 sts tog) around, join. *(16)*

Rnds 6–7: Ch 3, dc in each st around, join.

Rnd 8: Ch 1, sc in first st, (ch 5, sc next st) around, ch 2, join with dc in first sc.

Rnd 9: Ch 1, sc in first ch sp, (ch 5, sc in next ch sp) around, ch 2, join with dc in first sc. Fasten off.

Stuff rnds 1–7 of Sleeve. Sew at an angle slanting left over rnds 5–10 of Dress.

BONNET

Rnd 1: With lt. green, ch 4, 11 dc in fourth ch from hook, join with sl st in top of ch-4. *(12 dc made)*

Rnd 2: (Ch 3, dc) in first st, 2 dc in each st around, join with sl st in top of ch-3. *(24)*

Rnd 3: Ch 3, 2 dc in next st, (dc in next st, 2 dc in next st) around, join. *(36)*

Rnd 4: Ch 3, dc in next st, 2 dc in next st, (dc in each of next 2 sts, 2 dc in next st) around, join. *(48)*

Rnd 5: Ch 3, dc in each of next 2 sts, 2 dc in next st, (dc in each of next 3 sts, 2 dc in next st) around, join. *(60)*

Rnd 6: Ch 3, dc in next 7 sts, dc next 2 sts tog, (dc in next 8 sts, dc next 2 sts tog) around, join. *(54)*

Rnd 7: Ch 3, dc in next 6 sts, dc next 2 sts tog, (dc in next 7 sts, dc next 2 sts tog) around, join. *(48)*

Rnd 8: Ch 3, dc in each st around, join. Fasten off.

Rnd 9: Join white with sc in first st, (ch 5, sc in next st) around, ch 2, join with dc in first sc. *(48 ch sps)*

Rnds 10–12: Ch 1, sc in first ch sp, (ch 5, sc in next ch sp) around, ch 2, join with dc in first sc. At end of last rnd, fasten off.

ROSE (make 5)

With pink, ch 10, 5 dc in third ch from hook, 5 dc in each ch across. Fasten off.

Roll each Rose and tack bottom of stitches together to hold shape.

BOUQUET LACE

Rnd 1: With white, ch 5, (dc, ch 1) 7 times in fifth ch

Continued on page 132

Broom Dolls

Designed by Maggie Weldon

Continued from page 130

from hook, join with sl st in fourth ch of ch-5. *(8 ch sps made)*

Rnd 2: Ch 1, sc in first st, ch 4, sc in next ch sp, (ch 4, sc in next st, ch 4, sc in next ch sp) around, ch 1, join with dc in first sc. *(16)*

Rnd 3: Ch 1, sc in first ch sp, ch 4, (sc in next ch sp, ch 4) around, join with sl st in first sc. Fasten off.

Cut two 8" pieces of ⅛" ribbon. Holding both pieces together, tie in bow. Sew to center of rnd 1. Sew two Roses over center of bow. Sew Bouquet Lace to inside lower edge of Sleeve, folding back top of Sleeve opening.

FINISHING

Insert broom handle up through top opening of Dress. Weave 9" end through bottom of rnd 1, gather to fit around handle. Secure. Smooth and flatten Dress to shape of broom with Sleeve at the left *(this now becomes front of the doll)*.

Tack each end of the Ruffle just out of sight on each side of the Dress back. Make three scallops across front of Dress between rnds 14–22 forming two points at top, tacking along the bottom of rnd 1 of Ruffle to secure.

Cut two 6" pieces from ¼" ribbon, tie each in bows. Sew one to top of each point. Sew one Rose to center of each bow.

Glue small amount of fiberfill to top right of handle to shape head; glue curly hair about 1½" down from top of handle with short curls at the top and the longer curls cascading over top of Dress above Sleeve.

Tie remaining ¼" ribbon in bow. Sew over rnd 7 of Bonnet. Sew one Rose to center of bow. Place Bonnet at a right angle on top of handle with Rose at back of head.

For hanger, thread remaining ⅛" ribbon around three stitches on rnd 1 of Dress at back of broom and out the top of the Bonnet. Tie ends in knot. ❑❑

PINK DOLL

Finished Size: 12" tall.

Materials:
- ❑ Size 10 crochet cotton thread:
  - 300 yds. pink
  - 225 yds. white
- ❑ 6" piece of ¼" and 26" piece of ⅛" white ribbon
- ❑ 12" flat dried pine broom with 3½" handle
- ❑ Small amount curly doll hair
- ❑ Miniature basket with flowers
- ❑ White sewing thread
- ❑ Sewing and tapestry needles
- ❑ Craft glue
- ❑ Polyester fiberfill
- ❑ No. 7 steel hook or hook needed to obtain gauge

Gauge: 7 dc = 1"; 5 dc rnds = 1½".

Basic Stitches: Sl st, ch, sc, dc.

DRESS

Rnd 1: Leaving 9" end for gathering, starting at top, with white, ch 36, sl st in first ch to form ring, ch 3, dc in each ch around, join with sl st in top of ch-3. *(First 3 chs count as first dc—36 dc made.)*

Rnds 2–4: Ch 3, dc in each st around, join.

Rnd 5: (Ch 3, dc) in first st, dc in next 5 sts, (2 dc in next st, dc in next 5 sts) around, join. *(42)*

Rnd 6: (Ch 3, dc) in first st, dc in next 6 sts, (2 dc in next st, dc in next 6 sts) around, join. *(48)*

Rnd 7: (Ch 3, dc) in first st, dc in next 7 sts, (2 dc in next st, dc in next 7 sts) around, join. *(54)*

Rnd 8: (Ch 3, dc) in first st, dc in next 8 sts, (2 dc in next st, dc in next 8 sts) around, join. *(60)*

Rnd 9: (Ch 3, dc) in first st, dc in next 9 sts, (2 dc in next st, dc in next 9 sts) around, join. *(66)*

Rnd 10: (Ch 3, dc) in first st, dc in next 10 sts, (2 dc in next st, dc in next 10 sts) around, join. Fasten off. *(72)*

Rnd 11: Working this rnd in **back lps** *(see Stitch Guide)*, join pink with sl st in first st, ch 3, dc in same st, dc in next 11 sts, (2 dc in next st, dc in next 11 sts) around, join. *(78)*

Rnd 12: (Ch 3, dc) in first st, dc in next 12 sts, (2 dc in next st, dc in next 12 sts) around, join. *(84)*

Rnd 13: (Ch 3, dc) in first st, dc in next 13 sts, (2 dc in next st, dc in next 13 sts) around, join. *(90)*

Rnd 14: (Ch 3, dc) in first st, dc in next 14 sts, (2 dc in next st, dc in next 14 sts) around, join. *(96)*

Rnd 15: (Ch 3, dc) in first st, dc in next 15 sts, (2 dc in next st, dc in next 15 sts) around, join. *(102)*

Rnd 16: (Ch 3, dc) in first st, dc in next 16 sts, (2 dc in next st, dc in next 16 sts) around, join. *(108)*

Rnd 17: (Ch 3, dc) in first st, dc in next 17 sts, (2 dc in next st, dc in next 17 sts) around, join. *(114)*

Rnd 18: (Ch 3, dc) in first st, dc in next 18 sts, (2 dc in next st, dc in next 18 sts) around, join. *(120)*

Rnd 19: (Ch 3, dc) in first st, dc in next 19 sts, (2 dc in next st, dc in next 19 sts) around, join. *(126)*

Rnd 20: (Ch 3, dc) in first st, dc in next 20 sts, (2 dc in next st, dc in next 20 sts) around, join. *(132)*

Rnd 21: (Ch 3, dc) in first st, dc in next 21 sts, (2 dc in next st, dc in next 21 sts) around, join. *(138)*

Rnd 22: (Ch 3, dc) in first st, dc in next 22 sts, (2 dc in next st, dc in next 22 sts) around, join. *(144)*

Rnd 23: (Ch 3, dc) in first st, dc in next 23 sts, (2 dc in next st, dc in next 23 sts) around, join. Fasten off. *(150)*

Rnd 24: Join white with sc in first st, ch 4, skip next 2 sts, (sc in next st, ch 4, skip next 2 sts) around, join with sl st in first sc. Fasten off.

Overskirt

Rnd 1: Working in remaining **front lps** of rnd 10 on Dress, join white with sc in first st, ch 4, skip next st, (sc in next st, ch 4, skip next st) around, join with sl st in first sc. *(36 ch sps made)*

Rnd 2: Sl st in each of next 2 chs, sc in same ch sp, 8 dc in next ch sp, sc in next ch sp, (ch 5, sc in next ch sp, 8 dc in next ch sp, sc in next ch sp) around, ch 2, join with dc in first sc. *(12 8-dc groups)*

Rnd 3: Ch 1, sc in first ch sp, (dc in next dc; for **picot,** ch 3, sl st in third ch from hook—*picot made)* 7 times, dc in next dc, *sc in next ch sp, (dc in next dc, picot) 7 times, dc in next dc; repeat from * around, join with sl st in first sc.

Rnd 4: Ch 8, skip next 2 picots, sc in next picot, ch 5, skip next picot, sc in next picot, ch 5, skip next 2 picots, (dc in next sc, ch 5, skip next 2 picots, sc in next picot, ch 5, skip next picot, sc in next picot, ch 5, skip next 2 picots) around, join with sl st in third ch of ch-8. *(36 ch sps)*

Rnds 5–9: Repeat rnds 2–4 consecutively, ending with rnd 3. At end of last rnd, fasten off.

Sleeve

Rnd 1: With pink, ch 4, 11 dc in fourth ch from hook, join with sl st in top of ch-4. *(12 dc made)*

Rnd 2: (Ch 3, dc) in first st, 2 dc in each st around, join with sl st in top of ch-3. *(24)*

Rnd 3: (Ch 3, dc) in first st, dc in next st, (2 dc in next st, dc in next st) around, join. *(36)*

Rnd 4: Ch 3, dc in next st, 2 dc in next st, (dc in each of next 2 sts, 2 dc in next st) around, join. *(48)*

Rnd 5: Ch 3, dc in each st around, join.

Rnd 6: Ch 3, (dc next 2 sts tog) 23 times, skip last st, join. *(24)*

Rnd 7: Ch 3, dc in next st, dc next 2 sts tog, (dc in each of next 2 sts, dc next 2 sts tog) around, join. *(18)*

Rnd 8: (Ch 3, dc) in first st, 2 dc in each st around, join. *(36)*

Rnds 9–10: Ch 3, dc in each st around, join. At end of last rnd, fasten off.

Rnd 11: Join white with sc in first st, ch 4, skip next 2 sts, (sc in next st, ch 4, skip next 2 sts) around, join with sl st in first sc. Fasten off.

Stuff first six rnds at top of Sleeve. Weave 6" piece ⅛" ribbon through sts of rnd 7, pull to gather Sleeve, tie in bow. Sew at an angle over rnds 4–10 of Dress. Sew handle of basket to inside back edge of Sleeve opening.

BONNET

Rnd 1: With pink, ch 4, 11 dc in fourth ch from hook, join with sl st in top of ch-4. *(12 dc made)*

Rnd 2: (Ch 3, dc) in first st, 2 dc in each st around, join with sl st in top of ch-3. *(24)*

Rnd 3: (Ch 3, dc) in first st, dc in next st, (2 dc in next st, dc in next st) around, join. *(36)*

Rnd 4: Ch 3, dc in next st, 2 dc in next st, (dc in each of next 2 sts, 2 dc in next st) around, join. *(48)*

Rnd 5: Ch 3, dc in each of next 2 sts, 2 dc in next st, (dc in each of next 3 sts, 2 dc in next st) around, join. *(60)*

Rnd 6: Ch 3, dc in each of next 3 sts, 2 dc in next st, (dc in next 4 sts, 2 dc in next st) around, join. *(72)*

Rnd 7: Ch 3, dc in next 4 sts, 2 dc in next st, (dc in next 5 sts, 2 dc in next st) around, join. *(84)*

Rnd 8: Ch 3, dc in next 5 sts, 2 dc in next st, (dc in next 6 sts, 2 dc in next st) around, join. *(96)*

Rnd 9: Ch 3, dc in next 6 sts, 2 dc in next st, (dc in next 7 sts, 2 dc in next st) around, join. *(108)*

Rnd 10: Ch 1, sc in first st, skip next st, (sc in next st, skip next st) around, join with sl st in first sc. Fasten off. *(54)*

Rnd 11: Join white with sc in first st, ch 4, skip next st, (sc in next st, ch 4, skip next st) around, join with sl st in first sc. *(27 ch sps)*

Rnds 12–16: Repeat rnds 2–4 of Overskirt consecutively, ending with rnd 3. At end of last rnd, fasten off.

FINISHING

Insert broom handle up through top opening of Dress. Weave 9" end through bottom of rnd 1, gather to fit around handle. Secure. Smooth and flatten Dress to shape of broom with Sleeve at the right *(this now becomes front of the doll)*.

Glue small amount of fiberfill to top left of handle to shape head; glue curly hair about 1½" down from top of handle with short curls at the top and the longer curls cascading down back of Dress behind Sleeve.

Tie ¼" piece of ribbon in bow. Sew to rnd 10 of Bonnet. Place Bonnet at a left angle on top of handle with bow at center front of head.

For hanger, thread remaining ⅛" ribbon around three stitches on rnd 1 of Dress at back of broom and out the top of the Bonnet. Tie ends in knot. ❏❏

Filet Cafe Curtains

Continued from page 129

Row 16: Ch 3, block, (mesh 7 times, ch 2; with green, dc in next st, dc in each of next 2 sts; with white, dc in next st, mesh 5 times; with red, block 2 times, dc in each of next 2 sts; with white, dc in next st, mesh 7 times, block) across, turn.

Row 17: Ch 3, block, (mesh 9 times; with green, block; with white, mesh 5 times; with green, block; with white, mesh 8 times, block) across, turn.

Row 18: Ch 3, block, (mesh 8 times, ch 2; with green, dc in next st, 2 dc in next ch sp; with white, dc in next st, mesh 3 times; with green, block; with white, mesh 10 times, block) across, turn.

Row 19: Ch 3, block, (mesh 10 times, ch 2; with green, dc in next st, 2 dc in next ch sp; with white, dc in next st, mesh 2 times; with green, block 3 times, 2 dc in next ch sp; with white, dc in next st, mesh 6 times, block) across, turn.

Row 20: Ch 3, block, (mesh 5 times; with green, block 4 times, dc in each of next 2 sts; with white, dc in next st, mesh; with green, block; with white, mesh 12 times, block) across, turn.

Row 21: Ch 3, block (mesh 9 times; with green, block 5 times, dc in each of next 2 sts; with white, dc in next st, mesh 2 times; with green, block 2 times, 2 dc in next ch sp; with white, dc in next st, mesh 4 times, block) across, turn.

Row 22: Ch 3, block, (mesh 8 times; with green, block; with white, mesh, ch 2; with green, dc in next 6 sts; with white, dc in next st, mesh 11 times, block) across, turn.

Row 23: Ch 3, block, (mesh 14 times, ch 2; with green, dc in each of next 3 sts; with white, dc in next st, mesh 8 times, block) across, turn.

Rows 24–26: Repeat row 2 of Pear Valance.

Rows 27–31: Repeat rows 27–31 of Pear Valance.

PEAR OR CHERRY CURTAIN

Rows 1–27: Repeat rows 1–27 of matching Valance.

Rows 28–66: Or to 2" less than desired length; ch 3, block, mesh across to last 3 sts, block, turn.

Rows 67–71: Repeat rows 27–31 of matching Valance. ❏❏

133

Bedroom Beauties

Star Pillow
Designed by Ann Parnell

Box Cover
Designed by JoAnn Evans

Star Pillow

Finished Size: 13½" square without ruffle.

Materials:
- ❏ 625 yds. cotton hardware twine or size 5 crochet cotton
- ❏ ½ yd. fabric
- ❏ Off-white sewing thread
- ❏ Polyester fiberfill
- ❏ Sewing and tapestry needles
- ❏ No. 1 steel hook or hook needed to obtain gauge

Note: The cotton hardware twine, also called tobacco twine, used in *Star Pillow* can be obtained through farm supply companies or hardware stores.

Gauge: 9 sc = 2"; 9 sc rows = 2".

Basic Stitches: Ch, sl st, sc, dc.

Special Stitches:
For **extended sc (esc)**, insert hook in st or ch, yo, pull through st or ch, yo, pull through 1 lp on hook, yo, pull through 2 lps on hook.
For **popcorn (pc)**, 4 esc in st or ch, drop lp from hook, insert hook in top of first esc of group, pull dropped lp through st.
For **V st**, (dc, ch 2, dc) in st or ch sp.

FRONT
Row 1: Ch 62, **esc** *(see Special Stitches)* in each ch across, turn. *(61 esc made)*

Rows 2–8: Ch 1, esc in each st across, turn.

Row 9: Ch 1, esc in first 8 sts, **pc** *(see Special Stitches)* in next st, (esc in each of next 3 sts, pc in next st) 11 times, esc in last 8 sts, turn. *(12 pc, 49 esc)*

Rows 10–61: Ch 1, work according to graph on page 138, turn. At end of last row, **do not turn.**

Rnd 62: For edging, working around outer edge, ch 1, sc in end of each row and in each st around with 3 sc in each corner st, join with sl st in first sc. Fasten off. *(252 sc)*

BACK
Row 1: Ch 62, esc in each ch across, turn. *(61 esc made)*

Rows 2–61: Ch 1, esc in each st across, turn. At end of last row, **do not turn.**

Rnd 62: Repeat rnd 62 of Front.

PILLOW FORM
Using Front piece as pattern, from fabric, cut two pieces 1" larger on all sides.

Allowing ½" for seam, sew pieces right sides together, leaving 5" open for turning. Clip corners. Turn. Stuff. Sew opening closed.

RUFFLE
Rnd 1: Hold Front and Back pieces wrong sides together, with Back facing you and matching sts; working through both thicknesses, join with sc in any st, sc in each st around with 3 sc in center st of each corner and inserting Pillow Form before closing, join with sl st in first sc, turn. *(260 sc made)*

Rnd 2: Ch 1, sc in first st, ch 1, skip next st, (sc in next st, ch 1, skip next st) around, join.

Rnd 3: (Sl st, ch 5, dc) in first ch sp, skip next st, *V st *(see Special Stitches)* next ch sp, skip next st; repeat from * around, join with sl st in third ch of ch-5.

Rnd 4: (Sl st, ch 5, dc, ch 2, dc) in first ch sp, (dc, ch 2, dc, ch 2, dc) in each ch sp around, join.

Rnd 5: (Sl st, ch 5, dc) in first ch sp, V st in each ch sp around, join.

Rnd 6: (Sl st, sc, ch 2, sc) in first ch sp, (sc, ch 2, sc) in each ch sp around, join with sl st in first sc. Fasten off. ❏❏

Graph on page 138

Box Cover

Finished Size: Fits round wooden box with 4½" lid.

Materials:
- ❏ 70 yds. ecru size 10 crochet cotton thread
- ❏ 26" of ¼" ribbon
- ❏ Round wooden box 4½" across lid
- ❏ No. 5 steel hook or hook needed to obtain gauge

Gauge: Rnds 1–2 are 1½" across.

Basic Stitches: Ch, sl st, sc, dc.

Special Stitches:
For **beginning popcorn (beg pc)**, ch 3, 4 dc in same st as ch 3, drop lp from hook, insert hook in third ch of ch-3, pull dropped lp through ch.
For **popcorn (pc)**, 5 dc in st or ch sp, drop lp from hook, insert hook in top of first dc of group, pull dropped lp through st or ch sp.

COVER
Rnd 1: Ch 6, sl st in first ch to form ring, ch 3, 17 dc in ring, join with sl st in top of ch-3. *(18 dc made)*

Rnd 2: Beg pc *(see Special Stitches)*, ch 3, skip next st, *pc *(see Special Stitches)* in next st, ch 3, skip next st; repeat from * around, join with sl st in top of beg pc. *(9 pc, 9 ch sps)*

Rnd 3: Ch 3, 3 dc in first ch sp, (dc in next pc, 3 dc in next ch sp) around, join with sl st in top of ch-3. *(36 dc)*

Rnd 4: Ch 3, dc in same st as ch 3, dc in next st, (2 dc in next st, dc in next st) around, join. *(54)*

Rnds 5–6: Repeat rnds 2–3. *(108)*

Rnd 7: Ch 3, dc in next 7 sts, 2 dc in next st, (dc in next 8 sts, 2 dc in next st) around, join. *(120)*

Rnd 8: Working this rnd in **back lps** *(see Stitch Guide)*, ch 4, skip next st, (dc in next st, ch 1, skip next st) around, join with sl st in third ch of ch-4. *(60 dc, 60 ch sps)*

Rnd 9: Sl st in first ch sp, ch 1, sc in same ch sp, ch 5, (sc in next ch sp, ch 5) around, join with sl st in first sc. Fasten off.

Weave ribbon through sts of rnd 8. Pull ends of ribbon to fit lid, tie in bow. ❏❏

Hat Pincushion

Note: Work in continuous rnds; do not join or turn unless otherwise stated. Mark first st of each rnd.

HAT

Rnd 1: With white, ch 2, 6 sc in second ch from hook. *(6 sc)*

Rnd 2: 2 sc in each st around. *(12)*

Rnd 3: (Sc in next st, 2 sc in next st) around. *(18)*

Rnd 4: (Sc in each of next 2 sts, 2 sc in next st) around. *(24)*

Rnd 5: (Sc in each of next 3 sts, 2 sc in next st) around. *(30)*

Rnd 6: (Sc in next 4 sts, 2 sc in next st) around. *(36)*

Rnd 7: (Sc in next 5 sts, 2 sc in next st) around. *(42)*

Rnd 8: (Sc in next 6 sts, 2 sc in next st) around. *(48)*

Rnd 9: (Sc in next 7 sts, 2 sc in next st) around. *(54)*

Rnd 10: (Sc in next 8 sts, 2 sc in next st) around. *(60)*

Rnd 11: (Sc in next 9 sts, 2 sc in next st) around. *(66)*

Rnd 12: (Sc in next 10 sts, 2 sc in next st) around. *(72)*

Rnd 13: (Sc in next 11 sts, 2 sc in next st) around. *(78)*

Rnd 14: (Sc in next 38 sts, 2 sc in next st) around. *(80)*

Rnds 15–24: Sc in each st around. At end of last rnd, join with sl st in first sc.

Rnd 25: Ch 3, dc in each st around, join with sl st in top of ch-3.

Rnd 26: Ch 1, sc in each st around, join with sl st in first sc.

Rnd 27: Working this rnd in **front lps** *(see Stitch Guide)*, ch 3, dc in same st as ch-3, (*dc in next 5 sts, 2 dc in next st, ch 3, skip next st*, 2 dc in next st) 9 times; repeat between first and second *, join with sl st in top of ch-3. *(90 dc, 10 ch sps)*

Rnd 28: Sl st in next st, ch 3, *[dc in next 6 sts, ch 3, skip next st, (dc, ch 2, dc) in next ch sp, ch 3, skip next st], dc in next st; repeat from * 8 more times; repeat between [ ], join.

Rnd 29: Sl st in next st, ch 3, *[dc in next 4 sts, ch 3, skip next st and next ch sp, (2 dc, ch 3, 2 dc) in next ch sp, ch 3, skip next ch sp and next st], dc in next st; repeat from * 8 more times; repeat between [ ], join.

Rnd 30: Sl st in next st, ch 3, (*dc in each of next 2 sts, ch 3, skip next st and next ch sp, 10 tr in next ch sp, ch 3, skip next ch sp and next st*, dc in next st) 9 times; repeat between first and second *, join.

Rnd 31: Sl st in next st, ch 6, skip next st and next ch sp, *[dc in next tr, (ch 1, dc in next tr) 9 times, ch 3, skip next ch sp and next st], dc in next st, ch 3, skip next st and next ch sp; repeat from * 8 more times; repeat between [ ], join with sl st in third ch of ch-6.

Rnd 32: Sl st in next ch sp, ch 1, sc in same ch sp, ch 3, (sc in next ch sp, ch 3) around, join with sl st in first sc. Fasten off.

BASE

Rnd 1: With white, ch 4, 19 dc in fourth ch from hook, join with sl st in top of ch-3. *(20 dc made)*

Rnd 2: Ch 3, dc in same st as ch 3, 2 dc in each st around, join. *(40)*

Rnd 3: Ch 3, dc in each of next 2 sts, 2 dc in next st, (dc in each of next 3 sts, 2 dc in next st) around, join. *(50)*

Rnd 4: Ch 3, dc in each of next 3 sts, 2 dc in next st, (dc in next 4 sts, 2 dc in next st) around, join. *(60)*

Rnd 5: Ch 3, dc in next 4 sts, 2 dc in next st, (dc in next 5 sts, 2 dc in next st) around, join. *(70)*

Rnd 6: Ch 3, dc in next 5 sts, 2 dc in next st, (dc in next 6 sts, 2 dc in next st) around, join. *(80)* Fasten off.

Matching sts, sew rnd 6 of Base to **back lps** of rnd 26 on Hat, stuffing before closing.

FLOWER (make 2 of each flower color)

Ch 4, sl st in first ch to form ring, ch 1, (sc, 2 dc, ch 3) 5 times in ring, join with sl st in first sc. Fasten off.

Insert glass head pin through center of Flower and into Pincushion.

Tie ribbon in bow around crown of Hat. ❏❏

Flower Coasters

Note: Work in **back lps** *(see Stitch Guide)* throughout pattern unless otherwise stated.

HAT (make 1 each red, white and blue)
Brim

Rnd 1: Ch 6, sl st in first ch to form ring, ch 3, 19 dc in ring, join with sl st in top of ch-3. *(20 dc made)*

Rnds 2–3: Ch 3, 2 dc in next st, (dc in next st, 2 dc in next st) around, join. *(30, 45)*

Rnd 4: Ch 3, dc in same st as ch-3, dc in each of next 2 sts, (dc in next st, dc in each of next 2 sts) around, join. *(60)*

Rnd 5: Ch 3, dc in same st, dc in each of next 3 sts, (2 dc in next st, dc in each of next 3 sts) around, join. *(75)*

Rnd 6: Ch 3, dc in same st, dc in next 4 sts, (2 dc in next st, dc in next 4 sts) around, join. *(90)*

Continued on page 138

Fancy
Florals

Rnd 7: Ch 3, dc in same st, dc in next 5 sts, (2 dc in next st, dc in next 5 sts) around, join. *(105)*

Rnd 8: Ch 3, dc in same st, dc in next 6 sts, (2 dc in next st, dc in next 6 sts) around, join. *(120)*

Rnd 9: Ch 3, dc in same st, dc in next 7 sts, (2 dc in next st, dc in next 7 sts) around, join. *(135)*

Rnd 10: Ch 3, dc in same st, dc in next 8 sts, (2 dc in next st, dc in next 8 sts) around, join. *(150)*

Rnd 11: Ch 3, dc in same st, dc in next 9 sts, (2 dc in next st, dc in next 9 sts) around, join. *(165)*

Rnd 12: Ch 3, dc in same st, dc in next 10 sts, (2 dc in next st, dc in next 10 sts) around, join. *(180)*

Rnd 13: Ch 1, sc in first st, (ch 6, skip next 3 sts, sc in next st) around to last 3 sts, ch 3, skip last 3 sts, join with dc in first sc.

Rnds 14–15: Ch 1, sc in first ch sp, (ch 6, sc in next ch sp) around, ch 3, join with dc in first sc. At end of last rnd, fasten off.

Crown

Rnd 1: With last rnd facing you, working in **front lps** of rnd 7, join with sl st in first st, ch 3, dc in each st around, join with sl st in top of ch-3. *(105 dc made)*

Rnd 2: Ch 3, dc in each st around, join.

Rnd 3: Ch 3, dc in same st, dc in next 6 sts, (2 dc in next st, dc in next 6 sts) around, join. *(120)*

Rnds 4–5: Ch 3, dc in each st around, join. At end of last rnd, fasten off.

Matching sts, sew rnd 5 of Crown to **front lps** of rnd 8 on Brim, stuffing before closing.

FLOWER (make 4 shaded pinks, 2 red, 2 blue, 2 white, 2 shaded blues)

Rnd 1: Ch 8, sl st in first ch to form ring, ch 1, 14 sc in ring, join with sl st in first sc. *(14 sc made)*

Rnd 2: Ch 1, sc in first st; for **petal**, ch 2, (sc, dc, 3 tr, dc, sc) in second ch from hook *(petal made),* sc in same st, petal, (sc in next st, petal, sc in same st, petal) around, join. Fasten off.

LEAF (make 15)

With shaded greens, ch 2, sc in second ch from hook, (ch 12, sc in same ch) 4 times. Fasten off.

FINISHING

Sew two red and two shaded blue Flowers and five Leaves to one side of Brim on blue Hat.

Sew two white and two shaded pink Flowers and five Leaves to one side of Brim on red Hat.

Sew two blue and two shaded pink flowers and five Leaves to one side of Brim on white Hat. ⌐⌐

Star Pillow

Pattern instructions on page 135

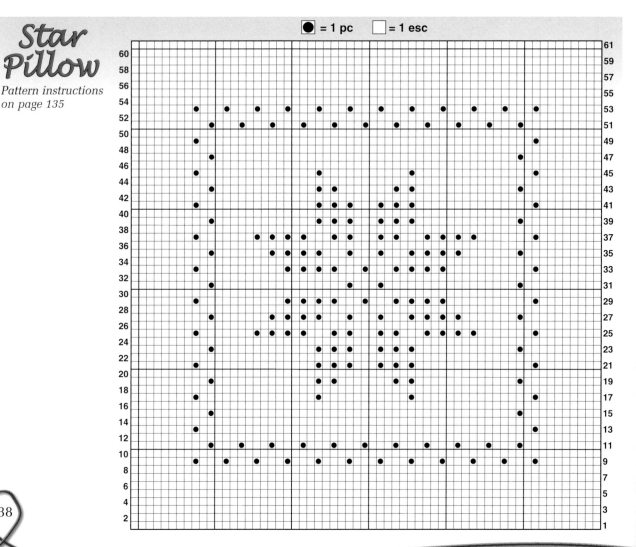

Fashion Favorites

Though sometimes overshadowed by other modes of clothing design such as sewing or knitting, crochet is a serious contender in the sphere of stylish wearables. Tailor-made for wardrobe aesthetics, thread crochet here exhibits its tasteful presence in a sophisticated beaded purse, a sensational jacket, a delicate ruffled dress or an ornate collar and filigree necklace that echo vintage looks. No matter what look is in vogue, crochet is always chic.

Beaded Clutch

Designed by Alma Shields

Finished Size: 5½" × 7¾"

Materials:
- ❑ 240 yds. size 20 crochet cotton thread
- ❑ White sewing thread
- ❑ 10 packages white pearl seed beads
- ❑ 18" × 30" piece white satin fabric
- ❑ 9" × 15" piece heavyweight interfacing
- ❑ 1 white ⁷⁄₁₆" shank button
- ❑ Beading and sewing needles
- ❑ No. 9 steel hook or hook needed to obtain gauge

Gauge: Rnds 1–2 = 1" across.

Basic Stitches: Ch, sl st, sc, hdc, dc.

Special Stitches:
For **bead ch (bch)**, pull up bead to hook, ch around bead.
For **bead sc (bsc)**, insert hook in st or ch sp, yo, pull lp through st or ch sp, pull up bead, complete as sc.
For **bead hdc (bhdc)**, yo, insert hook in st or ch sp, yo, pull lp through st or ch sp, pull up bead, complete as hdc.
For **bead dc (bdc)**, yo, insert hook in st or ch sp, yo, pull lp through st or ch sp, (pull up bead, yo, pull through 2 lps on hook) 2 times.
For **bead reverse popcorn (brpc)**, 3 bdc in st or ch sp, drop lp from hook, insert hook from back to front in top of first dc of group, pull dropped lp through st.

Note: *Back side of sts is right side of work.*

FIRST ROW
Motif No. 1
NOTE: *For each motif, thread 296 beads onto crochet cotton, push back along thread as you work until needed.*
Rnd 1: Ch 6, sl st in first ch to form ring, bch 2 times, ch 1, 15 bdc in ring, join with sl st in ch-1. *(16 bdc)*
Rnd 2: Ch 5, sc in next st, ch 2, (dc in next st, ch 2, sc in next st, ch 2) around, join with sl st in third ch of ch-5. *(8 dc, 8 sc)*
Rnd 3: Ch 1, sc in first st, ch 7, skip next 2 ch sps, (sc in next st, ch 7, skip next 2 ch sps) around, join with sl st in first sc. *(8 ch sps)*
Rnd 4: Ch 1; for **petals,** *(bsc, bhdc, 7 bdc, bhdc, bsc) in each ch sp around, join.
Rnd 5: Sl st in each of first 3 sts, ch 1, (sc in next st, ch 3, skip next st, sc in next st, ch 7, skip next 8 sts) around, join.
Rnd 6: (Sl st, ch 1, sc) in next ch-3 sp, *[ch 4, (brpc, ch 4) 3 times in next ch-7 sp, sc in next ch-3 sp, ch 4, (sc, ch 4, sc) in next ch-7 sp, ch 4], sc in next ch-3 sp; repeat from * 2 more times; repeat between [ ], join.
Rnd 7: (Sl st, ch 1, sc) in first ch sp, *[ch 4, brpc in next ch sp, ch 9, brpc in next ch sp, ch 4, sc in next ch sp], (ch 5, sc in next ch sp) 4 times; repeat from * 2 more times; repeat between [ ], (ch 5, sc in next ch sp) 3 times, ch 5, join. Fasten off.

Motif No. 2
Rnds 1–6: Repeat rnds 1–6 of Motif No. 1
Rnd 7: (Sl st, ch 1, sc) in first ch sp, ch 4, brpc in next ch sp; working on side of last Motif made, ch 4, sl st

in first marked ch-9 sp according to X's on joining diagram below, ch 4, brpc in next ch sp on this motif, ch 4, sc in next ch sp, (ch 2, sl st in next marked ch sp on last motif, ch 2, sc in next ch sp on this motif) 4 times, ch 4, brpc in next ch sp, ch 4, sl st in next marked ch-9 sp on last motif, ch 4, brpc in next ch sp on this motif, *ch 4, sc in next ch sp, (ch 5, sc in next ch sp) 4 times, ch 4, brpc in next ch sp, ch 9, brpc in next ch sp; repeat from *, (ch 5, sc in next ch sp) 3 times, ch 5, join. Fasten off.
Repeat Motif No. 2 one time.

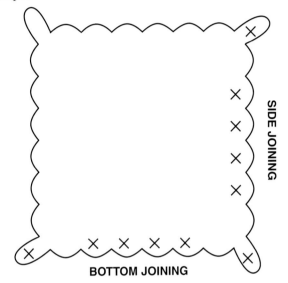

SIDE JOINING

BOTTOM JOINING

SECOND ROW
Motif No. 1
Working on bottom of Motif No. 1 of last Row *(see diagram)*, repeat Motif No. 2 of First Row.

Motif No. 2
Rnds 1–6: Repeat rnds 1–6 of Motif No. 1 on First Row.
Rnd 7: (Sl st, ch 1, sc) in first ch sp, *ch 4, brpc in next ch sp; working on bottom of next Motif on last Row, ch 4, sl st in next marked ch-9 sp, ch 4, brpc in next ch sp on this Motif, ch 4, sc in next ch sp, (ch 2, sl st in next marked ch sp on other Motif, ch 2, sc in next ch sp on this Motif) 4 times; working on side of last Motif on this Row, repeat from *, [ch 4, brpc in next ch sp, ch 9, brpc in next ch sp, ch 4, sc in next ch sp], (ch 5, sc in next ch sp) 4 times; repeat between [ ]. (ch 5, sc in next ch sp) 3 times, ch 5, join. Fasten off.
Repeat Motif No. 2 one time.

THIRD & FOURTH ROWS
Work Motifs same as Second Row.

FIFTH ROW
Center Motif
Working on bottom of second Motif on Fourth Row, repeat Motif No. 2 of First Row.

Half Motif
NOTE: *For each Half Motif, thread 144 beads onto crochet cotton.*
Row 1: For **first Half Motif,** for **outside edge,** ch 21; for **ring,** sl st in fifth ch from hook; ch 16. Fasten off.

Continued on page 145

141

Finished Size: Filigree design is 8½" long. Rose is 1¾" across, Large Violet is 1" across, Small Violet is ¾" across.

Materials:
- ❏ 150 yds. white size 10 crochet cotton thread
- ❏ One pair earring posts or clips
- ❏ Craft glue
- ❏ Tracing paper
- ❏ Tapestry needle
- ❏ No. 7 steel hook or hook needed to obtain gauge

Gauge: 10 sts = 1". Dc is ⅜" tall; tr is ½" tall.

Basic Stitches: Ch, sl st, sc, hdc, dc, tr.

NECKLACE
Right Bottom Scroll

Row 1: For **shaping cord,** cut two strands crochet cotton each 20" long; holding both strands together as you  work, beginning at center of cord, work 40 sc around shaping cord *(see illustration)*, turn. **Do not** cut excess ends from cord; they will be used again later.

Row 2: Ch 2, sc in next st, (ch 1, skip next st, sc in next st) 18 times, ch 1, skip next st, sl st in last st, turn. *(19 sc, 1 sl st, 20 ch lps made)*

Row 3: Ch 1, sc in first ch sp, (ch 1, skip next st, sc in next ch sp) 6 times, ch 2, skip next st, hdc in next ch sp, (ch 2, skip next st, dc in next ch sp) 3 times, (ch 3, skip next st, tr in next ch sp) 8 times, (ch 2, dc) 3 times in ch-2 sp at end of row 2, ch 2, sl st in side of sc at end of row 1, turn. *(23 sts, 22 ch sps)*

Row 4: Hold shaping cord behind sts and ch sps at top of last row; covering cord as you work, 4 sc in each of first 4 ch sps, 5 sc in each of next 8 ch sps, 4 sc in each of next 4 ch sps, 3 sc in each of next 6 ch sps, 2 sc in ch-1 sp at end of row 3, 2 sc around shaping cord, join with sl st in end of row 1. Fasten off. **Do not** cut shaping cord. Front of row 4 is right side of work. *(94 sc)*

Trace and cut pattern piece for Right Bottom Scroll. Place Scroll with right side up on pattern piece. Pull cord at end of row 1 to shape inner curve, pull cord at end of row 4 to shape outer curve if needed. Secure ends. Cut excess cord.

Left Bottom Scroll

Rows 1–3: Repeat rows 1–3 of Right Bottom Scroll. At end of last row, **do not turn.** Fasten off.

Row 4: Hold shaping cord behind sts and ch lps at top of last row; covering cord as you work, join with sl st in end of row 1, 2 sc around shaping cord, 2 sc in ch-1 sp at end of row 3, 3 sc in each of next 6 ch sps, 4 sc in each of next 4 ch sps, 5 sc in each of next 8 ch sps, 4 sc in each of last 4 ch sps, join with sl st in end of row 1. Fasten off. **Do not** cut shaping cord. Front of row 4 is right side of work. *(94 sc)*

Trace and cut pattern piece for Left Bottom Scroll. Shape same as Right Bottom Scroll.

Side Scroll (make 2)

Row 1: For shaping cord, cut two strands crochet cotton each 30" long; holding both strands together as you work beginning at center of cord, work 117 sc around shaping cord, turn. **Do not** cut excess ends from cord; they will be used again later.

Row 2: Working this row in **back lps** *(see Stitch Guide),* sl st in first st, sc in each st across leaving last st unworked, turn. Fasten off. *(115 sc, 1 sl st made)*

Continued on page 144

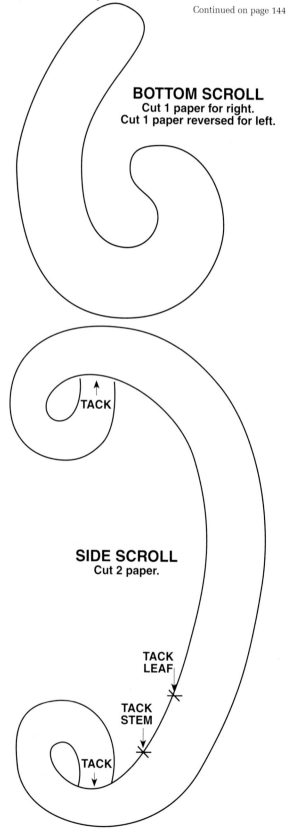

BOTTOM SCROLL
Cut 1 paper for right.
Cut 1 paper reversed for left.

TACK

SIDE SCROLL
Cut 2 paper.

TACK
LEAF

TACK
STEM

TACK

Fashion Favorites

Irish Filigree

An Original by Annie™

Row 3: Skip first 27 sc, join with sl st in next st, ch 3, skip next 2 sts, (dc in next st, ch 2, skip next 2 sts) 18 times, dc in next st, ch 3, skip next 2 sts, sl st in next st leaving last 27 sc unworked, turn. Fasten off.

Row 4: Hold shaping cord behind sts and ch lps at top of rows 2 and 3; covering cord as you work, join with sc in sl st at end of row 2, sc in same st, sc in next 27 sts, sc in next sl st, 4 sc in next ch sp, 3 sc in each of next 18 ch sps, 4 sc in last ch sp, sc in next sl st, sc in each st across with 2 sc in last st. Fasten off. **Do not** cut shaping cord. Front of row 4 is right side of work. *(121 sc)*

Trace and cut pattern pieces for Side Scrolls. Place each Scroll right side up on pattern pieces. Shape in same manner as Bottom Scrolls. Tack ends of Scrolls in place according to pattern piece.

Rose (make 2)

Rnd 1: Make **slip ring** *(see Stitch Guide)*, ch 3, 9 dc in ring, pull end tightly to close ring, join with sl st in top of ch-3. *(10 dc made)*

Rnd 2: Ch 1, sc in each st around, join with sl st in first sc.

Rnd 3: Ch 3, skip next st, (sc in next st, ch 2, skip next st) around, sc in joining sl st of rnd 2 *(5 ch sps).*

Rnd 4: For **petals,** (sl st, ch 2, 4 dc, ch 2, sl st) in each ch sp around. *(5 petals)*

Rnd 5: Working behind petals, ch 1, (sc in **back lp** of next skipped sc on rnd 2, ch 4) around, join with sl st in first sc. *(5 ch sps)*

Rnd 6: For **petals,** (sl st, ch 2, 7 dc, ch 2, sl st) in each ch sp around. *(5 petals)*

Rnd 7: Ch 2; *working behind next petal between 2 center dc *(see illustration),* sc around ch sp, ch 5; repeat from * around, join with sl st in first sc. *(5 ch sps)*

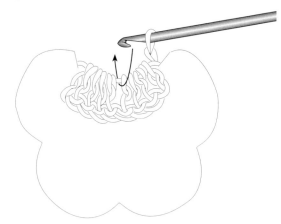

Rnd 8: For **petals,** (sl st, ch 2, 10 dc, ch 2, sl st) in each ch sp around. Fasten off.

Rose Leaf Spray (make 2)

Beginning at bottom of stem, ch 16, **do not fasten off.**

Row 1: For **first leaf,** 6 tr in fifth ch from hook, turn. *(7 tr made)*

Row 2: Ch 3, (dc next 2 sts tog) 2 times, dc in next st leaving last st unworked, turn. *(4 dc)*

Row 3: Ch 1, skip first st, sc next 2 sts tog

leaving last st unworked, **do not turn;** for **tip of leaf,** ch 3, sc in third ch from hook; working down side of leaf, ch 1, sl st in top of st at end of row 2, ch 2, sl st in top of st at end of row 1, ch 4, sl st in same ch as 6 tr of row 1, **do not turn or fasten off.**

For second leaf, ch 9, repeat rows 1–3 of first leaf; sc in next 4 ch below second leaf, **do not fasten off.**

For third leaf, ch 5, repeat rows 1–3 of first leaf; sc in each ch across stem. Fasten off.

Sew stem to back of rose with leaves extended past last rnd of petals.

Bud & Leaf Spray (make 2)

Beginning at bottom of stem, ch 13; for **first leaf,** sc in second ch from hook, hdc in next ch, dc in each of next 3 chs, hdc in next ch, sc in next ch, ch 9; for **second leaf,** sc in second ch from hook, hdc in next ch, dc in each of next 2 chs, hdc in next ch, sc in next ch; for **bud,** ch 8, bend ch-8 lp into small circle, sl st in first ch of ch-8 *(see illustration);* working in ch-8 lp just made (sc, hdc, 2 dc, 2 tr, ch 3), sl st in front lp and left bar at top of last tr made *(see Stitch Guide),* (2 tr, 2 dc, hdc, sc) in remainder of lp, sl st in last ch of ch-8 lp, ch 7; for **third leaf,** sc in second ch from hook, hdc in next ch, dc in each of next 2 chs, hdc in next ch, sc in next ch, sl st in side of sc on second leaf, sc in each of next 2 chs between second and first leaf, sl st in side of sc on first leaf, ch 8; for **fourth leaf,** sc in second ch from hook, hdc in next ch, dc in each of next 3 chs, hdc in next ch, sc in next ch; sc in each ch across stem. Fasten off.

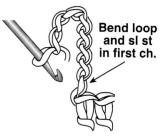

Bend loop and sl st in first ch.

Large Violet (make 7)

Rnd 1: Ch 2, 5 sc in second ch from hook. *(5 sc made)*

Rnd 2: (Sl st, ch 3, 2 tr, ch 3, sl st) in each st around. Fasten off.

Small Violet (make 4)

Rnd 1: Ch 2, 5 sc in second ch from hook. *(5 sc made)*

Rnd 2: (Sl st, ch 2, 2 dc, ch 2, sl st) in each st around. Fasten off.

Single Leaf

Row 1: Beginning at bottom of stem, ch 25, 4 tr in fifth ch from hook, turn. *(5 tr made)*

Row 2: Ch 3, dc next 2 sts tog, dc in next st leaving last st unworked, turn. *(3 dc)*

Row 3: Ch 3, sc in third ch from hook, skip first dc, sc in next dc leaving last st unworked **do not turn;** working down side of leaf, ch 2, sl st in base of st at end of row 2, ch 4, sl st in same ch as 4 tr on row 1, sl st in each ch across stem. Fasten off.

Assembly

Tack narrow end of each Bottom Scroll to each Side Scroll according to Diagram No. 1. Tack edges of bottom scrolls together where they meet according to diagram.

Tack end of stem and back of one bottom leaf on each

Bud & Leaf Spray to inner edge of each Side Scroll. Tack end of stem on Single Leaf to back side at top of left-hand Side Scroll. Tack center back of each flower to Side and Bottom Scrolls according to Diagram No. 2.

EARRING (make 2)
Flower
Work same as Small Violet of Necklace. Glue center back of Flower to earring post. ❑❒

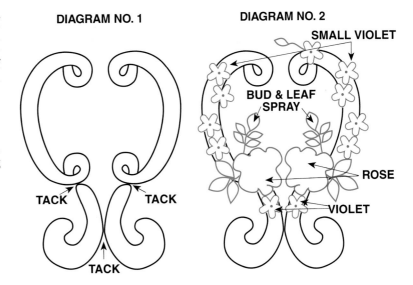

DIAGRAM NO. 1

TACK TACK

TACK

DIAGRAM NO. 2

SMALL VIOLET

BUD & LEAF SPRAY

ROSE

VIOLET

Beaded Clutch
Continued from page 141

Row 2: Join with sl st in 13th ch of starting ch, 7 bdc in ring, skip next 3 chs of ch-16, sl st in next ch, turn. *(7 bdc)*

Row 3: Ch 2, sc in first dc, (ch 2, dc in next st, ch 2, sc in next st) across, ch 2, skip next 2 chs of starting ch, sl st in next ch, turn. *(4 sc, 3 dc)*

Row 4: (Ch 7, skip next sc, sc in next dc) 3 times, ch 7, skip next sc, sl st in next ch, **do not turn.** Fasten off. *(4 ch sps)*

Row 5: Join with sl st in 11th ch of starting ch; for **petals,** (bsc, bhdc, 7 bdc, bhdc, bsc) in each ch sp across; skip next 2 chs, sl st in next ch, turn.

Row 6: Ch 4, skip first 4 sts, (sc in next st, ch 3, skip next st, sc in next st, ch 7, skip next 8 sts) 3 times, sc in next st, ch 3, skip next st, sc in next st, ch 4, skip last 4 sts and next 2 chs, sl st in each of next 3 chs, turn.

Row 7: (Bdc, ch 4, brpc) in first ch sp, ch 4, *sc in next ch-3 sp, ch 4, (sc, ch 4, sc) in next ch-7 sp, ch 4, sc in next ch-3 sp, ch 4*, (brpc, ch 4) 3 times in next ch-7 sp; repeat between first *, (brpc, ch 4, bdc) in last ch sp, skip next ch, sl st in next ch, **do not turn.** Fasten off.

Row 8: Join with sl st in first ch, sl st in bottom left-hand ch-9 sp on Center Motif, ch 4, brpc in first ch sp on this Motif, *ch 4, sc in next ch sp, (ch 2, sl st in next marked ch sp on other Motif, ch 2, sc in next ch sp on this Motif) 4 times, ch 4, brpc in next ch sp, ch 4, sl st in next marked ch-9 sp on other Motif,* ch 4, brpc in next ch sp on this Motif; working in Motif on row above, repeat between first *, sl st in last ch on this Motif. Fasten off.

For **second Half Motif,** working on third Motif on Fourth Row and opposite side of Center Motif, repeat first Half Motif.

EDGING

Rnd 1: Working around outer edge, evenly space 28 sc across first Half Motif, ch 2, 4 sc in each ch sp across Center Motif, ch 2, evenly space 28 sc across second Half Motif, ch 2, 4 sc in each ch sp around with (4 sc, ch 2, 4 sc) in each corner ch-9 sp, ch 2, join with sl st in first sc.

Rnd 2: Ch 1, sc in first 4 sts, (ch 4, sc in next 4 sts) 6 times, ch 4, 4 sc in next ch sp, ch 4, (sc in next 4 sts, ch 4) 3 times, ch 4, sc in each of next 2 sts; for **button loop,** ch 8, skip next 4 sts, sl st in next st, **turn,** ch 1, 10 sc in ch-8 lp, sl st in next st, **turn,** sl st in next 10 sts, sc in next sl st, sc in next st, (ch 4, sc in next 4 sts) 3 times, ch 4, 4 sc in next ch sp, (ch 4, sc in next 4 sts) 7 times, ch 4, 4 sc in next ch sp, sc in each st around with (2 sc, ch 2, 2 sc) in each corner ch sp, 4 sc in last ch-2 sp, ch 4, join. Fasten off.

FINISHING

For lining, using crocheted piece as pattern, from fabric and interfacing, cut two pieces ¼" larger around outer edge. Baste one piece interfacing to wrong side of each fabric piece. Allowing ¼" for seam, sew fabric right sides together leaving one short end open for turning. Clip corners. Turn. Sew opening closed. Press.

Sew lining to wrong side of purse.

With lining inside, fold First and Second Rows down over Third and Fourth Rows; working through both thicknesses, matching sts, join with sl st in first st at fold, sl st in each st across side leaving sts on Fifth Row unworked. Fasten off.

Repeat on other side.

Fold Fifth Row down. Sew bottom to purse below button loop. ❑❒

145

Dress & Gloves Ensemble

DRESS

Finished Sizes: Size 2 fits 20"-22" chest; size 4 fits 23"-25" chest.

Materials:
- ❏ Size 10 crochet cotton thread:
  - 1,575 yds. peach
  - 150 yds. white
- ❏ 2 small pearl buttons
- ❏ Embroidery needle
- ❏ No. 9 steel hook or hook needed to obtain gauge

Gauge: 9 sts = 1"; 3 dc and 3 sc rows = 1".

Note: Instructions are for size 2; changes for size 4 are in [ ].

SKIRT
First Ruffle
Foundation: With peach, ch 216 [240] *(make foundation chain loosely to prevent pulling),* sl st in first ch to form ring.

Rnd 1: Ch 3, dc in each ch around, join with sl st in top of ch-3. *(216 dc made)* [240 dc made]

Rnd 2: (Ch 5, skip next 2 dc, sc in next st) around, join with sl st in first ch of first ch-5. *(80 ch sps)*

Rnds 3–8: Sl st to center of first ch sp on previous rnd, (ch 5, sc in next loop) around, join. At end of last rnd, fasten off.

Rnd 9: Join white with sc in any ch sp on last rnd, *ch 5, sc in fourth ch from hook, ch 1, sc in next ch sp; repeat from * around, join with sl st in first sc. Fasten off.

Second Ruffle
Foundation: With peach, ch 225 [250], sl st in first ch to form ring.

Rnd 1: Ch 3, dc in each ch around, join with sl st in top of ch-3. *(225 dc made)* [250 dc made]

Rnds 2–4: Ch 3, dc in each st around, join.

Rnd 5: Ch 3, [dc in next st], (2 dc in next st, dc in next 28 [31] sts) around, join. *(233)* [258]

Rnd 6: Repeat rnd 2.

Rnd 7: (Ch 5, skip next 2 dc, sc in next dc) around, join with sl st in first ch of first ch-5.

Rnds 8–13: Sl st to center of first ch sp on previous rnd, (ch 5, sc in next loop) around, ch 5, join. At end of last rnd, fasten off.

Rnd 14: Join white with sc in any ch sp on last rnd, *ch 5, sc in fourth ch from hook, ch 1, sc in next ch sp; repeat from * around, join with sl st in first sc. Fasten off.

Remaining Ruffles
For each Ruffle *(make 5),* adding 9 chs to starting chain, repeat Second Ruffle *(make more Ruffles if additional length is desired on Skirt).*

Arrange Ruffles *(see photo),* having the smallest at the top and largest at bottom.

To join Ruffles, starting with bottom Ruffle, sew the edge of the foundation to the wrong side of the last dc rnd on Ruffle above.

BODICE
Lower Back
With right side of work towards you, work along other side of ch as follows:

Row 1: Working in remaining lps of foundation on First Ruffle, join peach with sc in first st, *ch 5, skip next 2 sts, sc in next st; repeat from * until 36 [40] ch sps have been made, turn.

Row 2: Sl st across to center ch of first ch sp, sc in same ch sp, (ch 2, sc in next ch sp) across, turn. *(35 ch sps)* [39 ch sps]

Row 3: Ch 3, dc in each ch and in each sc across, turn. *(106 dc)* [118 dc].

Row 4: Ch 1, sc in each st across, turn.

Row 5: Ch 3, dc in each st across, turn.

Rows 6–8: Repeat rows 4 and 5 alternately, ending with row 4.

Row 9: Ch 1, sc in first st, (ch 5, skip next 2 sts, sc in next st) across, turn.

Row 10: Sl st across to center ch of first ch sp, sc in same ch sp, (ch 2, sc in next ch sp) across, turn. *(34 ch sps)* [38 ch sps]

Row 11: For **armhole shaping,** sl st across first 3 ch-2 sps; for **first upper back,** ch 3, dc in each sc and in each ch across to middle of last row leaving remaining sts and chs unworked, turn. *(43 dc)* [49 dc]

Row 12: Ch 1, sc in each st across to last 3 sts, skip last 3 sts, turn. *(40 sc)* [46 sc]

Row 13: Ch 3, dc in each st across, turn.

Row 14: Ch 1, sc in each st across, turn.

Repeat rows 13 and 14 alternately until piece measures 3¼" up from armhole shaping, ending with row 13 at center back edge of piece. **Do not fasten off.**

First Shoulder
Row 1: Ch 1, sc in each st across leaving last 6 sts unworked, turn.

Row 2: Sl st in first 6 sts, ch 3, dc in each st across, turn.

Row 3: Sl st in first 18 sts, ch 1, sc in each st across leaving last 3 [6] sts unworked, turn.

Row 4: Sl st in first 3 sts, ch 3, dc in next 4 [7] sts. Fasten off.

Second Upper Back
Row 11: Join peach with sl st in next unworked st of row 10 on Lower Back, ch 3, dc in each st and in each ch across leaving last 3 sts unworked for **armhole shaping,** turn.

Row 12: Sl st in first 3 sts, ch 1, sc in each st across, turn.

Row 13: Ch 3, dc in each st across, turn.

Row 14: Ch 1, sc in each st across, turn.

Repeat rows 13 and 14 alternately until piece measures 3¼" up from armhole shaping, ending with row 13. **Do not fasten off.**

Second Shoulder
Row 1: Sl st in first 6 sts, ch 1, sc in each st across, turn.

Row 2: Ch 3, dc in each st across leaving last 6 sts unworked, turn.

Row 3: Sl st in first 3 [6] sts, ch 1, sc in each st across leaving last 18 sts unworked, turn.

Row 4: Ch 3, dc in next 4 [7] sts leaving last 3 sts unworked. Fasten off.

Front
With right side of work towards you, work along other side of ch as follows:

Row 1: Working in remaining lps of foundation on First Ruffle, join peach with sc in same st

Continued on page 148

147

Dress & Gloves Ensemble

Continued from page 147

as last sc on row 1 of Back, *ch 5, skip next 2 sts, sc in next st; repeat from * until 36 [40] ch sps have been made, sl st in ch-1 at beginning of row 1 on Back, turn.

Row 2: Sl st across to center ch of first ch sp, sc in same ch sp, (ch 2, sc in next ch sp) across, turn. *(35 ch sps) [39 ch sps]*

Row 3: Ch 3, dc in each ch and in each sc across, turn. *(106 dc) [118 dc].*

Row 4: Ch 1, sc in each st across, turn.

Row 5: Ch 3, dc in each st across, turn.

Rows 6–8: Repeat rows 4 and 5 alternately, ending with row 4.

Row 9: Ch 1, sc in first st, (ch 5, skip next 2 sts, sc in next st) across, turn.

Row 10: Sl st across to center ch of first ch sp, sc in same ch sp, (ch 2, sc in next ch sp) across, turn. *(34 ch sps) [38 ch sps]*

Row 11: For **armhole shaping,** sl st across first 3 ch-2 sps, ch 3, dc in each sc and in each ch across leaving last 3 ch sps unworked, turn.

Row 12: Ch 1, sl st in first 3 sts, sc in each st across to last 3 sts, skip last 3 sts, turn.

Row 13: Ch 3, dc in each st across, turn.

Row 14: Ch 1, sc in each st across, turn.

Repeat rows 13 and 14 alternately until piece measures 3" up from armhole shaping, ending with row 14. **Do not fasten off.**

First Neck Shaping
Row 1: Ch 3, dc in next 31 [37] sts leaving remaining sts unworked, turn.

Row 2: Ch 1, skip first 2 sts, sc in each st across, turn.

Row 3: Ch 3, dc in each st across to last st, skip last st, turn.

Rows 4–5: Repeat rows 2 and 3. **Do not fasten off.**

First Shoulder
Row 1: Ch 1, sc in each st across leaving last 6 sts unworked, turn.

Row 2: Sl st in first 6 sts, ch 3, dc in each st across, turn.

Row 3: Sl st in first 18 sts, ch 1, sc in each st across leaving last 3 [6] sts unworked, turn.

Row 4: Sl st in first 3 sts, ch 3, dc in next 4 [7] sts. Fasten off.

Second Neck Shaping
Row 1: Skip next 15 unworked sts past First Neck Shaping, join peach with sl st in next st, ch 3, dc in next 31 [37] sts, turn.

Row 2: Ch 1, sc in each st across leaving last 2 sts unworked, turn.

Row 3: Sl st in first 2 sts, ch 3 dc in each st across, turn.

Rows 4–5: Repeat rows 2 and 3. **Do not fasten off.**

Second Shoulder
Row 1: Sl st in first 6 sts, ch 1, sc in each st across, turn.

Row 2: Ch 3, dc in each st across leaving last 6 sts unworked, turn.

Row 3: Sl st in first 3 [6] sts, ch 1, sc in each st across leaving last 18 sts unworked, turn.

Row 4: Ch 3, dc in next 4 [7] sts leaving last 3 sts unworked. Fasten off.

Sew up side and shoulder seams.

For **button loops,** join peach with sc in end of last row on right back edge of Bodice, ch 3, sc evenly spaced across to middle of edge, ch 3, sc evenly spaced across to bottom of edge. Fasten off.

Sew buttons to correspond on opposite edge.

SLEEVES
Rnd 1: Join peach with sc at center bottom of armhole opening, (ch 5, sc) evenly spaced around armhole *(one loop to each dc row and enough to keep work from pulling along underarm shaping),* **do not join rnds.**

Rnds 2–18: (Ch 5, sc in next ch sp) around. At end of last rnd, ch 5, join with sl st in first sc.

Rnd 19: *Ch 1, sc in next loop; repeat from * around, join.

Rnd 20: Ch 3, dc in each sc around, join with sl st in top of ch-3.

Rnd 21: Ch 1, sc in each dc around, join.

Rnds 22–23: Repeat rnds 20 and 21. At end of last rnd, fasten off.

Repeat on other armhole.

COLLAR
Row 1: Working across neck edge of Bodice, join peach with sc in first st at corner of back opening, (ch 5, sc) evenly spaced across to opposite corner of back opening, turn.

Rows 2–9: (Ch 5, sc in next ch sp) across, turn. At end of last row, fasten off.

Row 10: Join white with sc in first ch sp on last row, *ch 5, sc in fourth ch from hook, ch 1, sc in next ch sp; repeat from * across. Fasten off. ❑❑

DRESS GLOVES

Finished Sizes: **Toddler's small.** Finished measurement: 4½" around open palm between thumb and fingers. **Toddler's large.** Finished measurement: 5" around open palm between thumb and fingers.

Gauge: **For Small—No. 10 steel hook,** 11 mesh = 2", 11 rows = 2". **For Large—No. 9 steel hook,** 5 mesh = 1", 5 rows = 1".

Materials:
- ❑ 120 yds. white size 10 crochet cotton thread
- ❑ 24" of ⅛" ribbon to match dress
- ❑ Large embroidery needle
- ❑ Steel hook stated for size or hook needed to obtain gauge for size

RIGHT GLOVE
Index Finger
Rnd 1: Ch 2, 9 sc in second ch from hook, join with sl st in first sc. *(9 sc made)*

Rnd 2: Ch 3, dc in each st around, join with sl st in top of ch-3.

NOTE: When working into dc, insert hook into center

of st below top three strands (see illustration).

Rnd 3: Ch 4, (dc in next st, ch 1) around, join with sl st in third ch of ch-4.

Rnds 4–9: Or to desired length; ch 4, (dc in next dc, ch 1, skip next ch) around, join. At end of last rnd, fasten off.

Middle Finger

Rnds 1–9: Repeat rnds 1–9 of Index Finger, **do not fasten off.**

Rnd 10: Repeat rnd 4 of Index Finger; to **join fingers,** hold Index Finger in front of Middle Finger with right sides together; working in last rnd on each finger, sl st in fifth dc on Index Finger, sl st in second dc on Middle Finger. Fasten off.

Ring Finger

Rnds 1–9: Repeat rnds 1–9 of Index Finger, **do not fasten off.**

Rnd 10: Repeat rnd 4 of Index Finger; sl st in sixth dc on Middle Finger, sl st in second dc on Ring Finger. Fasten off.

Little Finger

Rnd 1: Ch 2, 8 sc in second ch from hook, join with sl st in first sc. (8 sc made)

Rnds 2–7: Repeat rnds 2–7 of Index Finger. (8 dc) At end of last rnd, **do not fasten off.**

Rnd 8: Repeat rnd 4 of Index Finger; sl st in fifth dc on Ring Finger, sl st in second dc on Little Finger. Fasten off.

Palm

Rnd 1: Join with sl st in fifth unworked dc on Index Finger, ch 4, dc in next dc; for **mesh,** ch 1, skip next ch, dc in next st or ch (mesh made), mesh one more time; *skipping sts used in Finger Joining, ch 1, dc in first unworked dc on next Finger, mesh 2 more times*; repeat between first * 2 more times, mesh around to next joining; repeat between first * 3 more times, mesh, ch 1, join with sl st in third ch of ch-4. (26 mesh)

Rnds 2–4: Ch 4, dc in next dc, mesh around, join. At end of last rnd, **turn.**

Row 5: Working in rows, ch 4, dc in next dc, mesh 20 times leaving last 5 mesh unworked for thumb opening, turn (21 dc).

Row 6: Ch 4, dc in next dc, mesh across, **do not turn.**

Rnd 7: Working in rnds, ch 12; skipping thumb opening, dc in third ch of ch-4, mesh 20 times, ch 1, join with sl st in third ch of ch-12.

Rnd 8: Working in chs and in sts, ch 4, skip next ch, dc in next ch, mesh around, ch 1, join with sl st in third ch of ch-4. (26 mesh)

Rnds 9–12: Ch 4, dc in next dc, mesh around, ch 1, join.

Rnd 13: For **ruffle,** (sl st, ch 3, 2 dc) in first ch sp, 3 dc in each ch sp around, join with sl st in top of ch-3. (78 dc)

Rnd 14: Ch 4, dc in next dc, (ch 1, dc) in each dc around, ch 1, join with sl st in third ch of ch-4.

Rnd 15: Ch 4, dc in next dc, mesh around, ch 1, join.

Rnd 16: Ch 3, dc in each dc and in each ch sp around, join with sl st in top of ch-3. Fasten off.

Thumb

Rnd 1: Working around thumb opening, join with sl st in first unworked dc on rnd 4, ch 4, dc in next dc, (ch 1, dc in next dc) 2 times, *dc in next worked dc; working in tops of sts at ends of rows, (ch 1, dc) in each of next 2 rows, dc in next worked dc*; working on opposite side of ch on rnd 7, (ch 1, skip next ch, dc in next ch) across; repeat between first *, join with sl st in third ch of ch-4. (16 dc)

Rnd 2: Ch 3, dc in next dc, (mesh 2 times, skip next dc) 2 times, mesh 4 times, skip next dc, mesh 2 times, skip next dc, join with sl st in top of ch-3. (12)

Rnd 3: Ch 3, skip next dc, dc in next dc, mesh around to last dc, skip last dc, ch 1, join. (10)

Rnd 4: Sl st in next dc, ch 4, dc in next dc, mesh around, ch 1, join with sl st in third ch of ch-4. (9)

Rnds 5–6: Ch 4, dc in next dc, mesh around, ch 1, join.

Rnd 7: Ch 3; skipping ch sps, dc in each dc around, join with sl st in top of ch-3.

Rnd 8: Ch 1, sc in first st, (sc next 2 sts tog) around. Leaving 8" end for weaving, fasten off. (4 sc)

With embroidery needle, weave 8" end through each st of last rnd; pull tight, secure.

LEFT GLOVE
Index, Middle, Ring & Little Fingers

Work same as Index, Middle, Ring and Little Fingers for Right Glove.

Palm

Rnds 1–4: Repeat rnds 1–4 of Palm for Right Glove. At end of last rnd, **do not turn.**

Rows 5–6: Repeat rows 5–6 of Palm for Right Glove. At end of last row, **turn.**

Rnd 7: Working in rnds, ch 4, dc in next dc, mesh around, ch 9, join with sl st in third ch of ch-4. **Do not turn.**

Rnds 8–16: Repeat rnds 8–16 of Palm for Right Glove.

Thumb

Work same as Thumb for Right Glove.

Cut ribbon in half, weave one piece through rnd 12 of Palm on each Glove, tie in bow at back of hand. ❏❐

Finished Size: Lady's 30" to 38" bust. Finished measurements: 44" bust, 34" long.

Materials:
- ❏ 3,052 yds. gold size 10 crochet cotton thread
- ❏ Bobby pins for markers
- ❏ Embroidery needle
- ❏ No. 4 steel hook or hook needed to obtain gauge

Gauge: Large Motif is 11" across.

Basic Stitches: Ch, sl st, sc, hdc, dc, tr, dtr.

Special Stitches:

For **beginning cluster (beg cl)**, yo 2 times, insert hook in sp or st or ch, yo, pull through, (yo, pull through 2 lps on hook) 2 times, *yo 2 times, insert hook in same sp or st or ch, yo, pull through, (yo, pull through 2 lps on hook) 2 times; repeat from *, yo, pull through all 4 lps on hook.

For **cluster (cl)**, yo 2 times, insert hook in sp or st or ch, yo, pull through, (yo, pull through 2 lps on hook) 2 times, *yo 2 times, insert hook in same sp or st or ch, yo, pull through, (yo, pull through 2 lps on hook) 2 times; repeat from * 2 more times, yo, pull through all 5 lps on hook.

For **V st**, (dc, ch 2, dc) in next st or ch sp.

For **double V st (dV st)**, (dc, ch 2, dc, ch 2, dc) in next ch sp.

For **popcorn (pc)**, 5 dc in next st or sp, drop lp from hook, insert hook in top of first dc of group, pull dropped lp through st, ch 1.

For **beginning shell (beg shell)**, (sl st, ch 3, 2 dc, ch 2, 3 dc) in first st or ch sp.

For **shell**, (3 dc, ch 2, 3 dc) in next st or ch sp.

For **half shell**, (ch 3, 2 dc) in first ch sp or st.

For **end shell**, 3 dc in same ch sp or st as first half shell made.

For **sc joining**, ch 1, join with sc in top of ch-3 on first half shell made.

For **Motif joining**, you will be working into corresponding Motifs; 2 sc in next ch sp after 4-tr group on corresponding Motif, ch 2, sc in next ch sp on this Motif, (ch 2; working on corresponding Motif, sc in next ch sp, ch 2, sc in next ch sp on this Motif) 5 times, ch 2, 2 sc in next ch sp before next 4-tr group on corresponding Motif.

FIRST ROW
First Large Motif
Note: *Use the above instructions for working Special Stitches throughout pattern.*

Rnd 1: Ch 4, sl st in fourth ch from hook to form ring, ch 4, (dc, ch 1) 7 times in ring, join with sl st in third ch of ch-4. *(8 dc, 8 ch sps made)*

Rnd 2: Sl st in first ch sp, ch 3, **beg cl**, *(ch 4, beg cl in fourth ch from hook) 2 times, mark bottom of last beg cl made, cl in next sp; repeat from * 6 more times, ch 4, beg cl in fourth ch from hook, join with **cl** in top of first beg cl made. *(24 cls made)*

Rnd 3: Half shell, (ch 4, skip next cl, **shell** in marked cl, remove marker) 7 times, ch 4, skip last cl, **end shell, sc joining.** *(8 shells)*

Rnd 4: Half shell, (ch 7, skip next ch sp, shell in ch sp of next shell) 7 times, ch 7, skip last ch sp, end shell, sc joining.

Rnd 5: Half shell, *ch 3, **V st** in fourth ch of next ch-7, ch 3, shell in ch sp of next shell; repeat from * 6 more times, ch 3, **V st** in fourth ch of last ch-7, ch 3, end shell, sc joining. *(8 shells, 8 V sts)*

Rnd 6: Half shell, (ch 4, skip next ch sp, V st in ch sp of next V st, ch 4, skip next ch sp, shell in next shell) 7 times, ch 4, skip next ch sp, V st in ch sp of last V st, ch 4, skip last ch sp, end shell, sc joining.

Rnd 7: Half shell, (ch 5, skip next ch sp, V st in ch sp of next V st, ch 5, skip next ch sp, shell in next shell) 7 times, ch 5, skip next ch sp, V st in ch sp of next V st, ch 5, skip last ch sp, end shell, sc joining.

Rnd 8: Half shell, (ch 6, skip next ch sp, V st in ch sp of next V st, ch 6, skip next ch sp, shell in next shell) 7 times, ch 6, skip last ch sp, end shell, sc joining.

Rnd 9: Half shell, *ch 6, skip next ch sp, **dV st** in ch sp of next V st, ch 6, skip next ch sp, shell in next shell; repeat from * 6 more times, ch 6, skip next ch sp, dV st in ch sp of last V st, ch 6, skip last ch sp, end shell, sc joining. *(8 shells, 8 dV sts)*

Rnd 10: Half shell, *ch 6, skip next ch sp, V st in next ch sp of next dV st, ch 3, V st in next ch sp of same dV st, ch 6, skip next ch sp, shell in next shell; repeat from * 6 more times, ch 6, skip next ch sp, V st in next ch sp of next dV st, ch 3, V st in next ch sp of same dV st, ch 6, skip last ch sp, end shell, sc joining. *(8 shells, 16 V sts, 8 ch-3 sps)*

Rnd 11: Half shell, *[ch 6, skip next ch sp, cl in ch sp of next V st, (ch 4, beg cl in fourth ch from hook) 2 times, mark bottom of last beg cl made, cl in next ch-3 sp, (ch 4, beg cl in fourth ch from hook) 2 times, mark bottom of last beg cl made, cl in ch sp of next V st, ch 6, skip next ch sp], shell in next shell; repeat from * 6 more times; repeat between [ ], end shell, sc joining. *(8 shells, 56 cls)*

Rnd 12: Half shell, *[ch 7, skip next ch sp, skip next cl, (sc, ch 3, beg cl) in marked cl, ch 4, beg cl in fourth ch from hook, mark bottom of beg cl, skip next cl, sc in marked cl, ch 7, skip next ch sp], skip next 2 sts on next shell, 3 dc in next st, ch 2, 3 dc in ch sp of same shell, ch 2, 3 dc in next st on same shell; repeat from * 6 more times; repeat between [ ], skip next 2 sts on end shell, 3 dc in last st, ch 2, 3 dc in ch sp of same end shell, sc joining. *(72 dc, 16 cls, 16 ch-2 sps)*

Rnd 13: Half shell in first ch sp, *[ch 7, skip next ch-7 sp, skip next cl, dc in marked cl, remove marker, (ch 3, dc in same cl as last dc made) 3 times, ch 7, skip next ch-7 sp, shell in next ch-2 sp, ch 3], shell in next ch-2 sp; repeat from * 6 more times; repeat between [ ], end shell, sc joining. *(16 shells, 32 ch-3 sps)*

Rnd 14: Half shell, *[ch 5, skip next ch-7 sp, **pc** in next ch-3 sp, (ch 3, pc in next ch-3 sp) 2 times, ch 5, skip next ch-7 sp, shell in ch sp of next shell, ch 3, pc in second ch of next ch-3 sp, ch 3], shell in ch sp of next shell; repeat from * 6 more times; repeat between [ ], end shell, sc joining. *(16 shells, 32 pc, 16 ch-3 sps)*

Rnd 15: Half shell, *[ch 5, skip next ch-5 sp, sc in next ch-3 sp, ch 5, sc in next ch-3 sp, ch 5, skip next ch-5 sp, shell in ch sp of next shell, ch 3, pc in second ch of next ch-3 sp, ch 5, pc in second ch of next ch-3 sp, ch 3], shell in ch sp of next shell; repeat from * 6 more times; repeat between [ ],

Continued on page 152

Lace Motif Jacket

Designed by Ann Parnell

end shell, sc joining. *(16 shells, 16 pc, 16 ch-3 sps)*

Rnd 16: Half shell, *[ch 7, skip next ch-5 sp, sc in next ch-5 sp, ch 7, skip next ch-5 sp, shell in next shell, ch 3, pc in second ch of next ch-3, ch 5, V st in third ch of next ch-5, ch 5, pc in second ch of next ch-3, ch 3], shell in next shell; repeat from * 6 more times; repeat between [ ], end shell, sc joining. *(16 shells, 8 V sts, 16 ch-5 sps)*

Rnd 17: Half shell, *[ch 5, skip next ch-7 sp, V st in next sc, ch 5, skip next ch-7 sp, shell in next shell, ch 3, pc in second ch of next ch-3, ch 2, V st in third ch of next ch-5, ch 2, V st in ch sp of next V st, ch 2, V st in third ch of next ch-5, ch 2, pc in second ch of next ch-3, ch 3], shell in next shell; repeat from * 6 more times; repeat between [ ], end shell, sc joining. *(16 shells, 16 pc, 32 V sts)*

Rnd 18: Half shell, *[ch 3, skip next ch-5 sp, sc in ch sp of next V st, ch 3, skip next ch-5 sp, shell in next shell, ch 3, pc in second ch of next ch-3, (ch 5, skip next ch-2 sp, sc in ch sp of next V st) 3 times, ch 5, skip next ch-2 sp, pc in second ch of next ch-3, ch 3], shell in next shell; repeat from * 6 more times; repeat between [ ], end shell, sc joining. *(16 shells, 16 pc, 64 ch sps)*

Rnd 19: (Ch 4, 3 tr) in first ch sp, skip next ch-3 sp and next sc and next ch-3 sp, *[4 tr in ch sp of next shell, (ch 5, sc in next ch sp) 6 times, ch 5], 4 tr in ch sp of next shell; repeat from * 6 more times; repeat between [ ], join with sl st in top of ch-4. Fasten off. *(16 4-tr groups, 56 ch sps)*

Second Large Motif

Rnds 1–18: Repeat rnds 1–18 of First Large Motif.

Rnd 19: (Ch 4, 3 tr) in first ch sp, skip next ch-3 sp and next sc and next ch-3 sp, 4 tr in ch sp of next shell; working on corresponding Motif *(see Coat Assembly)*, work Motif joining *(see Special Stitches)*, *4 tr in ch sp of next shell on this Motif, skip next ch-3 sp and next sc and next ch-3 sp, 4 tr in ch sp of next shell, (ch 5, sc in next ch sp) 6 times, ch 5; repeat from * 6 more times, join with sl st in fourth ch of ch-4. Fasten off. *(16 4-tr groups, 56 ch sps)*

Next Large Motifs

Work same as Second Large Motif two more times for a total of four Motifs in First Row.

SECOND ROW
First Large Motif

Work same as Second Large Motif of First Row, working Motif joining on First Large Motif on Row below.

Second Large Motif

Rnds 1–18: Repeat rnds 1–18 of First Large Motif of First Row.

Rnd 19: (Ch 4, 3 tr) in first ch sp, skip next ch-3 sp and next sc and next ch-3 sp, 4 tr in ch sp of next shell; working on Second Large Motif of Row below *(see Coat Assembly)*, work Motif joining, *4 tr in ch sp of next shell on this Motif, skip next ch-3 sp and next sc and next ch-3 sp, 4 tr in ch sp of next shell, (ch 5, sc in next ch sp) 6 times, ch 5*, 4 tr in ch sp of next shell, skip next ch-3 sp and next sc and next ch-3 sp, 4 tr in ch sp of next shell; working on corresponding Motif, work Motif joining; repeat between first and second * 5 more times, join with sl st in fourth ch of ch-4. Fasten off. *(16 4-tr groups, 56 ch sps)*

Next Large Motifs

Work same as Second Large Motif two more times for a total of four Motifs in Second Row.

THIRD ROW
First Large Motif

Work same as Second Large Motif of First Row; working

COAT ASSEMBLY

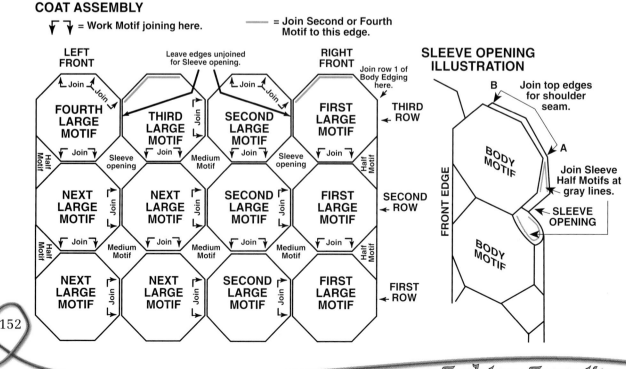

▼▼ = Work Motif joining here.
—— = Join Second or Fourth Motif to this edge.

Fashion Favorites

Motif joining on First Large Motif on Row below.

Second Large Motif
Rnds 1–18: Repeat rnds 1–18 of First Large Motif of First Row.

Rnd 19: (Ch 4, 3 tr) in first ch sp, skip next ch-3 sp and next sc and next ch-3 sp, 4 tr in ch sp of next shell; working on Motif of Row below, work Motif joining, *4 tr in ch sp of next shell on this Motif, skip next ch-3 sp and next sc and next ch-3 sp, 4 tr in ch sp of next shell on this Motif, (ch 5, sc in next ch sp) 6 times, ch 5*; repeat between first and second * one more time, 4 tr in ch sp of next shell, skip next ch-3 sp and next sc and next ch-3 sp, 4 tr in ch sp of next shell; working on corresponding Motif, for **shoulder joining,** work Motif joining between A and B arrows on Sleeve Opening Illustration, 4 tr in ch sp of next shell on this Motif, skip next ch-3 sp and next sc and next ch-3 sp, 4 tr in next ch sp of next shell, work Motif joining; repeat between first and second * 3 more times, join with sl st in fourth ch of ch-4. Fasten off. (16 4-tr groups, 56 ch sps)

Third Large Motif
Work same as Second Large Motif on Second Row.

Fourth Large Motif
Work same as Second Large Motif on Third Row.

MEDIUM MOTIF
Rnd 1: Ch 4, sl st in fourth ch from hook to form ring, ch 4, (dc in ring, ch 1) 7 times, join with sl st in third ch of ch-4. (8 dc, 8 ch sps made)

Rnd 2: Sl st in first ch sp, ch 3, beg cl, *(ch 4, beg cl in fourth ch from hook) 2 times, mark bottom of last cl made, cl in next sp; repeat from * 6 more times, ch 4, beg cl in fourth ch from hook, join with cl in top of first beg cl made. (24 cls made)

Rnd 3: Half shell, (ch 5, skip next cl, shell in marked cl, remove marker) 7 times, ch 5, skip last cl, end shell, sc joining. (8 shells, 8 ch sps)

Rnd 4: Half shell, (*ch 5, sc in next ch sp, ch 5, sc in ch sp of next shell, ch 5, sc in next ch sp, ch 5*, shell in ch sp of next shell) 3 times; repeat between first and second *, end shell, sc joining. (4 shells, 16 ch sps)

Rnd 5: Half shell, *(ch 5, sc in next ch sp) 4 times, ch 5, shell in ch sp of next shell; repeat from * 2 more times, (ch 5, sc in next ch sp) 4 times, ch 5, end shell, sc joining. (4 shells, 20 ch sps)

Rnd 6: Half shell, *(ch 5, sc in next ch sp) 5 times, ch 5, shell in ch sp of next shell; repeat from * 2 more times, (ch 5, sc in next ch sp) 5 times, ch 5, end shell, sc joining. (4 shells, 24 ch sps)

Rnd 7: (Ch 4, 3 tr) in first ch sp; working between adjacent Motifs (see Coat Assembly on page 152), *work Motif joining, 4 tr in ch sp of next shell on this Motif; repeat from * 2 more times, work Motif joining, join with sl st in fourth ch of ch 4. Fasten off. (Four 4-tr groups, 28 ch sps)

Work three more Medium Motifs between Large Motifs according to Coat Assembly.

HALF MOTIF
Row 1: Ch 5, dc in fifth ch from hook, (ch 1, dc, ch 1, dc, ch 1, dc, ch 4, sc) in same ch as first dc made, ch 4, sc in third ch of ch-5, turn. (6 ch sps made)

Row 2: Ch 3, beg cl in last sc made, *(ch 4, beg cl in fourth ch from hook) 2 times, mark bottom of last beg cl made, cl in next ch sp; repeat from * 4 more times, turn. (16 cls)

Row 3: Ch 4, sl st in marked cl, **beg shell** in top of first cl, (ch 5, skip next cl, shell in marked cl, remove marker) across, turn. (5 shells, 4 ch sps)

Row 4: Sl st in first 3 sts, beg shell in first ch sp, (ch 5, sc in next ch sp, ch 5, sc in ch sp of next shell, ch 5, sc in next ch sp, ch 5, shell in ch sp of next shell) 2 times, turn. (3 shells, 8 ch sps)

Rows 5–6: Sl st in first 3 sts, beg shell in first ch sp, *(ch 5, sc in next ch sp) across to next shell, ch 5, shell in ch sp of next shell; repeat from * across, turn. At end of last row (3 shells, 12 ch sps).

Row 7: Sl st in first 3 sts, (sl st, ch 4, 3 tr) in first ch sp; working on two Motifs between Rows (see Coat Assembly on page 152), work Motif joining, 4 tr in ch sp of next shell on this Motif, work Motif joining, 4 tr in next ch sp of last shell on this Motif. Fasten off. (Three 4-tr groups, 14 ch sps)

Work three more Half Motifs according to Coat Assembly.

SLEEVE
Sleeve Half Motif
Rows 1–6: Repeat rows 1–6 of Half Motif. At end of row 6, **do not turn.**

Rnd 7: Working across ends of rows, ch 5, skip next shell, sc in side of next shell, ch 5, skip next shell, sc in side of next cl, ch 5, sc in next cl, ch 5, skip center of row 1, sc in next cl, ch 5, sc in next cl, (ch 5, skip next shell, sc in side of next shell) 2 times, sl st across to ch sp of shell; working on two Motifs at **top** of Sleeve opening, work Motif joining, 4 tr in ch sp of next shell on this Motif, work Motif joining, sl st in ch sp of last shell on this Motif, sl st in next dc. Fasten off.

Repeat Sleeve Half Motif, joining to two Motifs at **bottom** of Sleeve opening.

SLEEVE ASSEMBLY

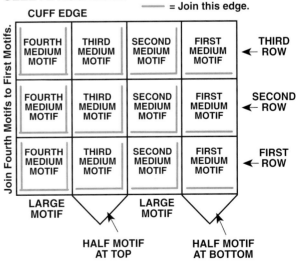

CUFF EDGE — = Join this edge.

Join Fourth Motifs to First Motifs.	FOURTH MEDIUM MOTIF	THIRD MEDIUM MOTIF	SECOND MEDIUM MOTIF	FIRST MEDIUM MOTIF	THIRD ← ROW
	FOURTH MEDIUM MOTIF	THIRD MEDIUM MOTIF	SECOND MEDIUM MOTIF	FIRST MEDIUM MOTIF	SECOND ← ROW
	FOURTH MEDIUM MOTIF	THIRD MEDIUM MOTIF	SECOND MEDIUM MOTIF	FIRST MEDIUM MOTIF	FIRST ← ROW

LARGE MOTIF — LARGE MOTIF

HALF MOTIF AT TOP — HALF MOTIF AT BOTTOM

First Row
First Medium Motif
Rnds 1–6: Repeat rnds 1–6 of Medium Motif on body.

Continued on page 154

Rnd 7: (Ch 4, 3 tr) in first ch sp; working on Half Motif at bottom of Sleeve opening, work Motif joining, *4 tr in ch sp of next shell on this Motif, (ch 5, sc in next ch sp) 6 times, ch 5; repeat from * two more times, join with sl st in fourth ch of ch-4. Fasten off. *(Four 4-tr groups, 28 ch sps)*

Second Medium Motif
Rnds 1–6: Repeat rnds 1–6 of Medium Motif on body.
Rnd 7: (Ch 4, 3 tr) in first ch sp; working on Motif just made, work Motif joining, 4 tr in ch sp of next shell on this Motif; working on adjacent Large Motif of Third Row on Coat, work Motif joining, 4 tr in ch sp of next shell on this Motif, (ch 5, sc in next ch sp) 6 times, ch 5, 4 tr in ch sp of next shell, (ch 5, sc in next ch sp) 6 times, ch 5, join with sl st in fourth ch of ch-4. Fasten off. *(Four 4-tr groups, 28 ch-sps)*

Third Medium Motif
Rnds 1–6: Repeat rnds 1–6 of Medium Motif on body.
Rnd 7: (Ch 4, 3 tr) in first ch sp; working on Motif just made, work Motif joining, 4 tr in ch sp of next shell on this Motif; working on adjacent Half Motif at top, work Motif joining, 4 tr in ch sp of next shell on this Motif, (ch 5, sc in next ch sp) 6 times, ch 5, 4 tr in ch sp of next shell, (ch 5, sc in next ch sp) 6 times, ch 5, join with sl st in fourth ch of ch-4. Fasten off. *(Four 4-tr groups, 28 ch sps)*

Fourth Medium Motif
Rnds 1–6: Repeat rnds 1–6 of Medium Motif on body.
Rnd 7: (Ch 4, 3 tr) in first ch sp; working on Motif just made, work Motif joining, 4 tr in ch sp of next shell on this Motif; working on adjacent Large Motif of Third Row on Coat, work Motif joining, 4 tr in ch sp of next shell on this Motif; working on First Motif on this row, work Motif joining, 4 tr in ch sp of next shell on this Motif, (ch 5, sc in next ch sp) 6 times, ch 5, join with sl st in fourth ch of ch-4. Fasten off. *(Four 4-tr groups, 28 ch sps)*

Second Row
First Medium Motif
Rnds 1–6: Repeat rnds 1–6 of Medium Motif on body.
Rnd 7: (Ch 4, 3 tr) in first ch sp; working on First Motif on last Row, work Motif joining, 4 tr in ch sp of next shell on this Motif, *(ch 5, sc in next ch sp) 6 times, ch 5, 4 tr in ch sp of next shell; repeat from * one more time, (ch 5, sc in next ch sp) 6 times, join with sl st in fourth ch of ch-4. Fasten off. *(Four 4-tr groups, 28 ch sps)*

Second Medium Motif
Rnds 1–6: Repeat rnds 1–6 of Medium Motif on body.
Rnd 7: (Ch 4, 3 tr) in first ch sp; working on Motif just made, work Motif joining, 4 tr in ch sp of next shell on this Motif; working on adjacent Motif, work Motif joining, 4 tr in ch sp of next shell on this Motif, (ch 5, sc in next ch sp) 6 times, ch 5, 4 tr in ch sp of next shell, (ch 5, sc in next ch sp) 6 times, ch 5, join with sl st in fourth ch of ch-4. Fasten off. *(Four 4-tr groups, 28 ch sps)*

Third Medium Motif
Work same as Second Medium Motif on Second Row.

Fourth Medium Motif
Rnds 1–6: Repeat rnds 1–6 of Medium Motif on body.
Rnd 7: (Ch 4, 3 tr) in first ch sp; working on Motif just made, work Motif joining, 4 tr in ch sp of next shell on this Motif; working on adjacent Motif, work Motif joining, 4 tr in ch sp of next shell on this Motif; working on adjacent Motif, work Motif joining, 4 tr in ch sp of next shell on this Motif, (ch 5, sc in next ch sp) 6 times, ch 5, join with sl st in fourth ch of ch-4. Fasten off. *(Four 4-tr groups, 28 ch sps)*

Third Row
Work same as Second Row.

FILL-IN MOTIF
Working one Fill-in Motif in holes on each side of underarm Half Motif, ch 6, sl st in sixth ch from hook to form ring, ch 3, 2 dc in ring; with right side facing you, ch 1, sc between center 2 sts on center 4-tr group in edge of opening, ch 1, 3 dc in ring, (ch 1, sc between center 2 sts on next 4-tr group, ch 1) 5 times, ch 1, join with sl st in top of ch-3. Fasten off.
Repeat in remaining underarm holes.

Cuff Edging
Rnd 1: With right side of work facing you; working in tr sts on last rnd of Fourth Motif on Third Row of Sleeve, skip 3 tr on 4-tr group, join with sl st in next tr, ch 4, dc in same st as last tr made; for **V st, (dc, ch 1, dc)** in center ch of next ch sp; V st in center ch of next 6 ch sps, V st in next tr, *skip next 6 tr, V st in next tr, V st in center ch of next 7 ch sps, V st in next tr; repeat from * 2 more times, join with sl st in third ch of ch-4. *(36 V sts made)*
Rnd 2: Ch 1, evenly space 49 hdc around, join with st st in top of first hdc, **turn.** *(49 hdc) (Ch-1 at beginning of rnds is not counted or used as a st.)*
Rnds 3–10: Ch 1, hdc in each st around, join, **turn.**
Rnd 11: Ch 1, sc in first 3 sts, ch 1, dc in next st, ch 1, (sc in next 3 sts, ch 1, dc in next st, ch 1) 11 times, sc in last st, join with sl st in first sc. Fasten off.
Repeat on other Sleeve opening.

BODY EDGING
NOTE: *When working between sts on 4-tr group, work between the second and third tr.*
Row 1: With right side facing you, working across neck and across Third Row of Motifs in 4-tr groups, join with sc between second and third tr on 4-tr group before shoulder joining on First Large Motif *(see Coat Assembly)*; working across ch sps, (ch 5, sc in next ch sp) 7 times, *ch 5, tr between 2 tr sts on next 4-tr group *(see above Note)*, skip next two 4-tr groups, tr between 2 tr sts on next 4-tr group, (ch 5, sc in next ch sp) 7 times; repeat from * 2 more times, ch 2, dc between 2 tr sts on next 4-tr group of last Motif, turn. *(36 sps)*
Rnd 2: *(Ch 4, sc in next ch sp) 6 times, ch 4, tr in next 2 ch sps; repeat from * 2 more times, (ch 4, sc in next ch sp) 7 times, ch 5, tr between same 2 tr sts

as first sc on row 1; working around ends of Motif rows, [tr between 2 tr sts on next 4-tr group, (ch 5, sc in next ch sp) 7 times, ch 5, tr between 2 tr sts on next 4-tr group, skip next 4-tr group; working across ends of rows on Half Motif, tr between 2 tr sts on next 4-tr group, (ch 3, sc in end of next row) 16 times, ch 5, tr between 2 tr sts on next 4-tr group, skip next 4-tr group]; repeat between [ ]; *to complete rnd, work steps A-D:*

A: Tr between 2 tr sts on next 4-tr group, *(ch 5, sc in next ch sp) 7 times, (ch 5, sc between 2 tr sts on next 4-tr group), 2 times; repeat from * 2 more times, (ch 5, sc in next ch sp) 7 times, ch 5, sc between 2 tr sts on next 4-tr group;

B: (Ch 5, sc between 2 tr sts on next 4-tr group) 3 times, *(ch 5, sc in next ch sp) 7 times, (ch 5, sc between 2 tr sts on next 4-tr group) 2 times; repeat from * one more time, (ch 5, sc in next ch sp) 7 times, ch 5, sc between 2 tr sts on next 4-tr group;

C: Repeat step B two more times.

D: Ch 5, sc between 2 tr sts on next 4-tr group, (ch 5, sc in next ch sp) 7 times, ch 5, tr between 2 tr sts on next 4-tr group; *working across ends of rows on Half Motif, skip next 4-tr group, tr between 2 tr sts on next 4-tr group, (ch 3, sc in end of next row) 16 times, tr between 2 tr sts on same 4-tr group; working across next Large Motif, skip next 4-tr group, tr between 2 tr sts on next 4-tr group, (ch 5, sc in next ch sp) 7 times, ch 5, tr between 2 tr sts on next 4-tr group; repeat from * one more time, tr between same 2 tr sts where last dc was worked on row 1, join with dtr *(see Stitch Guide)* in first ch sp, **turn. Do not fasten off.**

LEFT FRONT BAND

Row 1: With right side facing you, ch 1, sl st in next 2 tr, *(5 hdc in next ch sp) 8 times, (3 hdc in next ch-3 sp) 17 times; repeat from *, turn, leaving remaining ch sps unworked. *(182 hdc made) (Ch-1 at beginning of rows is not counted or used as a st.)*

Rows 2–6: Ch 1, hdc in first st, hdc in each st across, turn. At end of last row, fasten off.

RIGHT FRONT BAND

Row 1: With right side of work facing you, skip next 130 ch sps on bottom; starting at bottom of Half Motif, join with sl st in next ch sp, ch 1, *(3 hdc in next ch-3 sp) 17 times, (5 hdc in next ch sp) 8 times; repeat from *, turn. *(182 hdc made) (Ch-1 at beginning of rows is not counted or used as a st.)*

Rows 2–3: Ch 1, hdc in first st, hdc in each st across, turn.

Row 4: Ch 1, hdc in first 4 sts; for **Buttonhole,** ch 3, skip next 3 sts; (hdc in next 31 sts, ch 3, skip next 3 sts) 5 times, hdc in last 5 sts, turn. *(164 hdc, 6 Buttonholes)*

Row 5: Ch 1, hdc in first st, hdc in each st and in each ch across, turn.

Row 6: Ch 1, hdc in first st, hdc in each st across. Fasten off.

TRIM

With wrong side of work facing you, working on bottom of rnd 2 of Body Edging, skipping Right Front Band, join with sl st in first ch sp on Large Motif on First Row, ch 1, (2 sc, ch 1, dc, ch 1, 2 sc) in same ch sp as first sl st, *(2 sc, ch 1, dc, ch 1, 2 sc) in next ch sp; repeat from * 130 more times; [working in ends of rows on Band, sc in end of next row, ch 1, dc in same row as last sc made, ch 1, sc in ends of next 3 rows, ch 1, dc in end of next row, ch 1, sc in end of next row; working in sts across Band, ch 1, dc in first st, ch 1, (sc in next 3 sts, ch 1, dc in next st, ch 1) 45 times, sc in next 2 sts; working in ends of rows, sc in end of next row, ch 1, dc in end of next row, ch 1, sc in ends of next 2 rows, ch 1, dc in end of next row, ch 1, sc in end of next row]; working across rnd 2 on Edging at neck, ◆(2 sc, ch 1, dc, ch 1, 2 sc) in next ch sp; repeat from last ◆ 29 more times; working in ends of rows on Left Front Band; repeat between [ ], join with sl st in first sc. Fasten off.

BUTTON (make 6)

NOTE: Work in continuous rnds, do not join or turn unless otherwise stated. Mark first st of each rnd.

Rnd 1: Leaving 36" for stuffing, ch 2, 6 sc in second ch from hook. *(6 sc made)*

Rnd 2: Working in **back lps** *(see Stitch Guide)*, 2 sc in each st around. *(12 sc)*

Rnds 3–4: Sc in each st around.

Rnd 5: (Skip next st, sc in next st) around, stuff with 36" piece before closing, join with sl st in first sc. Leaving 8" for sewing, fasten off.

Sew Buttons on Left Front Band matching Buttonholes. ❏❐

1911 Yoke Collar

Designed by Barbara Dotzauer

Finished Size: 13" neckline. Changes for 15" and 17" are in [ ].

Materials:
- ❑ 220 yds. white size 20 crochet cotton thread
- ❑ Two hook and eye fasteners
- ❑ Sewing thread and needle
- ❑ No. 11 steel hook or hook needed to obtain gauge

Gauge: 5 tr groups = 3"; 4 pattern rows = 1".

Basic Stitches: Ch, sl st, sc, dc, tr.

YOKE
Row 1: Starting at bottom, ch 216, sc in ninth ch from hook, (ch 3, skip next 3 chs, sc in next ch, ch 4, skip next 4 chs, sc in next ch) across, turn. *(47 ch sps)*

Row 2: For **beginning shell (beg shell), ch 7, (tr, ch 3, tr) in first ch sp;** skip next ch-3 sp; *for **shell, (tr, ch 3, tr, ch 3, tr)** in next ch-4 sp, skip next ch sp; repeat from * across to last ch sp, (tr, ch 3, tr, ch 3) in last ch sp, tr in fifth ch of ch-8, turn. *(24 shells) Front of row 2 is right side of work.*

Row 3: Ch 1, sc in first st, ch 4, skip next ch sp and st, (sc in next ch sp, ch 3, skip next 2 sts, sc in next ch sp, ch 4, skip next st) across to last 3 ch sps, sc in next ch sp, ch 3, skip next 2 sts, sc in next ch sp, ch 4, skip next st, sc in fourth ch of ch-7, turn.

Row 4: Beg shell, skip next ch-3 sp, (shell in next ch 4-sp, skip next ch-3 sp) across to last ch sp; for **end shell, (tr, ch 3, tr, ch 2) in last ch-4 sp, tr in last st;** turn.

Rows 5–20: Repeat rows 3 and 4 alternately.

Row 21: For **first side,** ch 1, sc in first st, ch 4, skip first ch sp, sc in next ch sp, (ch 3, sc in next ch sp, ch 4, sc in next ch sp) 9 times leaving last 14 shells unworked, turn. *(19 ch sps)*

Row 22: Repeat row 4. *(10 shells)*

Row 23: Ch 1, sc in first st, ch 4, skip first ch sp, sc in next ch sp, (ch 3, sc in next ch sp, ch 4, sc in next ch sp) across to last shell, ch 3, sc in next ch sp leaving remaining sts and ch unworked, turn. *(18 ch sps)*

Row 24: Ch 4, skip first ch-3 sp, (shell in next ch-4 sp, skip next ch-3 sp) across to last ch-4 sp, end shell, turn. *(9 shells)*

Rows 25–28: Repeat rows 23 and 24 alternately. At end of last row *(7 shells).*

Row 29: Ch 1, sc in first st, ch 4, skip first ch sp, (sc in next ch sp, ch 3, sc in next ch sp, ch 4) 6 times, skip last ch sp, sc in last st leaving ch-4 unworked, turn. *(13 ch sps)*

Rows 30–37: Repeat rows 4 and 3 alternately.

Row 38: Ch 7, (tr, ch 3, tr, ch 3, tr) in first ch sp, skip next ch-3 sp, (shell in next ch-4 sp, skip next ch-3 sp) across to last ch sp, end shell, turn.

Row 39: Ch 1, sc in first st, ch 4, skip first ch sp, sc in next ch sp, (ch 3, sc in next ch sp, ch 4, sc in next ch sp) across to last 2 ch sps and ch 7, ch 3, (sc, ch 4, sc) in next ch sp, ch 3, sc in next ch sp, ch 4, sc in fourth ch of ch 7, turn. *(15 ch sps)*

Rows 40–43: Repeat rows 38 and 39 alternately. At end of last row *(19 ch sps).*

Rows 44–46: Repeat rows 4 and 3 alternately, ending with row 4 and 10 shells. Mark row 46 at neck edge.

Row 47: Ch 1, sc in first st, ch 4, skip first ch sp, sc in next ch sp, ch 3, sc in next ch sp, (ch 4, sc in next ch sp, ch 3, sc in next ch sp) across leaving remaining sts and ch unworked, turn. *(18 ch sps)*

Row 48: Ch 4, skip first ch-3 sp, (shell in next ch-4 sp, skip next ch-3 sp) across to last ch-4 sp, end shell, turn. *(9 shells)*

Rows 49–62: Repeat rows 47 and 48 alternately. At end of last row *(2 shells).*

Row 63: Ch 1, sc in first st, ch 4, skip first ch sp, sc in next ch sp, ch 3, sc in next ch sp leaving last ch sp unworked, turn. *(2 ch sps)*

Row 64: Ch 4, skip first ch-3 sp, end shell. Fasten off.

Row 21: For **second side,** with wrong side of row 20 facing you, skip next 4 unworked shells on row 20, join with sc in first tr of next shell, ch 4, skip next ch sp, sc in next ch sp, (ch 3, sc in next ch sp, ch 4, sc in next ch sp) across to last shell, ch 3, sc in next ch sp, ch 4, sc in fourth ch of ch-7, turn. *(19 ch sps)*

Row 22: Repeat row 4. *(10 shells)*

Row 23: Ch 4, skip first ch sp, sc in next ch sp, ch 3, sc in next ch sp, (ch 4, sc in next ch sp, ch 3, sc in next ch sp) across to last ch sp, ch 4, sc in fourth ch of ch-7, turn.

Row 24: Beg shell, (skip next ch-3 sp, shell in next ch-4 sp) across to last 2 ch sps, tr in next ch-3 sp leaving last ch-4 sp unworked, turn. *(9 shells)*

Rows 25–28: Repeat rows 23 and 24 alternately. At end of last row *(7 shells).*

Rows 29–37: Repeat rows 3 and 4 alternately, ending with row 3.

Row 38: Beg shell, skip next ch-3 sp, (shell in next ch-4 sp, skip next ch-3 sp) across to last ch-4 sp, (tr, ch 3, tr, ch 3, tr, ch 3) in last ch sp, tr in last st, turn.

Row 39: Ch 1, sc in first st, ch 4, skip first ch sp, sc in next ch sp, ch 3, (sc, ch 4, sc) in next ch sp), (ch 3, sc in next ch sp, ch 4, sc in next ch sp) across to last shell, ch 3, sc in next ch sp, ch 4, sc in fourth ch of ch-7, turn. *(15 ch sps)*

Rows 40–43: Repeat rows 38 and 39 alternately. At end of last row *(19 ch sps).*

Rows 44–46: Repeat rows 4 and 3 alternately, ending with row 4 and 10 shells. Mark row 46 at neck edge.

Row 47: Ch 4, skip first ch sp, sc in next ch sp, ch 3, sc in next ch sp, (ch 4, sc in next ch sp, ch 3, sc in next ch sp) across to last ch sp, ch 4, sc in fourth ch of ch-7, turn.

Row 48: Beg shell, (shell in next ch-4 sp, skip next ch-3 sp) across to last 2 ch sps, tr in next ch-3 sp leaving last ch-4 sp unworked, turn. *(9 shells)*

Rows 49–61: Repeat rows 47 and 48 alternately, ending with row 47 and 5 ch sps.

Row 62: Beg shell, skip next ch-3 sp, shell in next ch-4 sp, tr in next ch-3 sp leaving last ch-4 sp unworked, turn. *(2 shells)*

Row 63: Ch 4, skip first ch sp, sc in next ch sp, ch 3, sc in next ch sp, ch 4, sc in fourth ch of ch-7, turn.

Row 64: Beg shell, tr in next ch-3 sp, **do not turn.** Fasten off.

COLLAR
Row 1: Ch 0 [6, 12]; working in ends of rows and in ch sps across neckline, join with sc in row 46 on second side of yoke, (ch 3, sc) 51 times evenly spaced across neckline to row 46 on first side, ch 0 [13, 19], turn.

Row 2: For **size 13" only,** beg shell, skip next ch

157

Continued on page 158

sp, (shell in next ch sp, skip next ch sp) across to last ch sp, end shell, turn. *(26 shells)*

Row [2]: For **size 15"** only, tr in eighth ch from hook, ch 3, tr in same ch, skip next 2 chs, shell in next ch, skip last 2 chs, shell in first ch sp on collar, (skip next ch sp, shell in next ch sp) across to ch-6, (skip next 2 chs, shell in next ch) 2 times, turn. *(30 shells)*

Row [2]: For **size 17"** only, tr in eighth ch from hook, ch 3, tr in same ch, (skip next 2 chs, shell in next ch) 3 times, skip last 2 chs, shell in first ch sp on collar, (skip next ch sp, shell in next ch sp) across to ch-12, (skip next 2 chs, shell in next ch) 4 times, turn *(34 shells)*.

Row 3: For **all sizes,** repeat row 3 of Yoke.

Row 4: Skipping ch-3 sps, beg shell, shell in next 11 [13, 15] ch-4 sps, (tr, ch 3, tr) in each of next 2 ch-4 sps, shell in next 11 [13, 15] ch-4 sps, end shell, turn.

Row 5: Repeat row 3 of Yoke.

Row 6: Beg shell, shell in next 10 [12, 14] ch-4 sps, (tr, ch 3, tr) in each of next 2 ch-4 sps, shell in next 11 [13, 15] ch-4 sps, end shell, turn.

Row 7: Repeat row 3 of Yoke.

Row 8: Beg shell, shell in next 10 [12, 14] ch-4 sps, (tr, ch 3, tr) in next ch-4 sp, shell in next 11 [13, 15] ch-4 sps, end shell, turn.

Row 9: Ch 1, sc in first st, ch 4, skip next ch sp and st, (sc in next ch sp, ch 3, skip next 2 sts, sc in next ch sp, ch 4, skip next st) 11 [13, 15] times, ch 3, sc in next ch sp, ch 4, sc in same ch sp, ch 3, skip next 2 sts, sc in next ch sp, ch 4, skip next st; repeat between ( ) across to last 3 ch sps, sc in next ch sp, ch 3, skip next 2 sts, sc in next ch sp, ch 4, skip next st, sc in fourth ch of ch-7, turn.

Row 10: Ch 3, sc in first ch sp, *[ch 4, sl st in top of last sc made, ch 5, sl st in same st, ch 4, sl st in same st], (ch 3, sc in next ch sp) 2 times; repeat from * across; repeat between [ ], ch 3, sc in first st, **do not turn or fasten off.**

First Side Edging

Working in ends of tr rows and in ch sps on back opening, (ch 3, sc in next row) 8 times, ch 3; for **sizes 15" and 17"** only, working on opposite side of ch on collar, sc in first ch, *ch 3, skip next 2 ch, sc in next ch; repeat from * [0, 2] times, ch 3, skip next ch sp; for **all sizes,** sc in next ch sp, (ch 3, dc in next ch sp, ch 3, sc in next row, ch 3, sc in next ch sp) 9 times, ch 3, sc in end of row 64, (ch 3, sc in same row) 2 times, sl st in next sc row, sl st in next tr row. **Do not turn or fasten off.**

First Side Scallop

Row 1: Working in ends of rows across side of collar, tr in next tr row, (ch 2, tr in same row) 6 times, sl st in next tr row leaving remaining rows unworked, turn.

Row 2: Ch 1, sc in first tr, (2 sc in next ch sp, sc in next tr) 6 times, ch 4, sl st in next row or ch sp, turn.

Row 3: For **picot, ch-4, sl st in fourth ch from hook;** (tr in same st as ch-4, picot) 3 times, *skip next 2 sts, dc in next st, skip next 2 sts, (tr, picot) 4 times in next st; repeat from * 2 times; for **joining,** sl st in next tr row, **do not turn or fasten off.**

Second Side Scallop

Rows 1–2: Sl st across to top of second tr row from last joining *(see illustration);* repeat rows 1–2 of First Side Scallop.

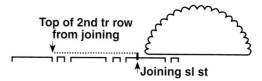

Top of 2nd tr row from joining

↑Joining sl st

Row 3: Picot, tr in same st as ch-4, ch 2, sl st in last picot of last scallop made, ch 2, sl st in last tr made, (tr in same st as last tr, picot) 2 times, *skip next 2 sts, dc in next st, skip next 2 sts, (tr, picot) 4 times in next st; repeat from * 2 more times, join with sl st in next tr row, **do not turn or fasten off.**

For **next Side Scallops,** repeat Second Side Scallop 4 times.

First Corner Scallop

Row 1: Sl st across to top of second tr row from last joining; working on opposite side of starting ch, tr in first ch-4 sp, (ch 2, tr in same sp) 9 times, skip next ch-3 sp, sl st in next ch-4 sp, turn.

Row 2: Ch 1, sc in first tr, (2 sc in next ch sp, sc in next st) 9 times, ch 4, sl st in next tr row, turn.

Row 3: Picot, tr in same st as ch-4, ch 2, sl st in last picot of last Scallop made, ch 2, sl st in top of last tr made, (tr, picot) 2 times in same st as last tr, dc in same st, skip next 2 sts, (tr, picot) 4 times in next st, *skip next 2 sts, dc in next st, skip next 2 sts, (tr, picot) 4 times in next st; repeat from * 3 times, **do not turn.**

Row 4: Skip next ch-3 sp, sl st in next ch-4 sp, sl st across to center of next ch-4 sp, **do not turn or fasten off.**

First Bottom Scallop

Row 1: Skip next ch sp, tr in next ch sp, (ch 2, tr in same ch sp) 6 times, skip next ch sp, sl st in next ch sp, turn.

Row 2: Ch 1, sc in first tr, (2 sc in next ch sp, sc in next tr) 6 times, ch 4, sl st in next ch sp, turn.

Row 3: Repeat row 3 of Second Side Scallop, **do not join or turn.**

Row 4: Repeat row 4 of First Corner Scallop.

Second Bottom Scallop

Rows 1–2: Repeat rows 1–2 of First Bottom Scallop.

Row 3: Repeat row 3 of Second Side Scallop, **do not join or turn.**

Row 4: Skip next ch-3 sp, sl st in next ch-4 sp, sl st across to center of next ch-3 sp, **do not turn or fasten off.**

Third Bottom Scallop

Rows 1–3: Repeat rows 1–3 of Second Bottom Scallop.

Row 4: Skip next ch-4 sp, sl st in next ch-3 sp, sl st across to center of next ch-4 sp, **do not turn or fasten off.**

For **Fourth and Fifth Bottom Scallops,** repeat First Bottom Scallop.

Second Corner Scallop

Row 1: Tr in last ch-4 sp, (ch 2, tr in same sp) 9 times, sl st in next tr row, turn.

Row 2: Ch 1, sc in first tr, (2 sc in next ch sp, sc in next st) 9 times, ch 4, sl st in next ch sp, turn.

Row 3: Repeat row 3 of First Corner Scallop, join with sl st in next tr row, **do not turn or fasten off.**

For Next Side Scallops, repeat Second Side Scallop six times.

Second Side Edging

Ch 3, sc in same row, (ch 3, sc in next ch sp) 2 times; working in ends of tr rows and in ch sps on back opening, (ch 3, dc in next ch sp, ch 3, sc in next ch sp, ch 3, sc in next ch sp) 8 times, ch 3, dc in next ch sp, ch 3, sc in next ch sp; for **sizes 15" and 17"** only, working on opposite side of ch on collar, ch 3, *skip next 2 ch, sc in next ch, ch 3; repeat from * [1, 3] times; for **all sizes,** working in ends of rows on collar, (sc in next row, ch 3) across, join with sl st in first ch of first ch-3 on row 10 of collar. Fasten off.

Sew hook and eye fasteners to first and last shell rows on collar. ❏❐

General Instructions

THREAD & HOOKS

When purchasing thread, be sure to check the label for the size specification. By using the size stated in the pattern, you will be assured of achieving the proper gauge. Size 10 cotton, commonly referred to as bedspread cotton, may not bear a size marking on the label. Sizes other than 10 should be clearly labeled.

The hook size suggested in the pattern is a guide to determine the size you will need. Always work a swatch of the type stitches stated in the gauge section of the pattern with the suggested hook. If you find your gauge is smaller or larger than what is specified, choose a different hook.

GAUGE

Gauge is measured by counting the number of stitches, chains, rows or rounds per inch. Each of the patterns featured in this book will have a gauge listed. In some, gauge for motifs or flowers is given as an overall measurement. Gauge must be attained in order for the project to come out the size stated and to prevent ruffling and puckering.

Before beginning your project, work up a small swatch with the stated thread to check your gauge. Lay the piece flat and measure the stitches or chains per inch. If you have more than specified, your gauge is too tight and you need a larger hook. Fewer stitches or chains per inch indicates a gauge that is too loose. In this case, choose the next smaller hook size.

Gauge is also affected by differing crochet techniques and hook styles. Slight adjustments can be made by pulling the loops a little tighter or looser on your hook as you work.

FINISHING

Patterns that require assembly will suggest a tapestry needle in the materials. This should be a #18 or #22 blunt-tipped tapestry needle. Sharp-pointed needles are not recommended as they can cut the thread and weaken the stitches.

Hiding loose ends is never a fun task, but if done correctly, may mean the difference between an item that looks great for years, or one that soon shows signs of wear. Always leave about 6" when beginning or ending. Thread the loose end into your tapestry needle and carefully weave it through the back of several stitches. Then to assure a secure hold, weave in the opposite direction, going through different strands. Gently pull the end, and clip, allowing the end to pull up under the stitches. A small amount of fabric glue may be placed on the end for extra hold.

If your project needs blocking, gentle steaming followed by spray starching works well. Lay your project flat on a surface large enough to spread it out completely. Smooth out wrinkles by hand as much as possible. Set your steam iron to the permanent press setting, then hold slightly above the stitches, allowing the steam to penetrate the thread. Do not rest the iron on the item. Gently pull and smooth the stitches into shape, spray lightly with starch, and allow to dry completely.

STIFFENING

There are many liquid products on the market made specifically for stiffening doilies and other soft items. For best results, carefully read the manufacturer's instructions on the product you select before beginning.

Forms for shaping can be many things. Styrofoam® shapes and plastic containers work well for items such as bowls and baskets. Glass or plastic drinking glasses can be used for vase-type items. If you cannot find an item with the dimensions given in the pattern to use as a form, any similarly sized item can be shaped by adding layers of plastic wrap. Place the dry crochet piece over the form to check fit, remembering that it will stretch when wet.

For shaping flat pieces, corrugated cardboard, Styrofoam® or a cutting board designed for sewing may be used. Be sure to cover all surfaces of forms or blocking board with clear plastic wrap, securing with cellophane tape.

If you have not used fabric stiffener before, you may wish to practice on a small swatch before stiffening the actual item. For proper saturation when using conventional stiffeners, work liquid thoroughly into the crochet piece and let stand for about 15 minutes. Then, squeeze out excess stiffener and blot with paper towels. Continue to blot while shaping to remove as much stiffener as possible. Stretch over form, shape and pin with rust-proof pins; allow to dry, then unpin.

Stitch Guide

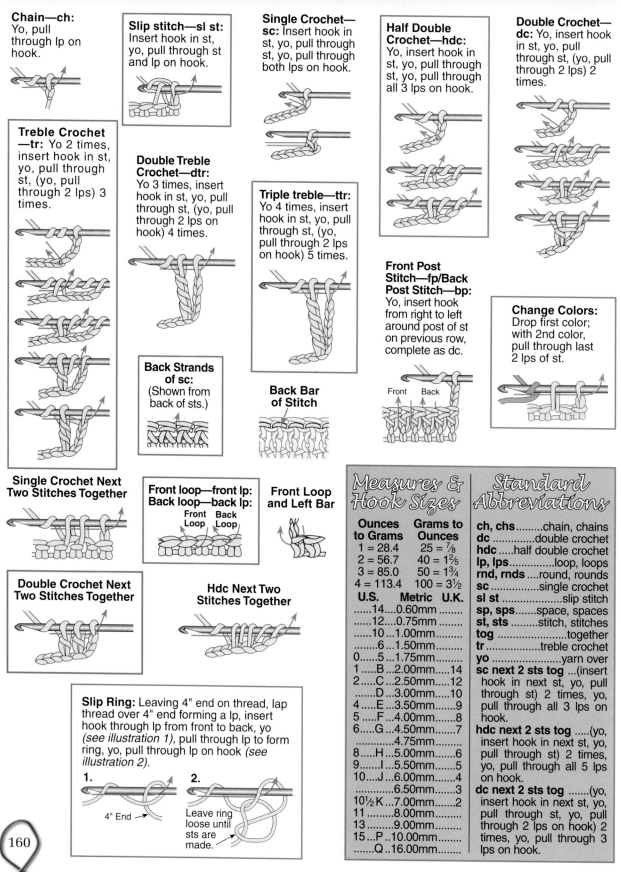

Chain—ch: Yo, pull through lp on hook.

Slip stitch—sl st: Insert hook in st, yo, pull through st and lp on hook.

Single Crochet—sc: Insert hook in st, yo, pull through st, yo, pull through both lps on hook.

Half Double Crochet—hdc: Yo, insert hook in st, yo, pull through st, yo, pull through all 3 lps on hook.

Double Crochet—dc: Yo, insert hook in st, yo, pull through st, (yo, pull through 2 lps) 2 times.

Treble Crochet—tr: Yo 2 times, insert hook in st, yo, pull through st, (yo, pull through 2 lps) 3 times.

Double Treble Crochet—dtr: Yo 3 times, insert hook in st, yo, pull through st, (yo, pull through 2 lps on hook) 4 times.

Triple treble—ttr: Yo 4 times, insert hook in st, yo, pull through st, (yo, pull through 2 lps on hook) 5 times.

Front Post Stitch—fp/Back Post Stitch—bp: Yo, insert hook from right to left around post of st on previous row, complete as dc.

Front   Back

Change Colors: Drop first color; with 2nd color, pull through last 2 lps of st.

Back Strands of sc: (Shown from back of sts.)

Back Bar of Stitch

Single Crochet Next Two Stitches Together

Front loop—front lp: Back loop—back lp:

Front Loop   Back Loop

Front Loop and Left Bar

Double Crochet Next Two Stitches Together

Hdc Next Two Stitches Together

Slip Ring: Leaving 4" end on thread, lap thread over 4" end forming a lp, insert hook through lp from front to back, yo *(see illustration 1)*, pull through lp to form ring, yo, pull through lp on hook *(see illustration 2)*.

1.

4" End

2.

Leave ring loose until sts are made.

Measures & Hook Sizes

Ounces to Grams	Grams to Ounces
1 = 28.4	25 = ⅞
2 = 56.7	40 = 1⅖
3 = 85.0	50 = 1¾
4 = 113.4	100 = 3½

U.S.	Metric	U.K.
14	0.60mm	
12	0.75mm	
10	1.00mm	
6	1.50mm	
0	5	1.75mm	
1	B	2.00mm	14
2	C	2.50mm	12
D	3.00mm	10
4	E	3.50mm	9
5	F	4.00mm	8
6	G	4.50mm	7
	4.75mm	
8	H	5.00mm	6
9	I	5.50mm	5
10	J	6.00mm	4
	6.50mm	3
10½ K	7.00mm	2
11	8.00mm	
13	9.00mm	
15	P	10.00mm	
Q	16.00mm	

Standard Abbreviations

ch, chs ....chain, chains
dc ....double crochet
hdc .....half double crochet
lp, lps ....loop, loops
rnd, rnds ....round, rounds
sc ....single crochet
sl st ....slip stitch
sp, sps.......space, spaces
st, sts ....stitch, stitches
tog ....together
tr ....treble crochet
yo ....yarn over
sc next 2 sts tog ...(insert hook in next st, yo, pull through st) 2 times, yo, pull through all 3 lps on hook.
hdc next 2 sts tog .....(yo, insert hook in next st, yo, pull through st) 2 times, yo, pull through all 5 lps on hook.
dc next 2 sts tog ....(yo, insert hook in next st, yo, pull through st, yo, pull through 2 lps on hook) 2 times, yo, pull through 3 lps on hook.